Mississippi Court Re

from the files

of the

High Court of Errors and Appeals

1799-1859

Compiled by

Mary Louise Flowers Hendrix

Southern Historical Press, Inc.
Greenville, South Carolina

This volume was reproduced
from a personal copy located in
the Publishers private library

Please direct all correspondence and book orders to:
SOUTHERN HISTORICAL PRESS, Inc.
PO Box 1267
Greenville, SC 29602-1267

Originally Published 1950
ISBN #0-89308-529-4
Printed in the United States of America

To my husband

THOMAS DEWITT HENDRIX

Whose sympathetic interest made it possible, this volume of Mississippi Court Records is affectionately dedicated.

INTRODUCTION

The compilation of this volume began because the writer wished to find the will of her great, great grandfather. The original will was destroyed when the courthouse in Franklin County, Mississippi, burned during the Reconstruction period.

As the work progressed, however, and it became more and more apparent that the files of the Mississippi High Court of Errors and Appeals contained a gold mine of names, dates, family connections and migrations of Pioneer Mississippians, self-interest diminished and the backbreaking, eye-straining work became a thrilling, exciting adventure.

As shown by the County History Chart incorporated in this book, many county records were destroyed in courthouse fires and except for the data contained in the files of the High Court sent up from the Probate Courts of these counties, there is nothing left of these early records. The wills included in this volume, filed with the High Court, are copies of the original wills and, in many instances, constitute the only existing evidence of family connections and relationships.

The cases herein indexed and abstracted pertain to will, administration, property settlement, guardianship, and divorce cases. Many cases filed with the High Court are missing. In some instances lawyers removed the files and did not return them; some were lost in moving the file cases from one place to another and possibly some fell into such a state of decay that they were discarded. As is the case with all old papers, the ink has dimmed, the penmanship is strange and sometimes very poor, names are misspelled or spelled in two or more ways, but for the most part they are in fair shape.

Among the High Court Judges of the period covered by this book were: William B. Shields, John P. Hampton, Powhatan Ellis, Joshua G. Clarke, Walter Leake, Louis Winston, Bela Metcalfe, Richard Stockton, Edward Turner, Joshua Child, Isaac Caldwell, John Black, John Winchester, William B. Griffith, Harry Cage, Isaac R. Nicholson, Alexander Montgomery, William L. Sharkey, George W. Smyth, Eli Huston, Cotesworth P. Smith, Daniel W. Wright, James F. Trotter, P. Rutillius R. Pray, Reuben Davis, Alexander M. Clayton, J. S. B. Thatcher, Collin S. Tarpley, William Yerger, Ephraim S. Fisher, Alexander H. Handy, and William L. Harris.

Prominently mentioned in the records are the following Probate Judges: Charles Wheaton, John Richards, William Doak, Halsey Townsend, P. A. Vandorn, John Phillips, John Cameron, Thos. Bilbo, Alexander McLeod, John McGuffie, Duncan McLaurin, Wm. P. Gadberry, Barnabus Allen, Jacob Remson Holmes, G. T. Lightfoot, A. M. Nelson, M. H. Peyton, Thomas Alexander Magee, J. W. Wilder, L. Lewis, Murdock McDonald, William K. Magee, H. Murray Quin, W. W. Whitehead, Richard M. Neilson, James A. Maxwell, Jackson Millsaps, Francis Gildart, and James A. Campbell.

Some "High Court Lawyers" of distinction of this period were: George Poindexter, Seargent S. Prentiss, Joseph Dunbar Shields, John A. Cheatham, Amos Whiting, William Dangerfield, Robert McGill, John Stafford, Enoch M. Lowe, John Lowry, Charles Clark (Governor of Mississippi 1863-1865), Marston H. Harper, Luther Stone, Oliver B. Hayes, Wiley Pope Harris, Hiram Cassidy, Sr., and Benjamin King.

We wish to acknowledge, with gratitude, the splendid work done with these old records by the Historical Records Survey of the Works Progress Administration. Under the supervision of Dr. W. D. McCain, Director of Mississippi's

Department of Archives and History, the workers recovered records from barrels and boxes scattered here and there in the Capitol Building. They were sorted, wrapped and tied securely, and each case was numbered and filed in proper order in steel filing cases. These records are now in the vaults of the Department of Archives and History in Jackson, Mississippi.

My sincere thanks go to Dr. W. D. McCain and his fellow workers in the Department of Archives and History and to Mr. C. S. Hudspeth for the many courtesies shown me during the preparation of this volume; also to Mrs. Bobbye Puryear who has rendered invaluable service in typing the manuscript for the printers.

We shall feel generously repaid for our efforts if only one person is made happy by finding a lost ancestor within the pages of this book. It is our fervent hope, however, that it will provide many missing links for many people, and will be a fore-runner of other volumes of genealogical records of the early families of my beloved State of Mississippi.

Mary Louise Flowers Hendrix
(Mrs. Thomas D. Hendrix)
408 Dunbar Street
Jackson, 32, Mississippi

April 12, 1950

MISSISSIPPI RECORDS — WHERE THEY MAY BE FOUND

In Mississippi, the Chancery Clerk of the County is the custodian of all Deed and Mortgage records, Will dockets, Administration of estates, Divorce actions, Contracts, Guardianships and all matters pertaining to equity.

The Circuit Clerk of the County is custodian of all Marriage records and County poll books.

Records of births and deaths from 1912 may be found in the Bureau of Vital Statistics, Old Capitol Building, Jackson, Mississippi.

The Department of Archives and History, War Memorial Building, Jackson, Mississippi has the census of Mississippi for 1820 in book form; the 1830-1840-1850-1860-1870-1880 Federal census records for Mississippi are on microfilm in this department. Mortality lists for 1850, 1860 and 1870, lists of educable children for the years 1878, 1885 and 1892 from some of the counties and early personal property tax lists for some of the counties may also be found in the Department of Archives and History.

The office of the State Land Commissioner, New Capitol Building has complete land grant records.

MISSISSIPPI COUNTIES.

County	When formed	County Seat	Records
Adams	April 1, 1779	Natchez	Complete
Alcorn	April 15, 1870	Corinth	Burned 1917
Amite	Feb. 24, 1809	Liberty	Complete
Attala	Dec. 23, 1833	Kosciusko	Burned (7-28-1858 (7-26-1896
Benton	July 15, 1870	Ashland	Complete
Bolivar	Feb. 9, 1836	(Rosedale (Cleveland	Complete 1836 Complete 1900
Calhoun	March 8, 1852	Pittsboro	Burned 12-22-1922
Carroll	Dec. 23, 1833	(Carrollton (Vaiden	Complete Complete
Chickasaw	Feb. 9, 1836	(Houston (Okalona	 Burned 1863
Choctaw	Dec. 23, 1833	(Chester (Ackerman	 Burned 1880 — some old records saved
Claiborne	Jan. 27, 1802	Port Gibson	Complete
Clarke	Dec. 23, 1833	Quitman	Complete
Clay	May 12, 1871	West Point	Complete
Coahoma	Feb. 9, 1836	(Clarksdale (Friars Point	Complete Complete
Copiah	Jan. 21, 1823	Hazlehurst	Complete
Covington	Jan. 5, 1819	Collins	Burned 1904 — some records saved
DeSoto	Feb. 9, 1836	Hernando	Burned 1940 — many records saved
Forrest	Jan. 6, 1908	Hattiesburg	Complete
Franklin	Dec. 21, 1809	Meadville	Burned 1877 — some deed books and marriage records saved.
George	March 16, 1910	Lucedale	Complete
Greene	Dec. 9, 1811	Leakesville	Burned 3-24-1875
Grenada	May 9, 1870	Grenada	Complete
Hancock	Dec. 14, 1812	Bay St. Louis	Burned 1860 — some records saved
Harrison	Feb. 5, 1841	Gulfport	Burned Jan. 1916. Chancery records saved. Some Circuit records.
Hinds	Feb. 12, 1821	(Raymond (Jackson	Complete from 1821 Complete from 1870
Holmes	Feb. 19, 1833	Lexington	Complete
Humphreys	1918	Belzoni	Complete
Issaquena	Feb. 23, 1844	Mayersville	Complete
Itawamba	Feb. 9, 1836	Fulton	Complete
Jackson	Dec. 14, 1812	Pascagoula	Burned 1875
Jasper	Dec. 23, 1833	(Paulding (Bay Springs	Burned 9-19-1932 Complete from 1904

County	When formed	County Seat	Records
Jefferson	Jan. 11, 1802	Fayette	Many probate records burned in 1901. Majority of records complete
Jeff Davis	May 9, 1906	Prentiss	Complete — see Covington and Lawrence
Jones	Jan. 24, 1826	(Ellisville (Laurel	Date of fire not known. First will dated 1894; First docket entry 2-5-1899
Kemper	Dec. 23, 1833	DeKalb	Burned 1882
Lafayette	Feb. 9, 1836	Oxford	Complete
Lamar	March 13, 1904	Purvis	Fire 1934. Records not burned but badly mixed.
Lauderdale	Dec. 23, 1833	Meridian	Complete
Lawrence	Dec. 22, 1814	Monticello	Two fires; many records complete
Leake	Dec. 23, 1833	Carthage	Complete
Lee	Oct. 26, 1866	Tupelo	Complete
Leflore	March 15, 1871	Greenwood	Complete
Lincoln	April 7, 1870	Brookhaven	Burned 1892
Lowndes	Jan. 30, 1830	Columbus	Complete
Madison	Jan. 29, 1828	Canton	Complete
Marion	Dec. 9, 1811	Columbia	Complete
Marshall	Feb. 9, 1836	Holly Springs	Complete-except two very early deed books
Monroe	Feb. 9, 1821	Aberdeen	Complete
Montgomery	May 13, 1871	Winona	Burned 1903. Some records saved. Records prior to 1871 in Carroll and Choctaw.
Neshoba	Dec. 23, 1833	Philadelphia	Complete
Newton	Feb. 23, 1836	Decatur	Burned 1877 and 1910
Noxubee	Dec. 25, 1833	Macon	Complete
Oktibbeha	Dec. 25, 1833	Starkville	Burned 1880
Panola	Feb. 9, 1836	(Batesville (Sardis	Land deeds Batesville from 1836. Other records from 1854. Records at Sardis burned 1886.
Pearl River	Feb. 23, 1890	Poplarville	Complete
Perry	Feb. 3, 1820	New Augusta	Burned 11-14-1877
Pike	Feb. 9, 1815	Magnolia	Burned 1882
Pontotoc	Feb. 9, 1836	Pontotoc	Complete
Prentiss	April 15, 1870	Booneville	Fire 1912 Chancery records saved. Circuit burned.
Quitman	Feb. 1, 1877	Marks	Complete
Rankin	Feb. 4, 1828	Brandon	Practically complete.

County	When formed	County Seat	Records
Scott	Dec. 23, 1833	Forest	Complete
Sharkey	March 29, 1876	Rolling Fork	Complete
Simpson	Jan. 23, 1824	Mendenhall	Burned 1840 and 1872
Smith	Dec. 23, 1833	Raleigh	Burned 1892 and 1912
Stone	1917	Wiggins	Complete
Sunflower	Feb. 15, 1844	Indianola	Complete
Tallahatchie	Dec. 23, 1833	(Charleston (Sumner	Complete Burned 1908
Tate	April 15, 1873	Senatobia	Complete
Tippah	Feb. 9, 1836	Ripley	Burned 1863. Few records for that year.
Tishomingo	Feb. 9, 1836	Iuka	Burned 6-30-1887
Tunica	Feb. 9, 1836	Tunica	Complete
Union	July 7, 1870	New Albany	Burned 1882
Walthall	March 16, 1910	Tylertown	Complete
Warren	Dec. 22, 1809	Vicksburg	Complete
Washington	Jan. 29, 1827	Greenville	Complete
Wayne	Dec. 21, 1809	Waynesboro	Burned 9-19-1892
Webster*	April 6, 1874	Walthall	Complete
Wilkinson	Jan. 30, 1802	Woodville	Complete
Winston	Dec. 23, 1833	Louisville	Complete
Yalobusha	Dec. 23, 1833	(Water Valley (Coffeeville	Complete Complete
Yazoo	Jan. 21, 1823	Yazoo City	Complete

* Data, as to completeness of records, was furnished by the various Chancery Clerks of the Counties.

* Webster County was first known as Sumner County.

1822 Marion Co. Miss. Drawer 65 Case #1

William Smith of Lawrence Co. Miss.

vs

Moses Cox, Thomas Banks, John Honey

****

1827 Franklin Co. Miss. Drawer 65 Case ....

Bond—Re: Estate of James Keith, Dec'd
James Witherspoon, Admr.
John F. Witherspoon and Jesse Guice, Bondsmen.

****

1845 Adams Co. Miss. Drawer 65 Case #2

Bond—Re: Eliza C. Wood, Guardian for
Mary Josephine Abercrombie, nee Bowmar, minor
Marriage contract between Charles Abercrombie and Mary Josephine Bowmar.

****

1823 Marion Co. Miss. Drawer 65 Case #4

Louise Ford, Relict of Solomon Ford, Dec'd

vs

Joseph Ford, Admr. Est. Solomon Ford, Dec'd
Solomon Ford died September 3, 1820.

****

1822 Pike Co. Miss. Drawer 65 Case #6

Hance Hamilton

vs

Darling McGraw, Executor Est. David McGraw Sr. Dec'd

Bondsmen: Richard Quin, Samuel Davis, John Lawrence, John Rippey, Isaac Boyd, Thos. King, Preston Bond, John Sistrunk, James Reed, Geo. M. Trotter, Thos. Gullege, Thos. Reeves.

****

1831 Wayne Co. Miss. Drawer 65 Case #6-a

Christopher Collins and Rachel Collins

vs

Ann Hendricks and Jacob Collins

Also named: Robert Collins, Christopher Collins, Jr., Joshua Collins, Jr., Benj. Collins, Jos. Collins, James Collins—all children of Christopher and Rachel Collins and all heirs of their grandfather, John Hendricks, Dec'd. Suit to void Will of John Hendricks, Dec'd.

****

1832 Wilkinson Co. Miss. Drawer 65 Case #6-99

Spencer Wood, Admr. Est. F. A. Browder, Dec'd.

vs

John F. Carmichael

Litigation involves property incorporated in marriage contract between Frederick Browder and Harriett Hooke. Harriett Hooke Browder died July 1830. Frederick Browder died December 1830.

****

1821 Lawrence Co. Miss. Drawer 65 Case #7

James Bailey

vs

Nancy Bailey

Divorce Petition.

****

1827 Pike Co. Miss. Drawer 65 Case #7-a

William Mellon, Admr. Est. Sam Mellon, Dec'd.

vs

J. B. Barker

****

1830 Amite Co. Miss. Drawer 65 Case #7-c

Robt. Stewart, Jr.

vs

Francis Wren, Exec. Estate James L. Collins, Dec'd.

****

1835 Madison Co. Miss. Drawer 65 Case #8

John D. Scott, Admr. de bonis non Est John Silverberg, Dec'd.

vs

Dr. Lewis Phoenis, Dan Sutherland, E. F. Devine, Alvis W. Harris, I. E. Gayden, David J. Bloom, Thos. J. Catchings, Edward Engelhard, Sarah Silverberg, Alford Easterling, John Montgomery, Joshua I. Parker and Charles J. Searles.

****

1824 Wilkinson Co. Miss. Drawer 65 Case #9

Daniel McGahey

vs

James F. Straughan

Litigation involving property of the heirs of Jonathan Ragan, late of Lawrence Co. Miss. and Wilson Nash, Admr. Estate of Jonathan Ragan, Dec'd.

****

1824 Hancock Co. Miss. Drawer 65 Case #10

Mary Colbert, nee Mary Oats of Hancock Co.

vs

Richmond Colbert of Covington Co.

Married November 27, 1814. Divorce Decree granted 1827.

****

1815 Adams Co. Miss. Territory Drawer 65 Case #10-a

Jeremiah Hunt and David Hunt, Execs. Est. Abjah Hunt, Dec'd.

vs

Robert Williams and wife, Elizabeth Williams.

****

1824 Lawrence Co. Miss. Drawer 65 Case #11

Francis Blair and Samuel Jayne, Gdns.; S. C. Williams

vs

Matthew Hubbert

****

1829 Lawrence Co. Miss. Drawer 65 Case #11-a

Stephen Williams

vs

Elizabeth Williams, nee Elizabeth Griffeth of Covington Co.

Divorce Petition. Marriage date: July 14, 1826 in Simpson Co.

****

1813 Co. of origin not given. Miss. Tr. Drawer 65 Case #12

Catherine Plowden, by next friend, Margaret Williams

vs

Banister Plowden

Divorce Petition. Married "about 1811" Decree October 1813.

****

1818 Adams Co. Miss. Drawer 65 Case #13

Thomas Dunbar

vs

Nancy Dunbar

Divorce Petition. Dates not shown.

****

1831 Pike Co. Miss. Drawer 65 Case #13-a

Gilbert Keen and wife, Elender Keen

vs

James Y. McNable, Guardian for: Nehemiah Williams, Nancy Williams, Floyd Williams, William Williams, all minor heirs of Reuben and Floyd Williams, Dec'd. See Will.

****

1824 Mobile Co. Miss. Drawer 65 Case #13-b

Benjamin McGaha

vs

Lavinia McGaha, nee Baxter of Jackson Co. Miss. Married April 15, 1819. Divorce Decree 1825.

****

1813 Adams Co. Miss. Territory Drawer 65 Case #14

Lydia A. Young

vs

Samuel C. Young

Divorce Petition.

Married in City of Natchez 1808. Divorce Decree April 1814.

****

1803 Adams Co. Miss. Territory Drawer 65 Case #14-a

Ebenezer Rees

vs

Ferdinand L. Claiborne, Exec. Est. Patrick Conely, Dec'd.

****

1813 Adams Co. Miss. Territory Drawer 65 Case #14-b

Stephen Minor, Admr. Est. Peter Walker, Dec'd.

vs

William T. Voss and Richard Coleman. Heirs of Peter Walker, Dec'd. not named.

****

1829 Warren Co. Miss. Drawer 65 Case #14-c

Gabriel Burnham

vs

Stephen Lewis, Admr. Est. Jonathan Powell, Dec'd. Heirs of Jonathan Powell: Mark Powell, Mary Nickerson, Nathan Green and William Aaron all of Kent Co. Delaware.

****

1825 Marion Co. Miss. Drawer 65 Case #15

Catherine Grantham of Jackson Co., By Wm. Leaman, Next Friend

vs

Ignatius Grantham

Divorce Petition. Marriage date: October 4, 1810.

****

1812 Co. not given. Miss. Territory Drawer 65 Case #15-a

Parthenia Judkins

vs

John Judkins

Married in State of Kentucky 1806. Div. Petition dismissed Oct. 1814.

****

1818 Claiborne Co. Miss. Drawer 65 Case #16

John Gibson

vs

William R. Chambliss, Admr. Est. Robt Trimble, Dec'd. late of Jefferson Co. Mississippi.

****

1820 Amite Co. Miss. Drawer 65 Case #18

James Duke

vs

Heirs of Jacob Curry, Dec'd.

Elizabeth Duke, nee Ragland, married Adam Duke (father of James) and later married Jacob Curry.

Heirs of Jacob Curry: Edmond Andrews and wife, Lucy; Thos. Bickham and wife, Polly; Abner O'Neal and wife, Betsy.

****

1815 Adams Co. Miss. Territory Drawer 65 Case #18-b

Henry Turner, Admr. Est. Daniel Clarke, Dec'd.

vs

Henry Hunt.

Bondsman: Jeremiah Hunt. Clarke heirs not named.

****

1832 Copiah Co. Miss. Drawer 65 Case #20

Henry Lewis of Copiah Co.

vs

Elizabeth Lewis, nee Moffitt of Madison Co.
Marriage date: Nov. 16, 1826.

****

1812 Adams Co. Miss. Territory Drawer 65 Case #21

Jacob Surget, Admr. Est. Catherine Surget, Dec'd.

vs

Francis Surget

****

1835 Co. not shown. Drawer 65 Case #22

Joseph Johnson and Daniel Williams

vs

Heirs of Daniel B. Pinson: David, Elizabeth and Nancy Pinson.

****

1813 Adams Co. Miss. Territory Drawer 66 Case #23

Catherine Townsend

vs

George Townsend

Divorce Petition. Marriage date: July 18, 1811. Decree April 27, 1814.

****

1827 Claiborne Co. Miss. Drawer 66 Case #23-a

Sarah Roads (Rhodes)

vs

Thomas Roads (Rhodes)

Divorce Petition. Marriage date: Jan. 1, 1808. Decree Dec. 5, 1828.

Bill recites there were five children, but were not named in bill.

****

1828 Adams Co. Miss. Drawer 66 Case #23-b

John Hopkins, Admr. Est. Colin Nutt, Dec'd.

vs

John Ker, Admr. Est. David Ker and Rush Nutt.

Rush Nutt was son of Richard Nutt of State of Virginia.

****

1830 Adams Co. Miss. Drawer 66 Case #23-c

Joseph E. Davis

vs

William B. Minor and Elizabeth Minor, Exec. and Exex. Est. Benj. M. Bullen.

****

1815 Franklin Co. Miss. Tr. Drawer 66 Case #24

Catharine Jones

vs

John J. Jones

Divorce Petition. Marriage date not given. Summons for trial May 1815.

****

1824 Adams Co. Miss. Drawer 66 Case #24-a

John Lombard, Admr. Est. Alexander Murray, Dec'd

vs

J. H. McCarn

Named as Commissioners: Nathaniel Perkins, William R. Richards, Joseph B. Lyons.

****

1817 Co. not shown. Drawer 66 Case #24-b

John Erwin

vs

Sarah Erwin, nee Sarah Slocum

Marriage date not given. Decree May 1821.

****

1820 Adams Co. Miss. Drawer 66 Case #25

Re: Winthrop Sargent's Estate. File contains numerous letters, accounts, etc., pertaining to his estate. No will in file.

****

1835 Co. not shown. Drawer 66 Case #25-b

Jefferson Nailer and Daniel N. Nailer

vs

Daniel Patterson, Mary Claiborne nee Patterson, Samuel Coburn, guardian for James and William Patterson.

****

1834 Pike Co. Miss. Drawer 66 Case #26

James C. Dickson

vs

David Dickson, Gdn. for his minor children: Thomas, Martha, Julia, David, Zebulon, Rankin and Mary Dickson. File also shows Elizabeth Hamilton as Admx. Est. Thomas Hamilton, Dec'd.

****

1822 Adams Co. Miss. Drawer 66 Case #26-c

John Richard, Admr. Est. Philip A. Engle, Dec'd

vs

Francis Gunnell and James Dunlap, Admrs. Estate James Kemp, Dec'd.

****

1828 Yazoo Co. Miss. Drawer 66 Case #29

George Hairston, Admr. Est. Henry Hairston, Dec'd

vs

Roderick Gary and Richard H. Weaver

Sureties: Alexander G. McNutt, William L. Anick.

****

1831 Wilkinson Co. Miss. Drawer 66 Case #30

Peterson G. Parham, Admr. Est. George H. Gordon, Dec'd

vs

Cotisworth P. Smith, Admr. Est. Prestwood Smith, Dec'd and Cotisworth P. Smith, Admr. Est. Thomas Kelsy, Dec'd.

****

1809 Wilkinson Co. Miss. Tr. Drawer 66 Case #31

Frederick Kimball, Exec. Est. Thomas Viles

File contains sundry papers of Est. of Thomas Viles including affidavits of: Dr. J. F. Carmichael, James Steel, Isaac Brumfield, William Blackwell, Zachaes Shaw, Samuel Davis.

Appraisers of Estate of Thos. Viles: Richard Davidson, Moses Hooke and Clarence Mulford.

****

1824 Jefferson Co. Miss. Drawer 66 Case #32

Thomas Hinds, William Green and Filmer Green, Execs. Est. Thomas M. Green, Dec'd

vs

Archibald Kirkland, Admr. Est. Chas. B. Howell, Dec'd and his widow, Pricilla Howell.

****

1839 Warren Co. Miss. Drawer 66 Case #32-c

Peter L. Burgett, Admr. Est. John Berry

vs

Peter Scrimshaw

****

1815 Adams Co. Miss. Tr. Drawer 66 Case #34

Jordon Johnson and William Hunt, Admr. Est. Henry Hunt, Dec'd

vs

Mary Brunner and Lydia M. Brunner

****

1808 Claiborne Co. Miss. Tr. Drawer 66 Gase #34-a

Ann Brashears

vs

Thos. Calvitt, Benj. Belk, William Brocus, Jr., Stephen B. Minor, William B. Minor and John Brocus

****

1829 Hinds Co. Miss. Drawer 66 Case #34-b

Stephen Duncan

vs

John Turnbull, Admr. Est. William Carson

****

1821 Franklin Co. Miss. Drawer 66 Case #35

Simon Simons for Abraham Luny

vs

Fannie Worland, Admx. Est. Levi Kendrick, Dec'd

File shows late Levi Kendrick had been Admr. Est. Wm. Pool, Dec'd.

****

1821 Rankin Co. Miss. Drawer 66 Case #35-a

Samuel M. Puckett, John W. King and D. W. Wright

vs

F. H. and L. W. Petrie, Executors (Estate not named).

****

1803 Jefferson Co. Miss. Tr. Drawer 66 Case #35-b

Willis Bonner (brother of Moses Bonner)

vs

Eliza Bonner (widow), William, Henry, Thos., and David Bonner, all heirs of Moses Bonner, Dec'd.

****

1828 Yazoo Co. Miss. Drawer 66 Case #37

Dr. John M. McMurrough

vs

Elizabeth McMurrough, formerly Elizabeth Carson, widow of Geo. Carson, Dec'd.

Divorce Petition. Marriage date: 1819 in State of Virginia. There were two children, but not named in bill.

****

1818 Adams Co. Miss. Drawer 66 Case #38

Sally Hardesty, heir at law, and John Anchord and wife, Cassandra, late wife of Thomas Hardesty, Admx. Est. Thomas Hardesty, Dec'd.

vs

William Thompson

****

1820 Co. not shown. Drawer 66 Case #38-a

William Parker

vs

Walter Irvin, Exec. Est. James McGravy, Dec'd.

****

1819 Adams Co. Miss. Drawer 66 Case #39

Elizabeth Littlepage

vs

John Littlepage

Divorce Petition. Marriage date not shown. Decree June 2, 1820.

****

1828 Jefferson Co. Miss. Drawer 66 Case #39

Halsey Townsend and wife, Ann Chambers Townsend

vs

Moses Odom, Admr. Est. John Chambers, Sr. Dec'd.

John Chambers, Sr. died May 1817. His heirs: Isaac Chambers, Elizabeth Odom (late wife of Moses Odom), John Chambers, Jr., Sebra Odom (widow of Moses Odom), Joseph Chambers and Mary Chambers.

****

1822 Adams Co. Miss. Drawer 66 Case #41

Robert S. Throckmorton and John S. Buck, Admrs. Est. James Ashley, Dec'd.

vs

Richard Terrele and William Stanton

****

1831 Wilkinson Co. Miss. Drawer 66 Case #46

Samuel Pilcher, Admr. Est. James Dickson, Dec'd.

vs

Fielding Davis

****

1817 Franklin Co. Miss. Drawer 66 Case #46-a

Joseph Forman and Henry Hunt, surviving partners of Wm. Gordon Forman, Dec'd.

vs

Joseph Montgomery

File contains separate answer of Elijah Smith, Admr. Estate of John Forman and William Gordon Forman, both dec'd.

****

1847 Franklin Co. Miss. Drawer 66 Case #47

Alfred King, Admr. Est. of Margaret Kimball, Dec'd, late wife of Timothy Kimball

vs

Timothy Kimball

Margaret Kimball was Margaret Ragan of Franklin Co. prior to her marriage to Timothy Kimball. Litigation involves marriage contract. Marriage date: 1828.

****

1819 Wilkinson Co. Miss. Drawer 66 Case #50

Frederick Cable, Abner Pipes and wife, Delilah, John Obrian and wife, Susan, James Watson and wife, Anna, devisees of Jacob Cable, Sr., Dec'd, and Abner Pipes, Exec. Estate Jacob Cable, Dec'd.

vs

Lewis Cable.

See Will.

****

1823 Amite Co. Miss. Drawer 66 Case #51

Sam W. Forman

vs

Estate of William R. Holmes

The Admr. of Est. of Holmes is referred to, but not named. File shows Elijah Smith as Admr. Est. Joseph Forman, Dec'd.

****

1819 Adams Co. Miss. Drawer 66 Case #55

Josiah Martin

vs

Walter Irvin, Admr. Estate Matthew Watson, Dec'd

****

1824 Adams Co. Miss. Drawer 66 Case #55-d

Edmund Shackelford

vs

Joseph E. Davis, Admr. Est. Lydia Tierman, Dec'd and B. C. Linsdale.

****

1815 Adams Co. Miss. Tr. Drawer 66 . Case #56

Roswell Valentine

vs

Polly Valentine of Jefferson Co.
Divorce Petition. Decree October 20, 1815.

****

1832 Wilkinson Co. Miss. Drawer 66 Case #57

Caleb Howell for use of William Stamps

vs

Dick H. Eggleston, Admr. Est. Horatio A. Gildart, Dec'd. Heirs: John W. Gildart, Robert S. Gildart, Sophia Gildart (widow), Sophia Gildart, Jr., Horatio N. Gildart.

****

1819 Adams Co. Miss. Drawer 66 Case #58

Elizabeth Roach, nee Elizabeth Greenfield

vs

Benjamin Roach

Divorce Petition. Marriage date: Feb. 1811. File also contains the marriage contract between Richard Roach and Martha McCausland of Wilkinson Co. and estate papers of

Martha McCausland Roach showing L. Gartley as only heir at law and Joseph Johnson, Admr.

****

1812 Adams Co. Miss. Tr. Drawer 66 Case #58-b

Phoebe Buford

vs

Henry Buford, late of State of Tennessee
Marriage date: 1808.

****

1834 Wilkinson Co. Miss. Drawer 67 Case #64

Cornelius Van Houston

vs

John Y. Reiley and Harry Cage, Admrs. Est. Samuel Reiley, Dec'd.
Heirs of Samuel Reiley not named.

****

1829 Claiborne Co. Miss. Drawer 67 Case #65

Charlotte Hail, lately widow of Archibald Evens

vs

Nathan Hail

Marriage date: May 1816. Decree Dec. 1829.

****

1829 Hinds Co. Miss. Drawer 67 Case #66

James Trahern

vs

William Trahern, Admr. Est. Wesley Trahern, Dec'd.

William, Wesley and James Trahern were brothers and were late of State of Virginia. Heirs not named.

****

1829 Warren Co. Miss. Drawer 67 Case #67

Edwin G. Cook, James W. Cook, Henry Felix Cook and Frances Ann Cook, heirs of Foster Cook, Dec'd and the following creditors: James Bland and wife Martha (lately wife of Foster Cook), R. M. McGinty, James Lambkin, B. H. Cook, D. H. Sills, James Woodbern, Joseph Hough, S. W. Oakley, Thos. B. Matthews, Evans Rogers, Samuel B. Slocumb, George W. Rogers and W. E. Rogers.

vs

William R. Ray, Admr. Est. Foster Cook, Dec'd.

****

1829 Monroe Co. Miss. Drawer 67 Case #69

Martin Sims, James Sims, Matthew Sims, Mary Sims and Geo. Sims, heirs of Parish Sims, Dec'd.

vs

Stephen Cocke and Benjamin Morrell.

****

1837 Adams Co. Miss. Drawer 67 Case 69-a

J. T. Griffeth and wife

vs

Charlotte C. Minor, Execx Est. Stephen Minor, Dec'd

File shows Mrs. Griffeth (not named) to be heir of Peter Walker and sole heir of her mother, Mrs. Ann B. Broughton.

****

1814 Adams Co. Miss. Tr. Drawer 67 Case #70

Edmund Andrews

vs

James and Patsy Curtiss, Admrs. Est. Richard Curtiss

Bondsman: Edmund, Even, Rees and George Andrews.

****

1836 Claiborne Co. Miss. Drawer 67 Case #72

Rebecca Cogan, Admx. Est. Thos. W. Cogan

vs

Eli Montgomery and Orange Clark

****

1831 Yazoo Co. Miss. Drawer 67 Case #72-a

Geo. W. Adams, Daniel W. Wright, Hiram G. Runnels, and .... Caldwell, survivors of Benjamin Johnson

vs

Richard Sparks, Nathan Hooker and Aaron B. Davis

****

1818 Adams Co. Miss. Drawer 67 Case #73

James Kempe

vs

John Richards, Admr. Est. Philip A. Engle, Dec'd.

****

1829 Rankin Co. Miss. Drawer 67 Case #73-b

Hannah Watson

vs

Harrison Watson

Married: Nov. 21, 1803 in Horey Dist. S. C. Children of Hannah and Harrison Watson: Coartney, Elizabeth, Appy Rosannah, Marguerite, Elijah, Sarah and James Watson. This litigation involves a deed of gift from Elizabeth Garroll of South Carolina to Hannah Watson.

****

1806 Jefferson Co. Miss. Tr. Drawer 67 Case #73-c

Wilson Hunt

vs

William, Timothy, James and Martha Murray, heirs of William Murray, Dec'd.

****

1839 Wilkinson Co. Miss. Drawer 67 Case #75

Daniel Woodward

vs

Hugh Connell, Admr. Est. William Connell, Dec'd.

****

1830 Hinds Co. Miss. Drawer 67 Case #75-a

William Ricks

vs

Martha Ricks

Witnesses: Sam M. Puckett, Hiram Coffee, William Dean. Decree Dec. 7, 1830.

****

1818 Adams Co. Miss. Drawer 67 Case #76

David Howard

vs

Elizabeth McClain, Admrx. Est. Charles McClain, Dec'd.

Before the case was concluded Elizabeth McClain married Nathaniel Wiltshire.

****

1831 Adams Co. Miss. Drawer 67 Case #76-a

R. M. Gaines, Admr. Est. John Richards, Dec'd

vs

William C. Conner

****

1834 Amite Co. Miss. Drawer 67 Case #77

Joel Tolar and Lewis Jackson, Admrs. de bonis non Est. John Rembert

vs

Samuel Tillson, William Stewart, Thos. McDonald, Sampson Batters and Soloman Weathersby.

Children of first marriage of John Rembert, Dec'd: James, Zachaes, John, Andrew, Judy and Charlotte. Of second marriage: (children of his wife, Sarah ....) Timothy, Tyre, Sarah (wife of Wm. Covington), Nancy (wife of Thomas Finlow), and Gadston Rembert.

****

1839 Covington Co. Miss. Drawer 67 Case #77-a

William M. C. Minning, Guardian for John C. Tuttle, Rebecca Ann Tuttle, Pinkney Tuttle, Daniel W. Jordan and wife, Emily Jordan (late widow of John Tuttle, Sr., Dec'd)

vs

Elam S. Ragan, Admr. Est. John Tuttle, Sr., Dec'd.

****

1816 Adams Co. Miss. Tr. Drawer 67 Case #79

William Brooks

vs

Edward Turner, Admr. Est. A. Moorehouse.

****

1820 Adams Co. Miss. Drawer 67 Case #80

Anne Weeks, Admx. Est. Levi Weeks, Dec'd

vs

Grove B. West and Elisha Brown

Heirs of Levi Weeks: Thomas Greenleaf Weeks, Sarah Katherine Weeks, Levi Hinkley Weeks.

****

1822 Wilkinson Co. Miss. Drawer 67 Case #80-a

Jesse H. Cartright

vs

Josiah F. Williams, Exec. Est. John Branch, Dec'd.

****

1834 Hinds Co. Miss. Drawer 67 Case #80-b

Caroline M. Mellon, Admx. and Isaac Caldwell, Admr. Est. Wm. Mellon

vs

John P. Gilbert, Admr. and Eliza Breckenridge, Admx. Est. Merideth S. Breckenridge, Dec'd.

****

1832 Madison Co. Miss. Drawer 67 Case #81

William Doake, Judge of Probate for use of Roderick B. Gary and Richard H. Weaver

vs

George Hairston, Sr. Admr. Est. Henry Hairston, Dec'd and William Gadberry and David W. Major.

****

1829 Monroe Co. Miss. Drawer 67 Case #83

Mary Cravens, alias Mary Sellers by next friend, D. W. Wright

vs

William Sellers

Divorce Petition. Decree granted June 3, 1829.

****

1830 Hinds Co. Miss. Drawer 67 Case #85

William White

vs

Elizabeth White

Divorce Petition. Marriage date: Feb. 1821 in Claiborne Co. Miss. Def't removed to State of Tennessee. Decree 1834.

****

1818 Adams Co. Miss. Drawer 67 Case #86

Jane E. Richardson

vs

Moses Richardson

Divorce Petition. Married: 1813 in Town of Washington, Miss. Decree: June 1820. Def't removed to City of New Orleans, La.

****

1830 Adams Co. Miss. Drawer 66 Case #87

Winston Gilmore, next friend for John and William Brooks, infants of William Brooks, Dec'd

vs

Samuel W. Lewis

Wm. Brooks, Sr. died 1822 in Wilkinson Co. Miss. His widow, Nancy, and Buford Brooks administered his estate. Nancy Brooks married Nazra Pool in 1823 or 1824.

****

1831 Wilkinson Co. Miss. Drawer 67 Case #87-a

A. B. Bradford, Admr. Est. Jacob Holmes, Dec'd

vs

Asher P. Slocumb, Admr. Est. Charles Slocumb, Dec'd.

****

1832 Hinds Co. Miss. Drawer 67 Case #88

Alfred C. Downs

vs

James R. Enloe, Admr. with Will attached of Philip Alston, Dec'd

Bill recites that Ziliah Ann Alston, wife of Philip, predeceased him. Litigation involving estate of Sally Downs, aunt of Alfred Downs and sister of Ziliah Ann Alston.

****

1827 Adams Co. Miss. Drawer 67 Case #89

James Moore

vs

Walter Irvin, Admr. Est. Matthew Watson, Dec'd.

****

1823 Franklin Co. Miss. Drawer 67 Case #92

Micajah Pickett, Admr. Est. James Knox, Dec'd

vs

Bartlett Ford, Exec. Est. Nathan King.
Heirs not named.

****

1832 Hinds Co. Miss. Drawer 67 Case #93

Michael King, James McKethan and wife, Flora Ann, George Thomas King, Nathan King, Jr., Henry R. King and Julia C. King, heirs of Nathan King, Sr.

vs

William Matthews, Admr. Est. Geo. McGuffie, Dec'd and William King, Peter Watkins and wife, Catherine, Margaret Buie, Unknown heirs of Archibald McGuffie residing in North Carolina, Archibald L., William, and Thos. Matthews, Mary Jane Puckett and husband, Samuel Puckett and the heirs of Nancy Torry.

****

1822 Franklin Co. Miss. Drawer 67 Case #94

John G. McConnell

vs

Agnes S. McConnell, nee Agnes S. Gibson of South Carolina
Married: 1809. Decree: 1823.

****

1828 Amite Co. Miss. Drawer 67 Case #95

John McNeill and John Rutherford, Jr. Admrs. Est. William Rutherford, Dec'd

vs

Henry Cassells, Agrippa Gayden, David Lea, Richard Hurst, Charles Davis, James Jones, John Burton, John Lowry, William Stewart, and John Burton, Admr. Est. Joseph King, successor to Wm. King, Admr.

****

1817 Adams Co. Miss. Drawer 67 Case #95-a

H. Turner, Admr. Est. D. Clark, Dec'd.

vs

Ann Eliza Claiborne, John F. H., Ferdinand L., Osman, Samuel H. and Charlotte Claiborne, heirs of Ferdinand L. Claiborne, Dec'd.

****

1799 Jefferson Co. Miss. Tr. Drawer 67 Case #96

William Collins, Jr. and James Collins by next friend, Wm. Collins, Jr., his guardian, and Martha A. Collins all heirs of Joshua Collins, Dec'd.

vs

William Collins, Sr. Exec. Est. Joshua Collins, Dec'd. and John McCaleb, Joseph Pipes and wife, Mary, and her children: Mary, James and Eliza Owens, heirs of __________ Owens, Dec'd.

****

1816 Adams Co. Miss. Tr. Drawer 67 Case #97

Executors of Estate of Alexander Murray, Dec'd.

vs

Thomas A. Claiborne.

Witness: Thomas H. Williams.

****

1807 Adams Co. Miss. Tr. Drawer 67 Case #99

Peter Vourdom and William Vourdom, sons of Samuel Vourdom, Dec'd. (Brother of William Vourdom), William Ward and wife, Ann, nee Vourdom, James Potter and wife, Elizabeth, nee Vourdom, Bartholomew Vourdom, Mark Vourdom, Hugh Kerry and wife, Elizabeth, nee Vourdom, Elizabeth Garry (sister of William Vourdom) all heirs of William Vourdom, Dec'd.

vs

William Brooks and wife, Elizabeth, and George Fitzgerald.

Suit to break will of William Vourdom, Dec'd. Peter, William, Ann, children of Samuel; Eleanor Kerry sister of William, Dec'd.

****

1818 Adams Co. Miss. Drawer 67 Case #100

Elijah Smith and David Hunt, Execs. Est. Abjah Hunt, Dec'd.

vs

Eliza R. Winn (widow) Nicholas C. Hall and wife, Caroline, Charles Winn and Minter Winn, children and heirs of Thos. W. Winn, Dec'd

****

1832 Pike Co. Miss. Drawer 67 Case #100-a

Susanna Newman

vs

Thomas Newman

Married: 1814, Decree 1833. Def't departed for State of Alabama.

****

-------- Yazoo Co. Miss. Drawer 67 Case #100-c

Elizabeth L. Barton, Admx. and widow of James L. Barton, Dec'd.

vs

George W. Parker

****

1821 Adams Co. Miss. Drawer 67 Case #101

Samuel Davis, Exec. Est. William Hill, Dec'd, late of New Orleans

vs

Eliza C. Wood and Eliza Wood, heirs of David Wood, Dec'd.

****

1829 Hinds Co. Miss. Drawer 67 Case #102

Nancy Bankston, by next friend, William Toney

vs

Thomas J. Bankston

Divorce Petition.
Married: January 1829—Decree: July 30, 1830.

****

1829 Marion Co. Miss. Drawer 68 Case #106

Samuel Spencer and wife, Arazamon, Richard Spencer and wife, Elizabeth

vs

James Garraway and wife Mary (late widow of Geo. Edrington formerly of State of South Carolina).

Arazamon and Elizabeth Spencer were sisters and the children of John Mansfield, Dec'd, of S. C. and of Elizabeth Mansfield, nee Griffin. After the death of John Mansfield, Elizabeth, his widow, married Geo. Edrington. The Edringtons moved from S. C. to Kentucky where Elizabeth died and subsequently daughter, Mary, married her stepfather, Geo. Edrington. Litigation involves estate of John Mansfield. Children of John and Elizabeth Mansfield: James, Arazamon G., Nancy, John and Elizabeth.

****

1831 Adams Co. Miss. Drawer 68 Case #107

Jacob Hackler

vs

Rhoda Hackler, alias Rhoda England, late wife of Wm. England of Jefferson Co.

Married: Oct. 5, 1820. Decree 1834

****

1833 Franklin Co. Miss. Drawer 68 Case #107-a

William Whitehead and wife Lydia (late wife of Stephen Cade) Admr. and Admx. Est. Stephen Cade, Dec'd.

vs

John Cade and John Baker

****

1824 Adams Co. Miss. Drawer 68 Case #108

Nancy Timberlake, Admx. Est. Samuel Timberlake, Dec'd.

vs

Thos. Ragan

****

1831 Franklin Co. Miss. Drawer 68 Case #108-a

James M. Owens, Jr., Gdn. for Benj. Franklin Owens (infant of Stephen Owens, Sr., Dec'd).

vs

Henry Owen, William O. Freeman and James M. Owen.

****

1809 Adams Co. Miss. Tr. Drawer 68 Case #109-a

Chas. Norwood, James Martin and Geo. Fezgurato, Exec. Est. William Stephens, Dec'd.

vs

James Erwin

****

1806 Adams Co. Miss. Tr. Drawer 68 Case #110

William Williams

vs

.... Kirk (Brother of James Kirk of the Kingdom of Ireland), Geo. Barnes of S. C., Mrs. .... Anderson (Sister) of Liverpool, Eng., and an unnamed sister of Geo. Barnes—all heirs of James Kirk.
Material witnesses: Abraham Ellis, Richard King.

****

1834 Hinds Co. Miss. Drawer 68 Case #111

Isaac Caldwell, Admr. Est. Samuel Ammen, Dec'd

vs

Thos. Woodridge, Admr. Est. Charles Anderson, Dec'd and Moses Hall.

****

1820 Adams Co. Miss. Drawer 68 Case #113

Elizabeth Morris

vs

Benjamin Morris

Divorce Petition.
Married: Jan. 15, 1817. Def't not found for service.

****

1830 Hinds Co. Miss. Drawer 68 Case 113-a

Elizabeth Hazlerigg, widow of Fielding Hazlerigg, Dec'd., Wm. Arthur, Amanda, and Ann Hazlerigg (children) and Moses Fay, Admr. Est. Fielding Hazlerigg, Dec'd. all of Fayette Co. Indiana

vs

Robert Y. Baucum and Bennett M. Hines

****

1817 Adams Co. Miss. Drawer 68 Case #113-b

William Engel

vs

Stephen Minor, Admr. Est. Joseph Suboys, Dec'd.

Heirs not named. Called as witnesses: Samuel Brooks, Joseph Newman, Wm. H. Beaumond, Esq., Michael Engel, Frances Rosset, Philip Engel, Jr., Peter Nordon, Lizette Robitaille, Manuel Texada, Francois Dallier, Judith Dallier, Matthew Tordiff, Frances Tordiff, Rosalie Emery.

****

1817 Adams Co. Miss. Drawer 68 Case #113-c

James C. Wilkins (son of John, Sr.)

vs

Mary Wilkins Murray and husband, Mangus M. Murray, Nancy Wilkins Butler and husband, James R. Butler, John Jr., George S., Henry, Robert, Jane and Catherine Wilkins, heirs of John Wilkins, Sr., Dec'd.

****

1877 Co. not shown. Drawer 68 Case #113-d

Geo. W. Faison, Admr. Est. S. A. C. Sapp

vs

C. H. Bell and Frank Johnson

****

1830 Madison Co. Miss. Drawer 68 Case #114

Newton L. Haxall

vs

John H. Cole and James Cobb, Exec. Est. Walter R. Johnson, Dec'd.

Litigation involves inheritance of Juliana Copeland of State of Virginia of Estate of Walter R. Johnson, Dec'd. See Wills.

****

1830 Rankin Co. Miss. Drawer 68 Case #116

Lenny Davis, widow of William Davis

vs

Nehemiah Magee, Admr. Est. William Davis, Dec'd.

****

1808 Adams Co. Miss. Tr. Drawer 68 Case #118

Francis Urrust

vs

Meange B. Urrest, nee Bruett
Divorce Petition.

****

1831 Hinds Co. Miss. Drawer 68 Case #119

James Ray

vs

Louisa Ray, nee Jelks, daughter of Dixon Jelks of Lawrence Co. Miss.
Divorce Petition.
Married: "about 1829"

****

1832 Washington Co. Miss. Drawer 68 Case #120

William Prince and wife Elizabeth of Washington Co. Miss., Joseph Macquillan and wife, Cynthia of Carroll Parish, La. and Joseph Macquillan, Gdn. for Mary and Eliza Ann Pennington

vs

Sally S. Prince, Admr. Est. William B. Prince, Dec'd

****

1835 Franklin Co. Miss. Drawer 68 Case #126

Thos. K. Pickett, Admr. de bonis non Est. Charles Pickett, Dec'd

vs

Rufus H. Pickett and William Pickett, Admrs. Est. William Pickett, Dec'd.

****

1805 Adams Co. Miss. Tr. Drawer 68 Case #127

Samuel Neill

vs

Peter A. Van Dorn

Litigation involving Spanish land grant to Richard Bell and later owned by Robert and Mordicai Throckmorton.

****

1816 Warren Co. Miss. Tr. Drawer 68 Case #129

Alexander McLeod, Harriet McLeod and Sarah McLeod, heirs of Martha Booker, by their Gdn. Murdock McLeod

vs

William Booker, Admr. Est Alexander Booker, Dec'd.

****

1816 Warren Co. Miss. Tr. Drawer 68 Case #129-a

Alexander, Harriet and Sarah McLeod, heirs of Martha McLeod, Dec'd, by Murdock McLeod, Gdn.

vs

William Brooks, Admr. Est. James Brooks, Dec'd

****

1839 Co. not shown. Drawer 68 Case #131

Charlotte Fisher, wife of Enoch Fisher, late Charlotte Stroud, Admr. Est. Holstein A. Stroud, Dec'd

vs

John Hampton for use of George W. Hampton

****

1808 Adams Co. Miss. Tr. Drawer 68 Case #132

David Ferguson and John Rabb

vs

Ferdinand L. Claiborne, Exec. and Pricilla Conely, widow of Patrick Conely, Dec'd.

****

1821 Franklin Co. Miss. Drawer 68 Case #132-a

Eliza King, widow of Nathan King

vs

Bartlett Ford, Exec. Est. Nathan King, Dec'd.

****

1823 Jackson Co. Miss. Drawer 68 Case #134

Stephen Gilmore

vs

Amy Gilmore, nee Amy Pearson

Divorce Petition.
Married: May 26, 1818 in Raleigh, N. C. Moved to Georgia and thence to Miss.

****

1808 Adams Co. Miss. Tr. Drawer 68 Case #134-a

Anthony Cavalier and Peter Pettit

vs

Sally, Polly and Margaret Tyler, Catherine Junkin, widow of Thomas Tyler, now wife of William Junkin.

****

1831 Jefferson Co. Miss. Drawer 68 Case #134-c

Mary N. Torry of Jefferson Co.

vs

David A. Torry

Divorce Petition.
Married: Dec. 11, 1830. Decree for dismissal 1834.

****

1835 Adams Co. Miss. Drawer 68 Case #134-d

Adam Bower, Admr. Est. Arthur Mahon, Dec'd

vs

Catherine Mahon, widow of Arthur Mahon, Dec'd.

****

1836 Wilkinson Co. Miss. Drawer 69 Case #139

Thomas H. Prisser

vs

David Leatherman, Admr. de bonis Est. Ephraim Fleshman, Dec'd for use of Jesse H. Hutchins.

****

1814 Adams Co. Miss. Tr. Drawer 69 Case #142

William Turner

vs

William Henry, Admr. Est. Robert Henry, Dec'd

Bondsmen: James Foster and Matthew Thomas. Heirs not named.

****

1831 Claiborne Co. Miss. Drawer 69 Case #143

Marsham F. Brashears

vs

Elizabeth Lee, John S. Gooch and wife Martha, David Lee, William Lindsey, Margaret Lindsey and Benjamin Lindsey, heirs of Gabriel Brashears, Dec'd.

****

1830 Claiborne Co. Miss. Drawer 69 Case #146

Joseph Harman, Admr. Est. James Harman, Jr. Dec'd and Nathan White

vs

William Murphree

****

1835 Lowndes Co. Miss. Drawer 69 Case #150-a

Moses Ayres

vs

Aureleus N. Jones, Admr. and Elizabeth Hendrick, Admx. Est. Gustavus Hendrick, Dec'd.

****

1837 Adams Co. Miss. Drawer 69 Case #152

David Phillips

vs

Nancy R. Phillips

Divorce Petition.
Married: Feb. 16, 1827. Decree Jan. 1837.

****

1839 Madison Co. Miss. Drawer 69 Case #152-c

Thomas Bowden and Nathan Tims, Admrs. Est. Simon Bowden, Dec'd

vs

John, Henry and David Shrock

****

1824 Marion Co. Miss. Drawer 69 Case #154

Catherine Oliver

vs

Charles B. Oliver

Divorce Petition.
Married: Sept. 1822
Witnesses: Abigail Cooper and Hugh McGowan.

****

1810 Adams Co. Miss. Tr. Drawer 69 Case #154-A

John Taylor Admr. Est. Gabriel Cerre, Dec'd.

vs

Elizabeth Burling (widow of Walter Burling) Catherine Junkin (widow of Thomas Tyler), Thomas, Sally, Polly, and Margaret Tyler, all heirs of Thomas Tyler, Dec'd.

****

1832 Wilkinson Co. Miss. Drawer 69 Case #156

Abram Iler

vs

Martha Ann Iler, Admx. Est. Jonas Iler, Dec'd.

****

1830 Warren Co. Miss. Drawer 69 Case #157

James McCarrel

vs

Frances Harvey, George Franklin and George Moore Admr. Est. Beverly Hughes, Dec'd.
Hughes heirs: John, Susan and Catharine Hughes.

****

1835 Warren Co. Miss. Drawer 69 Case #162

Burwell Vick

vs

Druscilla House, Admx. and Isaac N. Selser, Admr. Est. Archibald Douglass, Dec'd.

****

1831 Washington Co. Miss. Drawer 69 Case #163

Mary B. Shelby

vs

Mira Jane Knox, wife of Andrew Knox and sister of Alexander G. Prince, Dec'd.

Litigation involves estate of Robert Prince, Dec'd, brother of Mary B. Shelby, Comp't.

****

1870 Co. not shown. Drawer 69 Case #166

J. P. Henry, Lavinia Henry, Wm. Ray and John C. McKenzie

vs

J. M. Pearsons, Admr. de bonis non Est. Mrs. M. D. Smith and W. M. Beck, Admr. Est. Joseph Beck, Dec'd.

****

1831 Wilkinson Co. Miss. Drawer 69 Case #168

Daniel Slack, Admr. Est. Isaac Bush, Dec'd

vs

William Hail

****

1832 Amite Co. Miss. Drawer 69 Case #176

Admr. Est. Ambrose McDaniel, Dec'd (Admr. not named)

vs

Mary Gray, Admx. Est. John Gray, Dec'd and Mary Phillips, formerly Mary Watkins.

****

1839 Adams Co. Miss. Drawer 70 Case #183

Martha Tewksberry

vs

Timothy Tewksberry

Divorce Petition.

Martha Tewksberry was the widow of Jacob Newcomber, Dec'd. She married Timothy Tewksberry Oct. 22, 1835 in Natchez, Miss.

Witnesses: Wm. Russell, Dr. D. G. Benbrooke, John H. Newcomber and L. P. Brooks.

****

1829 Hinds Co. Miss. Drawer 70 Case #181

Joseph A. McRaven, Samuel Smith and Jeremiah Powell, Exec. Est. Charles M. Lawson, Dec'd

vs

James C. Dickson, Admr. Est. John McKay

Lawson heirs: Jeremiah Powell and wife, William Irvin and wife, Andrew Gamble and wife, and Hanna McIntyre

****

1810 Adams Co. Miss. Drawer 70 Case #186

Admr. John Andrews, Dec'd (not named)

vs

Charles McElhaney and wife Susannah and Eliza Reagh, heirs of John Reagh, Dec'd.

****

1831 Wayne Co. Miss. Drawer 70 Case #189

Mary Brewer

vs

Harris Mounger, Exec. Est. Ann Mounger, Dec'd

Ann Mounger, widow of Elijah Thompson married Sampson Mounger father of Harris Mounger.

****

1832 Hinds Co. Miss. Drawer 70 Case #189-a

Alfred C. Downs, Thos. D. Downs, Charlotte B. Haynes, Andrew Haynes (husband of Charlotte) Carolyn M. Ferguson and husband, Thos. Ferguson, all heirs of Henry Downs, Dec'd

vs

Zella Ann Alston, Henry D., John, William D. Jamison, Parham O'Neal and wife, Mary D., Francis Griffin and wife (not named), and the unknown heirs of Elizabeth Horton, all heirs of William Downs, Dec'd

****

1834 Wilkinson Co. Miss. Drawer 70 Case #191

Mary Conrad by next friend, Henry Conrad

vs

John Stevens, Admr. Est. David Barron.

Mary Conrad was the wife of Peter Conrad. Barron heirs not named.

****

1839 Holmes Co. Miss. Drawer 70 Case #191-a

William H. Johnson, Admr. Est. Charles Land, Dec'd.

vs

William Eggleston

****

1821 Jefferson Co. Miss.. Drawer 70 Case #191-b

Re: Estate papers John Shaw, Dec'd, Samuel G. Cloud, Admr.

****

1810 Adams Co. Miss.. Tr. Drawer 70 Case #191-c

William Foster, Admr. de bonis non Est. John Foster, Dec'd by Charles B. Green, Attorney

vs

Silas Dinsmore, John Foster and Isaac Morris

John Short, original Admr. died and Wm. Foster appointed in his place.

****

1834 Amite Co. Miss. Drawer 70 Case #192

John D. Brooks by next friend, William Gilmore; William Brooks, Jr. by next friend, W. T. Lewis

vs

Robert Pool, Admr. Est. Nazra Pool, Dec'd

John and William Brooks, Jr. were sons of William Brooks, Dec'd and step sons of Nazra Pool, Dec'd

****

1832 Yazoo Co. Miss. Drawer 70 Case #199

John F. Williams

vs

Thomas Jones, Admr. and Mary Dunton, Admx. Est. William Dunton, Dec'd

****

1848 Wilkinson Co. Miss. Drawer 70 Case #199-a

Justus Hurd and wife, Isabella and Carolyn Buford

vs

Robert Smith, Exec. Est. Samuel H. Buford, Dec'd

****

1826 Jefferson Co. Miss. Drawer 70 Case #199-b

John Tumbrell, Admr. Est. Armstrong Ellis, Dec'd, and James Berthe' and wife, Charlotte M. Berthe' lately widow of Armstrong Ellis, Dec'd

vs

John Hood

****

1816 Adams Co. Miss. Tr. Drawer 70 Case #201

Edmund Andrews and Robert Moore

vs

Samuel Postlethwaite and Love Baker, Execs. Est. Charles McKiernan, Dec'd

Heirs named in will: Emeline and Caroline Stephenson, daughters of Johnathan and Elizabeth Stephenson. Will provides for residue of estate to be used for a hospital for the City of Natchez, Miss. Book A. Register of Wills, Adams Co. Miss. Probated Nov. 13, 1810.

****

1837 Adams Co. Miss. Drawer 70 Case #206

Fountain Winston and David Lawson, Execs. Est. Christopher H. Kyle, Dec'd

vs

John Smith and Eli Montgomery.

****

1836 Yazoo Co. Miss. Drawer 70 Case #209

Elizabeth Castien (Caston)

vs

Samuel Castien (Caston), James W. and Edward Exum. Injunction suit.

Elizabeth and Samuel Castien were married in 1833.

****

1832 Warren Co. Miss. Drawer 70 Case #210

Frances Hyland, Admx. Est. James Hyland; Martha Howland, infant, by father and next friend, William Howland, daughter of Martha Howland, Dec'd, nee Martha Hyland, daughter of James Hyland, Dec'd; Henry Hyland, Minerva Hyland and John Hyland, all minor children of James Hyland, Dec'd

vs

Martha Hyland (widow of Jacob Hyland) Admx., and Claiborne Steel, Admr. Estate of Jacob Hyland, Dec'd.

****

1821 Adams Co. Miss. Drawer 70 Case #212

Anthony Campbell

vs

George Ralston, Admr. Est. James Fitzhugh, Dec'd.

Anthony Campbell married Mary Grafton, widow of Daniel Grafton and litigation involves Est. Daniel Grafton, Dec'd.

****

1831 Hinds Co. Miss. Drawer 70 Case #212-a

Moses Hall

vs

Susan E. Reilly, Admx. Est. James F. Reilly

****

1880 Winston Co. Miss. Drawer 70 Case #216

A. W. Welch

vs

M. A. Coleman, Admr. Est. Wm. C. Coleman, Dec'd

Wm. C. Coleman, father of Emeline Welch was guardian for Alexander Wm. Welch, Sallie, Robert Edward and Elizabeth Welch, minor children of Wm. B. Welch, Dec'd and Emeline Welch.

****

1830 Wilkinson Co. Miss. Drawer 70 Case #219

Martha Spears, Admx. Est. Richard Spears

vs

Admr. Est. Austin Spears

****

1832 Franklin Co. Miss. Drawer 70 Case #219-c

David Thompson

vs

John L. Thompson, Patsy Kell (wife of Thos. Kell), Catherine Slocumb and husband, Asher Slocumb and James Thompson, all children of David Thompson

****

1844 Warren Co. Miss. Drawer 70 Case #219-e

John I. Street of State of Virginia, Assignee of James Fisher and A. Burwell of Warren Co. Miss., Admr. Est. James Fisher, Dec'd

vs

Ambrose Knox, Andrew Knox, John G. Cocks and Thomas Grimes.

****

1836 Jefferson Co. Miss. Drawer 70 Case #221

William Barnes, Admr. Est. George Barnes, Dec'd

vs

William W. Loyd.

****

1834 Adams Co. Miss. Drawer 70 Case #222

John Dixon and wife Eunice (lately widow of Joseph Leonard, Dec'd) and Elizabeth, Joseph, Isreal G. Leonard, children of Jos. Leonard, Dec'd

vs

Margaret Reed, Execx Est. of Thomas P. Reed, Dec'd
See Will.

****

1832 Warren Co. Miss. Drawer 70 Case #223

Washington Ellington

vs

Sally Ellington, nee Sally Matthews

Divorce Petition.

Married: August 19, 1822 in Pendleton Dist. S. Carolina. Def't departed for State of Alabama. Decree December 5, 1832.

****

1836 Wilkinson Co. Miss. Drawer 70 Case #225

Lazarus Drake, Admr. Est. of Wills Drake, Dec'd

vs

George Gorton and wife, Maria Louisa, Clarrisa, Dorcas and Russell Curtis, all heirs of Charles Curtis, Dec'd

Bill recites that Charles Curtis married Polly (Mary) Randolph of Pinkneyville, Miss. in December 1824. Charles Curtis died in Alexandria in 1826.

****

1832 Adams Co. Miss. Drawer 70 Case #228

Martha Watts of Fort Adams, Miss.

vs

Robert Watts

Divorce Petition.
Married: March 13, 1828.

****

1823 Adams Co. Miss. Drawer 70 Case #229

John, Alexander and Thos. Henderson

vs

Charles B. Green, Jr. Admr. de bonis non Est John Hankinson, Dec'd, Frances Hankinson (widow of John), and Henry Fisk.

****

1832 Adams Co. Miss. Drawer 70 Case #230

Levi Foster, David McMillan and wife, Sarah, nee Foster, Nancy Wood, William K. Collins and wife, Mary, nee Foster, Samuel W. Wells and wife, Frances, nee Foster, William Barnard and wife, Barbara, nee Foster, David McIntosh and wife, Caroline, nee Foster, James Foster, Isaac H. Foster, Henry Nelson, Samuel Sojourner and wife, Sarah, nee Nelson, John F. Sapp and wife, Patsy, nee Nelson, Nancy Ligon, Thos. Nelson, Elizabeth Carr, Joseph Carr, Jr, John Carr, Joseph

Sorsby, Elizabeth Sorsby, Louisa Sorsby, Foster Sorsby, Thaddeus Sorsby, heirs of Cassandra Foster who was daughter of Thomas Foster, Sr., Dec'd and sister of Levi Foster, Sarah McMillan, Nancy Wood, Mary Collins, Frances Ann Wells, Bart Barnard, Caroline McIntosh, James Foster, Isaac H. Foster and Ellen Carr, Dec'd

vs

Cassandra Foster, widow of Ephraim Foster

Ephraim Foster died in 1824. His widow, Cassandra, married one John Speed in Feb. 1825. Comp'ts in this case charge that John Speed was a married man at the time of his marriage to Cassandra Foster, making the marriage to Speed void.

****

1832 Wilkinson Co. Miss. Drawer 70 Case #231

Mary A. Wamack

vs

John G. Wamack

Divorce Petition
Married: Sept. 16, 1830 in Wilkinson Co. Miss.

****

1832 Madison Co. Miss. Drawer 70 Case #234

Mary Luster of Madison Co. Miss., Benj ________ and wife, Lucy, Jesse Bailey of State of Virginia, James Daniel and wife, Milly, James Bailey of State of Kentucky.

vs

Mary Bailey, Execx. and Augustine Kearney, Exec. Est. David Bailey, Dec'd
See Will.

****

1822 Franklin Co. Miss. Drawer 71 Case #242

Edmund McGehee

vs

Bartlett Ford, Admr. Est. John Middleton, Jr.

****

1832 Franklin Co. Miss. Drawer 71 Case #245

Thos. K. Pickett

vs

Rufus K. Pickett and William Pickett, Jr. (son) Executors Est. William Pickett, Dec'd
William Pickett died 1826.

****

1832 Yazoo Co. Miss. Drawer 71 Case #246

Isaac Garrard (Girod), Admr. Est. William Garrard (Girod), Dec'd

vs

John D. Swain

William Garrard (Girod) died July 1832.

****

1822 Co. not shown. Drawer 71 Case #249

Susana Penny

vs

William Penny

Divorce Petition.
Bill recites: "Married upward of 20 years".

****

1835 Holmes Co. Miss. Drawer 71 Case #250

James C. Bole, Admr. Est. John Idem, Dec'd

vs

Soloman Wolfe, Joel A. George, Whitson H. George and Davis Isom.

****

1839 Holmes Co. Miss. Drawer 71 Case #250-a

John Lear, Admr. Est. James S. Goodwin, Dec'd.
vs
John Hall, Edward B. Walker and Joseph Watson

****

1832 Madison Co. Miss. Drawer 71 Case #251

James Montgomery, Admr. de bonis non Est. Charles Anderson, Dec'd
vs
Thos. Woolridge, original Admr. Est. Charles Anderson, Dec'd.

****

1833 Claiborne Co. Miss. Drawer 71 Case #258

Daniel G. Humphreys
vs
John Briscoe and wife, Elizabeth, nee Lee, John L. Gooch and wife, Martha, nee Lee, William L. Irish and wife, Catherine, nee Lee, David Lee, William B. Lindsey, Benj. Lindsey, James Lindsey, Eugene A. Thorbourne and wife, Margaret, nee Lindsey, Wm. Bush and wife, Lucinda, alias Elizabeth Brashear, and Elizabeth Maury, all heirs of Marshall F. Brashear and David Lee and Tobias Brashear.

****

1822 Adams Co. Miss. Drawer 71 Case #268

Richard Fletcher, Washington, Miss.
vs
Rachel Boyce, widow and Admx. Est. Daniel Boyce, Dec'd

****

1833 Franklin Co. Miss. Drawer 71 Case #277

John Temple and wife, Elvira (late Elvira Coleman, posthumous child of Richard Coleman, Dec'd)
vs
John McNace

Heirs of Richard Coleman, Dec'd: Nancy Coleman (widow but later wife of John McNace), Richard T. Coleman, Indiana Coleman, Wm. D. Coleman and Elvira Coleman (Temple)

See Will.

****

1829 Marion Co. Miss. Drawer 71 Case #278

Calvin Sumrall and wife, Elizabeth, Purson Powell and wife, Sarah, and Thomas Gibson

vs

William Graham and wife, Nancy (late Nancy Gibson, widow of Stafford Gibson.)

Elizabeth Sumrall, Sarah Powell and Thos. Gibson were children of Stafford and Nancy Gibson (Graham). Stafford Gibson died in North Carolina in 1805 and Nancy Gibson obtained letters of Adm. in Chesterfield Dist. of South Carolina. Nancy Gibson married William Graham in 1809

****

1834 Lawrence Co. Miss. Drawer 71 Case #280

Wilson Cooper, Admr. with will attached, Est. William McIntyre, Dec'd

vs

Joseph Stephenson of Hinds Co., Hanson Alsbury, Elam Regan and Henry J. White all of Covington Co.

****

1834 Madison Co. Miss. Drawer 71 Case #285

Ira E. Hobbs and Benj. W. Macklin

vs

Sterling R. Cockrill, Admr. Est. Washington J. Cockrill, Dec'd

Washington J. Cockrill of Madison Co. Miss. married Mary E. Macklin, dau. Thos. Macklin of Limestone Co.

Ala. in Dec. 1831. Washington J. Cockrill died July 8, 1832, and Mary Macklin Cockrill died July 5, 1832.

****

1832 Claiborne Co. Miss. Drawer 71 Case #288

Simon Gentry

vs

Rhody Gentry, nee Gibson

Divorce Petition.
Married: 1814. Decree: Jan. 9, 1835.

****

1837 Wilkinson Co. Miss. Drawer 71 Case #291

William Butler Hooke, Francis Fitzhugh Hooke, Richard Butler Hooke and Moses Josiah Hooke, heirs of Moses Hooke, Dec'd, and Harriet Hooke, Dec'd

vs

Spencer Wood, Admr. Est. Frederick Avery Browder, Dec'd

Moses Hooke died 1821. His widow, Harriet, married Frederick Avery Browder Sept. 6, 1826. She died July 16, 1830, and Frederick A. Browder died March 1, 1831. Only issue of this marriage: Mary Jane Browder, infant.

****

_____ Hinds Co. Miss. Drawer 71 Case #292

Mary E. McLaughlin by next friend, James Compton

vs

Thos. E. Helm, James Kirkpatrick, Michael McLaughlin (husband of Mary E.) and W. F. Fitzgerald.

Litigation involving "The Mansion House" in City of Jackson, Miss.

****

1833 Lawrence Co. Miss. Drawer 72 Case #292

Thompson V. Berry

vs

Catherine Berry, nee Magee

Divorce Petition
Married Feb. 1831 in Covington Co. Decree July 1833.

****

1837 Yazoo Co. Miss. Drawer 72 Case #295

Nancy Ann Brown, Admx. and Geo. Fisher and Beverly R. Grayson, Admx. with will attached, Est. Jesse S. Brown, Dec'd

vs

Arthur Moseley

****

1840 Rankin Co. Miss. Drawer 72 Case #311

John McKain, Exec. Est. Andrew Gounly, Dec'd

vs

Samuel M. Puckett

****

1813 Adams Co. Miss. Tr. Drawer 72 Case #314

Love Baker, Execx. and S. Postlewaite, Exec. Est. Chas. McKiernan, Dec'd

vs

Theodore J. H. Richey

****

1834 Hinds Co. Miss. Drawer 72 Case #318

Amanda Terrell, widow of James Terrell, Dec'd

vs

Samuel Terrell, Exec. Est. James Terrell, Dec'd

****

1840 Hinds Co. Miss. Drawer 72 Case #319

Abner G. A. Beasley, Admr. Est. James F. Beasley, Dec'd

vs

Robert A. Patrick

****

1840 Hinds Co. Miss. Drawer 72 Case #322

Harmon Stidger

vs

Augustus L. Dabney, Admr. Est. Benj. F. Dabney, Dec'd

****

1833 Wayne Co. Miss. Drawer 72 Case #336

Charity Whiddon

vs

Max Whiddon

Divorce Petition
Married: 1790 in State of North Carolina

****

1834 Wilkinson Co. Miss. Drawer 72 Case #338

Benj. N. Rogers, Admr. Est. Hayes G. White, Dec'd, Sarah N. Shaw (late widow of Hayes G. White) and her husband John A. Shaw, and Benj. N. Rogers, Gdn. for Anna Jane White, infant

vs

Asa Sapp and Nathan E. Raymond

****

1823 Adams Co. Miss. Drawer 72 Case #339

Howell Moss, Admr. Est. George Johnson, Dec'd late of Fredericksburg, Va.

vs

Michael Snyder

****

1834 Simpson Co. Miss. Drawer 72 Case #343

John Cupp

vs

Catherine Cupp, nee Sullivan

Divorce Petition
Married: April 20, 1822 Jefferson Co. Miss.

****

1832 Hinds Co. Miss. Drawer 72 Case #344

H. T. Wiggins

vs

Jesse Bass and Counsel R. Bass and Joseph Brittain, Admrs. Est. Edmund P. Bass, Dec'd

****

1823 Claiborne Co. Miss. Drawer 72 Case #345

Robert C. Evans and Thos. L. Evans, infant sons of Lewis Evans, Dec'd by Gdn. Gabriel Tichenor, James C. Wilkins and Gabriel Tichenor Execs. Est. Lewis Evans Dec'd

vs

Thos. Freeland, Admr. Est. Davis Christian, Dec'd. Christian heirs: William and Nicholas H. Christian.

****

1834 Pike Co. Miss. Drawer 72 Case #347

John Keigler, Exec. Est. Margaret Payne alias Margaret Holliman, Dec'd

vs

Thomas C. Payne

****

1841 Lafayette Co. Miss. Drawer 72 Case #360

Samuel Hayter, Admr. Est. Jefferson Hayter, Dec'd

vs

John N. Houston, Robert B. Houston and James F. Smith

****

1834 Monroe Co. Miss. Drawer 72 Case #392

Griffin Roberts and wife, Mary, nee Martin, James M. Martin, Eliza Jane Martin and William Martin

vs

Samuel A. Edmunson and James M. Hawkins, Admr. Est. Jane Edmunson, Dec'd (late Jane Martin, mother of Comp'ts.)

William Martin, father of Comp'ts died in Monroe Co. in 1826 or 1827 and his widow, Jane, subsequently married S. A. Edmunson.

****

1823 Adams Co. Miss. Drawer 72 Case #364

Elizabeth Q. Keen

vs

Thomas Keen

Divorce Petition.
Married: June 17, 1818.

****

1851 Wilkinson Co. Miss. Drawer 72 Case #366

John J. Bryant, Mary Bryant, Tiberius J. Bryant, Mordicia J. Bryant, Ann Bryant and Geo. Bryant, children and heirs of Thos. Bryant, Dec'd. Timothy Walker and wife, Ann, nee Bryant, heirs of Thos. Bryant, Dec'd. Mary F. Laverty, Thomas B. Laverty, Honora Laverty, Alice Laverty, children and heirs of Alice and Kenner Laverty, both deceased (Alice Laverty, Dec'd daughter of Thos. Bryant, Dec'd) all heirs of Moses Bryant, Dec'd. William Hazlett and wife Ann, nee Fletcher, Robert Fletcher, Phoebe Fletcher and Benj. Fletcher, children of John and Phoebe Fletcher, both deceased (said Phoebe Fletcher, Dec'd being only heir of Benj. Bryant, Dec'd), Ann S. Holt, widow of Wm. Holt, Dec'd, and only heir of Mary Dickerson, Dec'd, nee Mary Bryant, Phoebe Hunter, widow of Dr. George Hunter, Dec'd (said Phoebe formerly Phoebe Bryant). The said Phoebe Hunter, Thos. Bryant, Dec'd, Moses Bryant, Dec'd, Benj. Bryant, Dec'd and Mary Dickerson, Dec'd, all legal heirs of John Hare, Dec'd.

vs

John C. Jenkins, Admr. Est. John F. Carmichael, Dec'd.

****

1856 Wilkinson Co. Miss. Drawer 72 Case #366-b

John Henderson, Admr. de bonis non Est. Phoebe Hunter, Dec'd

vs

Isaiah Winchester, Admr. Est. John Jenkins, Dec'd

****

1834 Hinds Co. Miss. Drawer 72 Case #369

John D. Carriel

vs

Isaac Caldwell, Admr. de bonis non Est. Thos. D. Downs, Dec'd

Lucy Downs widow, relinquished administratrixship of Est. of Thos. D. Downs, Dec'd

****

1836 Madison Co. Miss. Drawer 72 Case #370

Charles C. Garner

vs

Heirs of Marce Wadlington, Dec'd.

Marce Wadlington died April 24, 1833, leaving Polly Wadlington (widow), Irvin C. Wadlington, James M. Wadlington, Maria Wadlington, wife of Felix G. Wadlington, John T. Wadlington, Mary Wadlington, wife of John H. Walker, Beulah Wadlington, wife of Chas. C. Garner (Comp't in this case), William Presley Wadlington, Wallace W. Wadlington, Eliza Ann Wadlington, Nancy Wadlington, Cordell N. Wadlington, Margaret Wadlington, Mary Louise and Thomas Garner, infant heirs of Cynthia C. Garner, Dec'd, nee Cynthia Wadlington.

****

1835 Jefferson Co. Miss. Drawer 72 Case #372

Nathaniel Harrison

vs

James, David, Isaac, Polly, Lotty and Sarah Ann Harrison, infants of James Harrison Dec'd, by John B. Thrasher, Gdn.

****

1824 Adams Co. Miss. Drawer 72 Case #376

Andrew Williams

vs

Rebecca Brant, Admx. Est. Joseph Brant, Dec'd

****

1814 Adams Co. Miss. Tr. Drawer 73 Case #388

John Taylor, Admr. Est. John Shaw, Dec'd

vs

Isaiah Packard

****

1834 Adams Co. Miss. Drawer 73 Case #390

James H. McCoy, Admr. Est. John Eldergill, Dec'd

vs

Joseph Nichols and wife, Elizabeth, nee Carney, daughter of Arthur Carney, Dec'd

Arthur Carney died July 6, 1804. John Eldergill died 1802.

****

1825 Adams Co. Miss. Drawer 73 Case #392

White Turpin, Admr. de bonis non Est. Samuel Hutchins, Dec'd

vs

Magdaline H. Claiborne (widow), John H., F. L., Benigah O., and Charlotte Claiborne, heirs of Ferdinand Claiborne, Dec'd.

This file also shows that King H. Holmes and George Dent were Execs. Est. Benjamin Dent, Dec'd.

****

1823 Amite Co. Miss. Drawer 73 Case #393

Robert McClure, Gdn. for Brice G. Scarlett, infant

vs

James M. Dowell. Admr. Est. John Scarlett, Dec'd

James Scarlett, father of Brice Scarlett, died in 1815 leaving as heirs: Merritt Scarlett, John D. Scarlett, Emily D. Scarlett, Leonia Scarlett and Brice Scarlett (children), and John Scarlett (brother). John Scarlett (the brother and uncle) died June 3, 1823 leaving considerable estate to same heirs.

****

1834 Adams Co. Miss. Drawer 73 Case #396

Theodore Stark

vs

Heirs of Francis and Sophia Gildart, Dec'd

Heirs: Robt. S., John W., Francis, Horatio N. Gildart and Mary Jane, wife of Samuel Pitcher, Elizabeth, wife of Dick H. Eggleston, Sophia, wife of John Fox and Frances wife of William Ruffin (both deceased), and Francis Gildart Ruffin, infant of William and Frances Ruffin, Dec'd

****

1834 Yazoo Co. Miss. Drawer 73 Case #397

John Alston and Elbert H. Harrison and wife, Elizabeth Ann Harrison, lately Cobb, Admrs. and Admx. Est. James Cobb, Dec'd

vs

William Bishop

****

1834 Wilkinson Co. Miss. Drawer 73 Case #400-a

Jane Butler Browder by Gdn. Augustine Bourgcat

vs

Moses S. Hooke, Richard B. Hooke, William B. Hooke, Francis F. Hooke, Harriet S. Hooke and Margaret A. Sheppard, nee Hooke, wife of Charles W. Sheppard.

****

1872 Carroll Co. Miss. Drawer 73 Case #403

Daniel Mayes, Admr. Est. John H. McIntyre, Dec'd, Mary G. Fox, lately widow of John H. McIntyre and John A. Fox, her husband

vs

John H. Davis

****

1823 Adams Co. Miss. Drawer 73 Case #407

Stephen Dunn, Admr. Est. Robert Daniels, Dec'd (late of Tennessee)

vs

William Mayben, John Nichols and John Smith
Robert Daniels died in 1821.

****

1834 Warren Co. Miss. Drawer 73 Case #407-a

William Torry and wife, Mary, nee Hammond

vs

Mary Pace (widow) and Elijah H., James and Lorenzo D. Pace, children and heirs of Royal Pace, Dec'd

Royal Pace died in Warren Co. in 1824. Mary Hammond Torry was child of an unnamed daughter of Royal and Mary Pace.

****

1834 Franklin Co. Miss. Drawer 73 Case #409

Edward Turner

vs

Rev. James D. Tyler and wife, Sarah, lately Sarah Turner, widow of Henry Turner, Dec'd

Rev. James D. Tyler was a resident of New Jersey and his wife, Sarah was a resident of Adams Co. Miss. They married March 1826 and this litigation involves a marriage contract.

****

1838 Lawrence Co. Miss. Drawer 73 Case #410

Lawrence D. Williams and wife, Sally Jane, nee Smith

vs

Irvin Scarbrough, Okey Powell, and wife, Mary Ann Clarinda, Frances Thompson Smith, Matthew B. Cannon and Abel Stringer.

Francis Smith, father of Sally Jane Smith Williams, died in 1822.

Heirs of Francis Smith: Holland Smith, Amycatina Smith (widow), James Randolph Smith, Nancy B. Smith, Sally Jane Smith, Mary Ann Clarinda Smith and Frances Thompson Smith.

****

1840 Franklin Co. Miss. Drawer 73 Case #412

Tillett Porter

vs

Sutton Byrd, Admr. Est. Nancy Porter, Dec'd.

Heirs: Ferdinand Porter, Abednago Porter (now dec'd), Elan—wife of Abednago—now married to John Miley, Samuel and Harriet Porter, children of Abednago and Elan Porter, Sarah Hollaway, nee Porter, wife of Robert Hollaway, Jane Holloway, nee Porter, wife of George Hollaway, Caroline Hollaway, nee Beck, wife of James Hollaway, daughter of Letha Beck, a daughter of Nancy Porter, Dec'd, David Porter and Tillet Porter (Comp't.)

****

1837 Simpson Co. Miss. Drawer 73 Case #414

Susan O'Neal, nee Smith

vs

Tyre O'Neal

Divorce Petition
Married: December 15, 1834

****

1819 Wilkinson Co. Miss. Tr. Drawer 73 Case #415

J. F. Carmichael

vs

Samuel Davis, Admr. Est. Thos. Viles, Dec'd

Thos. Viles died 1808 leaving: Mary Viles (widow), Betsy Viles and Nancy Viles Magness, wife of James Magness. James and Nancy V. Magness married 1812. Mary Viles, widow Thos. died 1808 or 1809. James F. Carmichael was Gdn. for Elizabeth (Betsy) Viles and of Peregrin Magness, infant heir of James and Nancy Viles Magness, Dec'd.

****

1843 Adams Co. Miss. Drawer 73 Case #416

Re: William Bisland, Trustee for infants of his brother, James Bisland, Dec'd. James Bisland died April 4, 1835 leaving Children: Martha Jane, Douglas S., Thomas A., Susanah E. and Mary L. Bisland.

Petition to distribute trust fund to heirs.

****

1823 Adams Co. Miss. Drawer 73 Case #419

Benard McCropen

vs

Robert McCullough, Admr. Est. Martha (alias Elizabeth) Harmon, Dec'd

****

1835 Wilkinson Co. Miss. Drawer 73 Case #420

Hezekiah B. Hull

vs

Sarah H. White (widow) and Benj. N. Rogers, Admr. Est. Hayes G. White, Dec'd.

Heirs of Hezekiah Hull: Galman, Lydia Ann and Theophilus Hull.

Heirs of Hayes G. White: Sarah H. (widow) and Anna Jane White (Dau.)

****

1840 Warren Co. Miss. Drawer 73 Case #421

Talbot I. Peck and wife, Helen, lately widow of Anthony Glass, Dec'd

vs

James Glass (brother of Anthony) James Glass, M. D., Isaac Webster and wife, Mary, Francis Rapolge, Mary Rapolge, Augustus Glass, William and Eliza Bittner, Mary Jane, John and Eliza Kirkwood—all heirs of Anthony Glass, Dec'd
Anthony Glass died November 9, 1834.
See Will.

****

1840 Madison Co. Miss. Drawer 73 Case #423

William J. Brown and wife, Elizabeth, Admr. and Admx. Est. Charles McCarroll, Dec'd

vs

Lewis Campbell, D. Hardeman, James C. Mitchell and Mitchell Calhoun.

****

1824 Wilkinson Co. Miss. Drawer 73 Case #427

Sarah E. Fulsom

vs

William Fulsom

Divorce Petition.

Married: December 1821. Sarah Fulsom was daughter of J. N. Pessioners, Dec'd and of Ellen Carr, late Ellen Pessioners.

****

1840 Hinds Co. Miss. Drawer 73 Case #431

Thomas M. Weathersby and wife, Margaret, nee Owens

vs

James Addkison of Marion Co. Miss.

Margaret O. Weathersby was daughter of James Owens of Limestone Co. Ala. and niece of William Owens.

James Owens died 1830 and litigation involves slave, Sidney, who was conveyed by deed of gift from William Owens to Margaret Owens in 1823. Margaret Owens married Thos. Weathersby in April 1837 in Marion Co. Miss.

****

1824 Franklin Co. Miss. Drawer 73 Case #437

Walter Cornett and wife, Sarah, late Cobia, James C. Walker and wife, Anna, late Gilly, Chas. G. Brunson and wife, Susanah, late Cobia, John Cobia, William H. Barchett and wife, Unity, late Cobia, all devisees under the will of Claudius Richbourg, late of Clerendon Co. Sumpter Dist. South Carolina

vs

George Lambright

Litigation involving slaves purchased by George Lambright from George Evans. Claudius Richbourg died February 10, 1778.

See Lambright will.

****

1826 Wilkinson Co. Miss. Drawer 73 Case #439

William Monks, Admr. Est. John Yeizer, Dec'd

vs

Gabriel Winter and Samuel G. Wright

****

1824 Claiborne Co. Miss. Drawer 73 Case #440

John Trimble, Admr. Est. Robert Trimble, Dec'd

vs

Joseph Moore, Exec. Est. William R. Chambliss, Dec'd

Robert Trimble died 1818

****

1836 Jefferson Co. Miss. Drawer 73 Case #442

Eliza McDougal

vs

William C. McDougal

Divorce Petition.

Eliza McDougal was daughter of Everard and Elizabeth Green, Dec'd. Everard died in 1814 and Elizabeth died Nov. 5, 1833. Their heirs: Martha, wife of Ebenezer E. Kebridge of Louisiana, Louisa, wife of Anthony M. Perriman, Abner E. Green and Samuel K. Sorsby, son of Elizabeth Green by previous marriage. Eliza Green married Thomas Baker Jan. 1, 1818 and had Thomas Francis and Everard Green Baker. Thomas Baker, Sr. died March 15, 1832 and Eliza G. Baker married William McDougal June 13, 1833.

****

1834 Adams Co. Miss. Drawer 73 Case #443

Ayers P. Merrill, Admr. Est. Elizabeth Whittle, Dec'd

vs

James B. Moore, Samuel Moore, John F. Girault, Eliza W. Girault, Mary H. Girault infant children of Anna Eliza Girault, Dec'd; A. P. Merrill and William N. Mercer, Execs. Est. James Moore, Dec'd and A. P. Merrill, Admr. de bonis non Est. Robert Moore, Dec'd

James Moore died May 29, 1829. Anna M. Moore died Feb. 27, 1829. Children of James and Anna Moore: Jane Sarah Merrill, Ann Eliza Girault, Margaret Moore, James Burling Moore and Samuel Moore. Children of Anna Eliza Girault: John, Mary H., and Eliza W. Girault. Anna Eliza Girault died 1830.

****

1830 Yazoo Co. Miss. Drawer 73 Case #445

Nancy Bain, Admx. and John W. Penny, Admr. Est. James Bain, Dec'd, Elam Bain, Robert Bain, Dana Bain, Alexander Bain, Margaret Bain, Katherine Bain, and Nancy Bain, infant heirs of James Bain, Dec'd

vs

John Jenkins and John W. Rogers.

****

1825 Adams Co. Miss. Drawer 73 Case #450

Gabriel Tichenor and James C. Wilkins, Exec. Est. Lewis Evans, Dec'd

vs

George R. Williams and wife, Mary Ann, and James Foster

****

1824 Adams Co. Miss. Drawer 73 Case #452

Cassandra Foster

vs

Ephraim Foster

Divorce Petition
Cassandra Foster was daughter of Thomas Foster.

****

1835 Wilkinson Co. Miss. Drawer 74 Case #463

Hazlewood M. Farish and William Stamps, Admrs. Est. Edward T. Farish, Dec'd

vs

Charles H. Stone

Edward T. Farish died October 7, 1833.

****

1824 Amite Co. Miss. Drawer 74 Case #465

James L. McKnight and Margaret H. McKnight, heirs of James McKnight, Dec'd

vs

Thomas Torrance

Margaret H. McKnight was widow of James Sr. and James L. McKnight, son.

James McKnight Sr. died in 1815.

****

1824 Jefferson Co. Miss. Drawer 74 Case #471

Samuel Calvit

vs

Eliza Lucretia Calvit (formerly known as Elizabeth Covington)

See Wills.

****

1835 Hinds Co. Miss. Drawer 74 Case #472

Pliney S. Black

vs

Thos. Robertson and wife, Caroline, Admr. and Admx. Est. William Mellon, Dec'd.

Caroline Robertson was widow of William Mellon who died in 1831.

****

1836 Jefferson Co. Miss. Drawer 74 Case #473

John James Cowden

vs

Ann H. Cowden, widow of James Cowden, Thos. L. Dobyns and wife, Columbia E. Dobyns.

John James Cowden was son and only child of James Cowden, Dec'd. James Cowden married Mrs. Ann H. Stanard, relict of Dr. Hugh Stanard, on Dec. 9, 1824. Mrs. Cowden had one child of her marriage to Josiah Simpson, Columbia E. Simpson, wife of Thos. L. Dobyns.

See will of Obediah Jones.

****

1834 Hinds Co. Miss. Drawer 74 Case #475

Harriet Ann Baird

vs

Felix W. Baird

Divorce Petition.

Married: January 1826 in Hinds County. Miss.

****

1824 Jefferson Co. Miss. Drawer 74 Case #481

J. B. Norrell

vs

Mary Norrell, nee Grubbs

Divorce Petition.
Married 1815. Case terminated by death of Comp't

****

1840 Carroll Co. Miss. Drawer 74 Case #482

William Windle

vs

Abram A. Halsy, Admr. Est. Stephen D. Miller, Dec'd.

****

1824 Adams Co. Miss. Drawer 74 Case #484

Lydia Bradley

vs

Calvin Bradley

Married: June 1823. Lydia Bradley was widow of Gabriel Swayze.

****

1835 Warren Co. Miss. Drawer 74 Case #484-a

Hiram Coffee

vs

Nathan Seymour, Admr. Est. Ruel A. Watson, Dec'd.

****

1829 Adams Co. Miss. Drawer 74 Case #485

John W. Brocus

vs

Betsy Tappan (formerly Betsy Frazer) Eliza Frazer, Eliphalet Frazer, Daniel Vertner, Abram and John Willis

****

1824 Jefferson Co. Miss. Drawer 74 Case #489

John Vanderall, William Scott (adults) Samuel Scott, Thomas Scott, Osborne Scott and Eliza L. Calvit, infants, all children and heirs of Huldy L. Calvit, Dec'd, late of Jefferson Co.

vs

John Kerr, William Terry, Rush Nutt, Eliza Nutt and Mary Terry, heirs of David Kerr, Dec'd.

Huldy L. Calvit, formerly Covington, was widow of Thos. Calvit, Dec'd.

****

1824 Adams Co. Miss. Drawer 74 Case #497

Sylvia Ann Stutson

vs

John S. Stutson

Divorce Petition. Bill dismissed.

****

1824 Wilkinson Co. Miss. Drawer 74 Case #498

Stephen Minor Kerchevel, by next friend, John W. Gildart

vs

Abram M. Scott

Stephen Minor Kerchevel was son of James Kerchevel, Dec'd. His mother (not named) later married John W. Gildart. Litigation involves a promissory note of John Minor, Esq. to Est. James Kerchevel, Dec'd.

****

1825 Adams Co. Miss. Drawer 74 Case #507

Robert Stewart

vs

Andrew Marschalk and wife, Sidney

Robt. Stewart married Susan, daughter of Andrew and Sidney Marschalk on May 14, 1818, and had a son, George Stewart

****

1826 Adams Co. Miss. Drawer 74 Case #508

Judith Williams, by next friend, Adam L. Benjamin

vs

James C. Williams, Exec. Est. David Williams, Dec'd.

Judith was widow of David Williams, Dec'd.

****

1836 Wilkinson Co. Miss. Drawer 74 Case #509

Jane Davis, William Stamps and Ananias Dunbar

vs

Eldred G. Robert, Admr. Est. Matilda Vaughn, Dec'd.

Jane Davis was appointed Gdn. for Matilda Vaughn in Jan. 1830 and Matilda Vaughn died March 16, 1834.

****

1820 Franklin Co. Miss. Drawer 74 Case #511

Adaliza Pickett by Richard Bein

vs

Macajah Pickett and William Pickett

Depositions of Needham Lee, Hiram Pickett, Rufus Pickett, Adam Cloy and James Witherspoon.

****

1835 Hinds Co. Miss. Drawer 74 Case #512

Susan Kersee, late Susan Davis

vs

William Kersee

Divorce Petition
Married in Hinds Co. June 1, 1834.

****

1872 Amite Co. Miss. Drawer 74 Case #512-a

Chas. E. Washburn and M. S. Shirk and Hiram Van Norman

vs

Wm. L. Johns and Wm. L. Ewell, Execs. Est. John Reeve, Dec'd.

****

1835 Madison Co. Miss. Drawer 74 Case #518

Vicey Myers, nee Wood

vs

Dennis Myers

Divorce Petition.
Married in Copiah Co. July 27, 1834.

****

1824 Adams Co. Miss. Drawer 74 Case #520

Hannah Paleske (widow)

vs

James Chambers, Exec. Est. Charles Paleske, Dec'd, late of Pennsylvania, but more recently of Mississippi.

Charles Paleske, son of Charles G. Paleske of Pa. died 1820.

****

1825 Adams Co. Miss. Drawer 74 Case #529

Calvin Bradley, Exec. Est. Lydia Bradley, Dec'd.

vs

Gabriel Swayze, Jr. and Matthew Losley, Admrs. de bonis non Est. Gabriel Swayze, Sr. Dec'd.

Gabriel Swayze, Jr. was son of Lydia Bradley (formerly Swayze), Dec'd.

****

1821 Holmes Co. Miss. Drawer 74 Case #529-a

William H. Johnson, Admr. Est. Thomas Land, Dec'd

vs

Charles A. Lancaster, Levin R. Marshall, John T. McMurran, John C. Jenkins (Admr. Est. J. F. Carmichael), Isaac B. McCorkle, Margaret S. Land, Thos. Land (infant), William and Silas Land.

****

1837 Claiborne Co. Miss. Drawer 74 Case #532

Wm. Ferriday, Admr. ad colligendum of William Bullitt, Dec'd

vs

John S. Roland and John S. Gooch, Admrs. Est. Parson B. Griffin, Dec'd, J. Susan Roland, Moses Goff and wife, Mary, heirs of Parson B. Griffin, Dec'd, Lemuel Brewster, Dewey Babcock, Chas. Gardince, Thos. Smith, Ralph Dubbard, Charles Smith and Madison Bruce.

Parson B. Griffin died 1833 leaving as his sole surviving heirs, Susan, wife of John Roland, and Mary, wife of Moses Goff, all of Claiborne Co.

****

1825 Adams Co. Miss. Drawer 74 Case #533

Gabriel Tichenor and James C. Wilkins, Execs. Est. Lewis Evans, Sr.

vs

Geo. R. Williams and wife, Mary Ann, and David Lattimore

****

1835 Rankin Co. Miss. Drawer 74 Case #536

John P. Stewart and wife, Jane, late Jane Watson of Hinds Co.

vs

Norvel Granberry, Admr. Est. Laughlin McLaurine, Dec'd., Mary McLaurine (widow), and James, Isabella, Launa

Laomi, and Jemima Jane McLaurine, children and heirs of Laughlin McLaurine.

Jane Watson Stewart was a cousin of Laughlin McLaurine.

****

1835 Hinds Co. Miss. Drawer 74 Case #537

Malcolm B. Terrell

vs

Philemon Terrell, (widow), Admx Est. John R. Terrell, Dec'd., Margaret Terrell and Samuel Terrell, children of John R. Terrell, Dec'd.

John R. was a nephew of Malcolm B. Terrell.

****

1825 Franklin Co. Miss. Drawer 74 Case #538

Peter Corbell

vs

Richard Dunn, Admr. Est. Lewis Dunn, Dec'd.

****

1825 Adams Co. Miss. Drawer 74 Case #539

Joseph Tidball, Citizen of Virginia

vs

Jane Ferguson (widow), Ann Ferguson, wife of David Hunt, George C. Ferguson, Charlotte and Margaret Ferguson, children of David Ferguson, Dec'd.

****

1827 Wilkinson Co. Miss. Drawer 74 Case #540

William Hammett

vs

John Stevens, Admr. de bonis non Est. Robt. B. Hammett, Dec'd.

Mary Hammett was widow and Elizabeth Hammett, infant daughter, of Robert B. Hammett who died Feb. 19,

1814. William, Comp't, was father of Robert Hammett, Dec'd. and Benj. Eccles was Gdn. for Elizabeth Hammett.

****

1835 Yazoo Co. Miss. Drawer 75 Case #541

Henry H. Pease

vs

Josef M. Cardosa, Lewis G. Galloway, John C. Richardson, Mary J. Davis, widow of Wiley Davis, Dec'd; Maria Harrington formerly Maria Higgins, widow of James Higgins, Dec'd, wife of I. C. Harrington; Wm. H. Johnson, Joseph M. Copes, and wife, Maria Ann, lately Maria Ann Davis, widow of Aaron B. Davis, Dec'd; Edmund Pursell and wife, Margaret, lately Margaret G. Hall, widow of Harden G. Hall Dec'd; Wm. H. Johnson and Charles F. Fisher, Admrs. Est. Thos. M. Hemlock, Dec'd; John Sehr and Hamilton M. Wright, Admrs. Est. James S. Goodwin, Dec'd and of William Hewes, Dec'd; John Sehr, Wm. H. Johnson and James R. West, Admrs. Est. James Higgins, Dec'd; Mary J. Davis, Admx. Est. Wiley Davis and Parham Buford, Sheriff of Yazoo Co.

****

1837 Smith Co. Miss. Drawer 75 Case #543

William H. Flowers of Smith Co. Miss.

vs

William Johnson

****

1825 Claiborne Co. Miss. Drawer 75 Case #545

Amos Whiting

vs

Richard Sessions, Admr. Est. Archibald Evans, Dec'd.

Archibald Evans, late of Claiborne Co. Miss. left as heirs: Charlotte Evans, widow, William O. Evans, son, and a daughter, not named, who was the wife of George L. Gayden.

****

1833 Jefferson Co. Miss. Drawer 75 Case #546

Louisa Holmes, nee Taylor

vs

William Holmes

Divorce Petition
Married: May 1826 in Adams Co. Miss.

****

1836 Amite Co. Miss. Drawer 75 Case #549

Sarah Faust (widow of James Faust)

vs

Peter Faust, Admr. Est. James Faust, Dec'd.

****

1836 Warren Co. Miss.. Drawer 75 Case #550-a

Re: Estate John Sevier, Dec'd.

Petition by James Smitheart for appointment of Henry Pender, Samuel Templeton, Charles A. Harris, Samuel Welsh and James R. Blunt as Commissioners to divide real and personal estate of John Sevier, Dec'd.

****

1835 Amite Co. Miss. Drawer 75 Case #553

Nathan D. Young and Isabella Young (husband and wife)

vs

Isabella Williams, Sr., Richard Williams and James Williams.

Isabella Young was daughter of Isabella Williams. Richard and James were brothers of Isabella Young and they were niece and nephews of Joseph Williams, Dec'd. who died intestate in Amite Co. Miss. in 1830. All formerly of State of Maryland.

****

1825 Wilkinson Co. Miss. Drawer 75 Case #554

Francis A. Bynum, Admr. Est. Austin J. Davis, Dec'd.

vs

Susan Davis, widow of Austin J. Davis
Austin J. Davis died in State of Louisiana in 1823.

****

1841 Marshall Co. Miss. Drawer 75 Case #555

Delilah Moore, widow

vs

Leander R. Guy, Exec. Est. John B. Moore, Dec'd.

****

1825 Wilkinson Co. Miss. Drawer 75 - Case #558

Mary Singleton, an infant, by next friend, Samuel Wright, Gdn.

vs

Hiram Singleton.

See will of Richard Singleton.

****

1830 Adams Co. Miss. Drawer 75 Case #559

Charles Miles of State of Kentucky

vs

Robert Fletcher, Lionel Fletcher and Rebecca Fletcher, Execs. Est. Richard Fletcher, Dec'd. and Richard M. Gains, Admr. Est. John Richards, Dec'd.

****

1839 Hinds Co. Miss. Drawer 75 Case #559-a

Robert Sims and wife, Nancy

vs

William Nichols, Joshua Howard and Elender Nichols, widow of Henry Nichols, Dec'd.

Henry Nichols, died May 1833 in Hinds Co. Heirs: Henry, William and Nehemiah Nichols, Elizabeth Nichols, wife of Jacob Lott, Jeremiah and Hezekiah Nichols, Nancy Nichols, wife of Robert Sims and Elender Nichols, widow of Henry.

****

1824 Wilkinson Co. Miss. Drawer 75 Case #564

Martha Ann Berry and William Augustus Berry, infants of Nancy Berry, Dec'd (late of Columbia Co. Ga.) by next friend, Wm. McGehee of Pulaski, Ga.

vs

Archibald McGehee of Wilkinson Co. Miss., Admr. Est. Nathan McGehee, Dec'd.

Nancy Berry was sister of Nathan McGehee who died in Wilkinson Co. in 1821, unmarried and intestate. Heirs: William McGehee (brother), Martha Ann and William Augustus McGehee (niece and nephew) and Archibald McGehee (brother).

****

1825 Wilkinson Co. Miss. Drawer 75 Case #568

Elizabeth Quick by next friend Thos. Smith

vs

John C. Quick

Divorce Petition
Married: May 17, 1822 in Wilkinson Co. Miss.

****

1836 Washington Co. Miss. Drawer 75 Case #570

Benj. F. Perryman and wife, Rachel, lately Dempsey

vs

William H. Dempsey

William H. Dempsey was son of Rachel Perryman.

****

1825 Claiborne Co. Miss. Drawer 75 Case #572

Sally Pryor

vs

William Pryor

Divorce Petition.
Married: 1816 in Claiborne Co. Miss.

****

1826 Hinds Co. Miss. Drawer 75 Case #573

William Morehead

vs

Heirs of David Smith, Dec'd

David Smith died in 1834 leaving heirs: Elizabeth, widow and seven children, Mary, wife of Joshua Peters of State of La., Lee, Henry H., Elizabeth, wife of Hezekiah Rester of Carroll Co.; Dicy Smith and Daniel Russell, infant son of Charity Smith Russell and Ann, wife of William Morehead (Comp't.)

****

1825 Adams Co. Miss. Drawer 75 Case #573-a

Robert H. Cummings and wife Emma F., Melvina Forman, Emma Longstreet, James Nelson, heirs at law of General David Forman, Dec'd

vs

Elijah Smith, Admr. de bonis non Est. William Fordon Forman, Dec'd; and George Salked, Thos. B. Barclay, George P. Barclay, Frederick M. Barclay.

Heirs of Gen. David Forman: Anna, Emma, Eliza, Melvina, Ravin, Sarah (dau. William Forman) and his wife—not named and represented as insane.

****

1836 Madison Co. Miss. Drawer 75 Case #591

Cynthia Sulcer

vs

Josiah Sulcer

Divorce Petition. Decree July 1837.

****

1871 Warren Co. Miss. Drawer 75 Case #592

Richard Frederic and William Anderson, Jr. and Nathaniel F. Bowe, all of State of Virginia

vs

John M. Chilton and Jane Magee (widow) Admr. and Admx. Est. Eugene Magee, Dec'd.

Heirs: Virginia M. and Eugene Magee and widow, Jane Magee.

****

1825 Adams Co. Miss. Drawer 75 Case #594

Elijah Smith, Admr. Est. Jeremiah Hunt, Dec'd

vs

Eliza D. Gorrell, relict of Phillip Gorrell

****

1836 Yazoo Co. Miss. Drawer 75 Case #599

James Buford, Admr.

vs

William Wilson and Henry Turney

John Wilson died June 1833 and Samuel Wilson died. Sept. 1833. William Wilson was appointed Admr. of Est. John Wilson and Mary Wilson (widow of Samuel), later Mary Young, was Admr. with will attached of Est. of Samuel Wilson, Dec'd. William and Samuel were brothers.

****

1838 Claiborne Co. Miss. Drawer 75 Case #610

Duncan C. McLeod and wife, Mariah

vs

W. Hiram Selser, Exec. Est. Pierce B. Tutt, Dec'd

****

1826 Adams Co. Miss. Drawer 75 Case #611

Charles B. Green and John B. Nevitt

vs

Francis B. Hankinson and Louis Miller, Admrs. Est. John Hankinson, Dec'd.

****

1837 Yazoo Co. Miss. Drawer 75 Case #611-a

William S. Eskridge, Admr. Est. Ignatius P. Eskridge

vs

Thos. F. Collins, Gdn. ad litem for Benj. B. and Mary Eskridge, infant heirs of Thos. P. Eskridge and for William, Robert and Edwin Wall, infant heirs of Eleanor Wall, Dec'd.

****

1841 Pike Co. Miss. Drawer 75 Case #612

Michael McAnulty, Gdn. of minor heirs of James Leggett, Dec'd

vs

Adam S. Bingaman

Heirs not named.

****

1826 Jefferson Co. Miss. Drawer 75 Case #613

Ephraim Forman, Admr. and Charlotte Forman, Admx Est. of Amos Gaskin, Dec'd.

vs

Mary Ann Gaskin, Admx. Est. Ferdinand B. Gaskin, Dec'd. Charlotte Forman was the relict of Amos Gaskin.

Ferdinand and Amos Gaskin were brothers. Amos died in 1823. John Gaskin was the father of Amos and Ferdinand.

****

1826 Adams Co. Miss. Drawer 76 Case #624

William B. Fowler and Nathaniel Ogden, Admr. Est. John P. Garino, Dec'd

vs

John W. Purvis and Nathan H. Luce.

****

1826 Adams Co. Miss. Drawer 76 Case #628

William Vangrevson and Howell Moss

vs

John Patton, Admr. Est. William Patton, Dec'd.

John Patton was a brother of William and a resident of Charlottesville, Virginia.

****

1826 Adams Co. Miss. Drawer 76 Case #633

Joseph E. Davis, Admr. Est. Isaac Gaillard, Dec'd

vs

James C. Wilkins, Admr. Est. Milton Burling, Dec'd

****

1826 Copiah Co. Miss. Drawer 76 Case #634

Margaret Boyd by next friend, John Boyd

vs

William Boyd

Divorce Petition.

Married: 1804 in South Carolina. Bill states Comp't and Def't were parents of twelve children, but children were not named, except John Boyd who was a son.

****

1836 Claiborne Co. Miss. Drawer 76 Case #635

Sarah H. Ludlow of Claiborne Co.
vs
B. A. Ludlow of Hinds Co.

Divorce Petition.
Married: Sept. 10, 1830.

****

1826 Adams Co. Miss. Drawer 76 Case #639

Jacob T. Swayze and wife, Cynthia
vs
R. R. Grayson, Exec. Est. Robert Ford, Dec'd.

****

1829 Pike Co. Miss. Drawer 76 Case #653

Elizabeth Lowry
vs
Francis Wren and John Collins, Execs. Est. James L. Collins, Dec'd.

Morgan Davis and Gabriel Felder, Commissioners; Depositions of Thos. McDowell, Darling Jones, Hezekiah Newman, Charles Davis, Agrippa Gayden, William Lowry, Jr. and Thomas Torrance.

****

1839 Jefferson Co. Miss. Drawer 76 Case #654

Anthony Hamberlain and wife, Berlinda, John Scribner and wife, Eleanor, Michael W. Trimble and wife, Catherine, all of Jefferson Co. Miss.
vs
Stephen Terry, Exec. Est. John Pickens, Dec'd.

John Pickens, an unmarried man, was a brother of Berlinda Hamberlain, Eleanor Scribner and Catherine Trimble.

****

1837 Marshall Co. Miss. Drawer 76 Case #655

Ann V. Martin, Exec. Est. Andrew S. Martin, Dec'd

vs

Hannibal Harris

****

1827 Claiborne Co. Miss. Drawer 76 Case #656

Thomas Maples

vs

Pheriby Maples

Divorce Petition. Married 1812.

****

1841 Adams Co. Miss. Drawer 76 Case #656-a

Commercial Bank of Natchez

vs

John Routh, Elias Ogden and Mary M. Ellis, Admrs. and Admx. Est. Thomas G. Ellis, Dec'd.

****

1836 Adams Co. Miss. Drawer 76 Case #657

Susan B. Patton

vs

Matthew Patton

Divorce Petition.
Married: 1824 in State of Kentucky

****

1837 Warren Co. Miss. Drawer 76 Case #659

Aaron Jones and wife, Margaret of N. C.; James Ward of Indiana; Thos. Ward of Tennessee; Isabella Hearth of Indiana; Thos. Alexander and Minus Ward of Virginia; ________ Field and wife, Nancy, William Alexander, ________ Gomley and wife, Jane, Minus Alexander, Mary Alexander and Margaret Alexander (infant) all of Tennessee and all heirs of William Ward, Dec'd.

vs

Thos. T. Merryman, Admr. Est. Wm. Ward, Dec'd and Henry Moore.

William Ward died in New Orleans, July 1830. Wm. L. Hearth was guardian for Margaret Alexander.

****

1826 Franklin Co. Miss. Drawer 76 Case #664

Sarah G. Rowan, nee Witherspoon

vs

Beal B. Rowan

Divorce Petition.

Married: Franklin Co. August 17, 1814. Sarah Rowan was the daughter of John F. and Mary A. Witherspoon of Franklin Co.

****

1826 Claiborne Co. Miss. Drawer 76 Case #674

Elizabeth Fitzman

vs

Sabastian Fitzman

Divorce Petition—Married 1818.

****

1848 Marshall Co. Miss. Drawer 76 Case #675

Eliza White of Washington Co. Virginia, Admr. Est. James White, Dec'd.

vs

Joseph Trotter, Mrs. P. D. Mayers, Silas Trotter and James M. Pearsall.

****

1839 Jefferson Co. Miss. Drawer 76 Case #676

John Gilliland and wife, Margaret, Abraham B. .... and wife, Mary and Martha Norwood

vs

Mary Frisby, John M. Jones and wife, Carolyn, John Frisby, Leanora Gardner, Levi Harris and Thompson Shaw all of Jefferson Co.

****

1841 Simpson Co. Miss. Drawer 76 Case #676-a

Joseph Chapman and wife, Elizabeth, late Elizabeth Brown of Rankin Co.; John Thomas and wife, Kirah, late Kirah Brown of Washington Co. Georgia; and Littleberry Brown

vs

Isham Brown, Exec. Est. Samuel Brown, Dec'd
Samuel Brown died Sept. 1837.
See Will.

****

1841 Adams Co. Miss. Drawer 76 Case #679

Robert W. Wood, Admr. Est. John Irby, Dec'd (an unmarried man)

vs

Elizabeth Butcher, a free colored woman.

****

1837 Green Co. Miss. Drawer 76 Case #681

John Futch, Sr., John Futch, Jr., Isaac Futch, Luke Lott, Proctor Bayard and Stephen Lewis all of Green Co.

vs

Lavinia Futch

Divorce Petition.
Married in State of Georgia. Property settlement litigation.

****

1827 Adams Co. Miss. Drawer 76 Case #683

Susan Foster

vs

Thos. Foster, Jr.

Divorce Petition.
Married: June 29, 1821. Susan Foster was daughter of James Carson.

****

1827 Adams Co. Miss. Drawer 76 Case #692

Adeline Witherspoon, nee Chaney

vs

Charles S. Witherspoon

Divorce Petition
Married: January 1, 1824.

****

1841 Adams Co. Miss. Drawer 76 Case #694

Daniel Hunt

vs

Frederick Stanton and Adam L. Benjamin, Execs. Est. Benjamin Harmon, Dec'd

****

1827 Monroe Co. Miss. Drawer 76 Case #696

Roger McGraw

vs

Sarah McGraw, nee Williams

Divorce Petition.
Married: 1824 in Monroe Co. Miss.

****

1827 Adams Co. Miss. Drawer 77 Case #704

Elizabeth O. Keene

vs

Thomas Keene

Divorce Petition.
Married: June 17, 1818 in Adams Co.

****

1827 Jefferson Co. Miss. Drawer 77 Case #706

Henry King and Susannah King, Exec. and Exex. Est. Prosper King

vs

Elizabeth Chaney, relict of Bailey E. Chaney

****

1827 Jefferson Co. Miss. Drawer 77 Case #710

Aaron Goodson

vs

Judith Goodson

Divorce Petition

Married in Jefferson Co. Jan. 4, 1827. Judith Goodson was daughter of Lemon Wilkes of Jefferson Co.

****

1827 Adams Co. Miss. Drawer 77 Case #716

Sarah Hough, Admx. Est. Lewis H. Hough, Dec'd

vs

Alexander Kennedy and wife, Leonora of State of Louisiana

Heirs: Sarah (widow), John A., Cassandra and Thos. H. Hough (infants)

****

1832 Hinds Co. Miss. Drawer 77 Case #722

William Wing, Admr. Est. Philip Hoff, Dec'd

vs

Letitia Dickson

****

1827 Amite Co. Miss. Drawer 77 Case #724

James W. Dickey

vs

Samuel McGehee, Wm. McGehee, James McGehee, David McGehee, Jeptha Day and wife, Nancy, Pope McGehee, Reuben Holloway and wife, Polky, Charles Rhodes and wife Olive, B. B. Wills and wife, Eliza, and Lewis McGehee.

****

1827 Wilkinson Co. Miss. Drawer 77 Case #727

Nancy Fanner

vs

Joseph D. Fanner

Divorce Petition
Married: April 8, 1813 in Wilkinson Co.

****

1828 Franklin Co. Miss. Drawer 77 Case #732

Mary R. King

vs

Isaac L. King

Divorce Petition
Married in Amite Co. Jan. 17, 1825. Mary King was a daughter of Samuel Moore of Amite Co. The Kings had one child, Genoa, at the time of the filing of this bill.

****

1842 Claiborne Co. Miss. Drawer 77 Case #737

James P. Parker, Admr. Est. A. W. P. Parker, Dec'd

vs

George Luke and Jeremiah M. Rhodes, Admrs. Est. Amos Whiting, Dec'd

Jeremiah Rhodes was husband of Maria L. Rhodes, late Maria Whiting,

****

1827 Wilkinson Co. Miss. Drawer 77 Case #738

William Mayes and wife, Emily

vs

Samuel W. Lewis, William Carson, John L. Wall and John C. Sims, Admr. Est. Peter Presler, Sr., Dec'd

Emily Mayes was Emily Marsellus, daughter of Ephraim Marsellus and Catherine Marsellus. Catherine Marsellus married after Ephraim's death one William Mc-

Nulty on Feb. 4, 1819. She died May 12, 1822, leaving one child of her second marriage, Thos. P. McNulty. Peter Presler was the father of Catherine Marsellus McNulty and Admr. of Est. of Ephraim Marsellus.

****

1838 Warren Co. Miss. Drawer 77 Case #739

Everett Stillwell, Exec. Est. Lewis Hood, Dec'd

vs

William H. Sims

****

1830 Madison Co. Miss. Drawer 77 Case #752

Peter Legrand and Pinckney E. Stuart

vs

James S. Ewing and James Hannah

****

1842 Hinds Co. Miss. Drawer 77 Case #760

Malachi B. Hamer and Daniel Bleu, Admrs. Est. Chas. A. Weston, Dec'd

vs

Joseph Marlow

****

1842 Hinds Co. Miss. Drawer 77 Case #762

William Clark, Admr. de bonis non Ests. Edwin Perry, Dec'd and Bridges A. Williams, Dec'd

vs

Peter Murphy and Thos. Cook

****

1828 Co. not shown. Drawer 77 Case #764

William Kelly

vs

Mary Smith, Admx. Est. William Smith, Dec'd

****

1828 Wilkinson Co. Miss. Drawer 77 Case #765

Ruffin, Eliza, Celia Ann, Matilda, John and Jane McGraw, infant heirs of Peter McGraw, Dec'd by Gdn. Jesse Bell

vs

John McAlpin, Exec. Est. Peter McGraw, Dec'd.
Peter McGraw died November 1825.

****

1828 Amite Co. Miss. Drawer 77 Case #769

Mary McRae, relict, and John McRae, Wm. McRae, Daniel McRae, Anthony T. Simmons and wife, Margaret, nee McRae, Elizabeth McRae and Thos. McRae, all infant heirs of John McRae, Dec'd; Robt. Frierson and wife, Ester D., nee McRae, Mary Willingham, infant of Mary Willingham, Dec'd, nee McRae, by next friend Mary McRae (her grandmother) and Sarah A. Dunham, wife of Samuel B. Dunham, all heirs of John McRae, Dec'd.

vs

Thomas B. Dunham

Mary McRae, relict of John, was daughter of Daniel Dubose, Sr. of Darlington Dist. South Carolina. Thos. B. Dunham married Frances McRae, daughter of John and Mary McRae.

****

1843 Adams Co. Miss. Drawer 77 Case #769-a

Horace D. Kellogg, Leonard K. Barbe and T. W. Leonard, Exec. Est. George W. Kellogg

vs

Marvin B. Street

****

1830 Co. not shown. Drawer 78 Case #777

Charles C. Campbell, Admr. Est. Vinson Carter, Dec'd.

vs

Samuel McKay and Amariah Nichols

****

1838 Wilkinson Co. Miss. Drawer 78 Case 777-a

A. L. Geiser, Admr. Est. John Geiser, Dec'd

vs

Isabella Semple, Admx. Est. Robert Semple, Dec'd

****

1839 Yazoo Co. Miss. Drawer 78 Case #781

Ransom Cook

vs

Malinda Cook, formerly Malinda Arnold

Divorce Petition.
Married: August 9, 1832 in Yazoo Co. Miss.

****

1840 Warren Co. Miss. Drawer 78 Case #785

Elijah H. Pace

vs

Katherine Pace

Divorce Petition
Married Jan. 17, 1828.

****

1829 Adams Co. Miss. Drawer 78 Case #795

William N. Mercer, Admr. Est. Benjamin Farrar, Dec'd

vs

James K. Cook

****

1838 Washington Co. Miss. Drawer 78 Case #803

Missouri H. Kilpatrick by next friend, Samuel Terrell

vs

Elihu Kilpatrick

Divorce Petition

****

1842 Rankin Co. Miss. Drawer 78 Case #808

Merel J. Smith

vs

Thompson J. Berry, Admr. Est. N. Touchstone, Dec'd

****

1828 Wilkinson Co. Miss. Drawer 78 Case #809

Joseph E. Walker

vs

Mary Walker

Divorce Petition
Married: May 1806

****

1828 Amite Co. Miss. Drawer 78 Case #822

Elisha Freeman

vs

Elizabeth Freeman, formerly Elizabeth Strange

Divorce Petition
Married: March 1823

****

1839 Hinds Co. Miss. Drawer 78 Case #825

Azariah D. Evans

vs

Mary Ann Evans, formerly Mary Ann Kellum

Divorce Petition

Married: March 2, 1823 in Camdem Dist. North Carolina

****

1837 Franklin Co. Miss. Drawer 78 Case #826

William W. Hendricks

vs

Jefferson C. Porter, James R. Porter, and William Porter, Execs. Est. John Porter, Dec'd.

William Hendricks was the father and only heir of Lucius J. Hendricks, Dec'd and the husband of Martha Porter Hendricks, Dec'd who was a daughter of John and Mary Porter. John Porter died in 1834. Heirs: Jefferson C., James R., William, Albert Quincy and Elvira Porter and Lucius J. Hendricks, infant child of Martha Porter Hendricks, Dec'd. See will of John Porter.

****

1873 Chickasaw Co. Miss. Drawer 78 Case #826

C. P. Hill, Admr. Est. Charles M. Polk, Dec'd

vs

H. L. Hill, Eaton Pullen and John J. Hodges

****

1828 Adams Co. Miss. Drawer 78 Case #834

Mary B. Martin (relict) Admx. Est. Moses Martin, Dec'd

vs

Edmond Shackleford

****

1829 Franklin Co. Miss. Drawer 78 Case #842

Dempsey P. Cain

vs

James C. Cain

Dempsey P., James C., Hardy, John, E. R., Knox, Susan and Rebecca Cain were heirs of James Cain, Dec'd. Nathan Cain was Exec. Est. James Cain, Dec'd.

****

1829 Wilkinson Co. Miss. Drawer 78 Case #844

James Garraway

vs

Mary Garraway, formerly Mary Tenner

Divorce Petition
Married: 1826 in Wilkinson Co. Miss.

****

1829 Franklin Co. Miss. Drawer 79 Case #862

Freeman Ford, late of Franklin Co. Miss. now of East Baton Rouge, La.

vs

Celia Ford

Writ of Injunction
Freeman Ford was son of Hezekiah Ford who died in 1818.

****

1842 Jefferson Co. Miss. Drawer 79 Case #868

Eliza Beck

vs

Andrew Montgomery, Gdn. for James, Emily and Patrick Norris, infant heirs of Mrs. Mary Norris. See will of Mary Norris.

****

1842 Copiah Co. Miss. Drawer 79 Case #870

Alex R. Kilcrease, Frances B. Kilcrease, David D. Kilcrease and Cornelius B. Kilcrease all of Claiborne Co.

vs

Mary Kilcrease (relict) Exex. Est. William Kilcrease, Dec'd

William Kilcrease died July 1818. He was a brother of the Comp'ts in this case.

****

1816 Warren Co. Miss. Tr. Drawer 79 Case #876

Murdock McLeod, Harriet McLeod, Alexander McLeod and Sara McLeod

vs

William Booker, Admr. Est. James Booker, Dec'd

****

1829 Wilkinson Co. Miss. Drawer 79 Case #889

Eliza O'Connell Powell

vs

Garston Powell

Divorce Petition

Eliza O'Connor Powell was Eliza O. Walsh, sister of Simon Walsh.

Married: May 1824

****

1842 Adams Co. Miss. Drawer 79 Case #902

Pharo Carter, Admr. Est. Absolum Griffin, Dec'd and Admr. de bonis non Est. James Cole, Dec'd

vs

Judge of Probate for use of Absolum Griffin.

James Cole died intestate in 1812. His widow, Synthia Cole, was Admx. and Lidon Hopkins was Admr. of his estate. Synthia subsequently married Absolum Griffin and died in 1833 or 1834. Children of James and Synthia Cole: Clarissa Cole, Hiram Cole, Caroline Cole and Felix Cole. Clarissa married John Wood and Caroline married John D. Ford.

****

1830 Adams Co. Miss. Drawer 79 Case #903

Austin Holbrook and wife, Magdeline, James Tyler and James Clark, all heirs of Margaret Nelson, formerly Margaret LeFleur

vs

James Williams and wife, Margaret, Morrison Holbrook and wife, Jane, Catherine Tyler, Littleton Monday and wife, Catherine, all of Franklin Co. Miss.; John Duvall and wife, Anna, Elijah Duvall and wife, Margaret, Abram Inlow and wife, Elizabeth, and Susan Tyler all of Wilkinson Co. Miss.; Anne, Joseph, Peter, Thomas, Abraham and Abjah Clarke all of Claiborne Co. Miss.; Peter Nelson, Jr., Lewis Shaverson and wife, Margaret, Molly Craven, John Craven, Daniel Walker and Tom Walker, all of Adams Co. Miss.

****

1830 Adams Co. Miss. Drawer 79 Case #934

George Newman

vs

Richard M. Gaines, Admr. Est. John Richards, Dec'd

****

1842 Rankin Co. Miss. Drawer 79 Case #934-a

Isaac F. Alexander, Admr. Est. Andrew R. Morrison, Dec'd

vs

Samuel Prestridge, Admr. and Eliza Pendleton, Admx. Est. Zebulon E. Pendleton, Dec'd.

****

1838 Warren Co. Miss. Drawer 79 Case #950

Robert A. Warren of Warren Co. Miss.

vs

Martin Anding of Copiah Co. Miss. and Lucy Carriel, Exec. Est. John D. Carriel, Dec'd of Warren Co. Miss.

****

1841 Co. not shown. Drawer 80 Case #953

J. B. Williamson and wife, Culea M.

vs

Culea Wren, widow of Jones Wren; Susan Spann, daughter of Jones and Culea Wren and widow of Robert Spann; Jane Spann, daughter of J. and C. Wren and wife of Charles Spann; Eliza Spann, daughter of J. and C. Wren and wife of Frederick Spann; Sarah R. Newman, widow of John R. Pettway, the infant son of James E. Pettway; Henry Williamson and wife, Louisa, formerly Louisa Spann, daughter of Robert Spann; Jones W. Spann; Richard Spann; Caroline Spann, Susan Spann, all children and heirs at law of Robert Spann, Dec'd.

****

1832 Adams Co. Miss. Drawer 80 Case #958

Re: Lucy Perkins, Admx. Est. Nathaniel Perkins

vs

Woodson Wren

Nathaniel Perkins, Dec'd and Woodson Wren were partners.

****

1842 Tippah Co. Miss. Drawer 80 Case #959

James P. Peters and Thos. Peters

vs

John H. Moss, Admr. Est. Aaron McLaughlin, Dec'd

****

1830 Western Dist. of Miss. Drawer 80 Case #963

Hugh Connell and Eliza Davis, Admr. and Admx. Est. John Davis, Dec'd

vs

Daniel McGahee, Charley McMicken and Ananias Dunbar Daniel McGahee is shown as Admr. Est. Robert Braden, Dec'd.

****

1833 Jefferson Co. Miss. Drawer 80 Case #972

William A. Young and wife

vs

Eli W. Harding and Elihu Kilpatrick

Litigation involves estates of Benj. W. Bullin and Susan Chamberlain. Elizabeth Minor, wife of William B. Minor named as material witness.

****

1845 Adams Co. Miss. Drawer 80 Case #974

Joseph Bonnell

vs

Anna Elizabeth Bonnell

Divorce Petition

Joseph Bonnell was Lt. in Army of United States and stationed at Fort Jessup, Louisiana

****

1830 Adams Co. Miss. Drawer 80 Case #975

Thomas Alexander, John, William, Jacob, Isaac and Abraham Alexander, minors by next friend, Asee Kinne, Gdn. for the heirs of Isaac Alexander, Dec'd

vs

Archibald Terrell, Richard Lipions, Amos Alexander and Thomas Alexander, Execs. Est. Isaac Alexander, Dec'd

****

1832 Adams Co. Miss. Drawer 80 Case #992

Mary Ann Forsythe

vs

Dempsey Jackson and Sturges Sprague, Admrs. Est. John Forsythe, Dec'd

****

1832 Adams Co. Miss. Drawer 80 Case #992-a

Abijah Hull

vs

Alonzo Wattles and Mary Ann Forsythe Wattles

Mary Ann was widow of John Forsythe and this litigation involves dowry rights.

****

1831 Adams Co. Miss. Drawer 80 Case #993

P. M. Lapice, Admr. Est. Josiah Morris, Dec'd

vs

Earl Clapp, Exec. Est. R. Caldwell, Dec'd

****

1831 Adams Co. Miss. Drawer 80 Case #998

James Cowden and Sarah Calvit, Exec. and Exex. Est. Samuel Calvit, Dec'd

vs

Wm. F. Markham, Peter C. Goosey and Christopher Dart

****

1839 Co. not shown. Drawer 80 Case #1003

Sarah Callender by next friend, Joseph Callender

vs

Estate of Drury W. Brarcole

****

1838 Claiborne Co. Miss. Drawer 80 Case #1004

Eli C. Briscoe

vs

John W. Thompson, John B. Thrasher, Jacob Hoover

****

1843 Holmes Co. Miss. Drawer 80 Case #1006

James G. McGee and wife, Mary Ann, daughter of David Ford, Dec'd

vs

Everett S. Ford (brother) and James S. Barnes (brother in law) Admrs. Est. David Ford, Dec'd

Other Ford heirs: Charlotte, wife of J. S. Baines, Everett, John Q., Albert, Rufus and Betsy Ford.

****

1839 Claiborne Co. Miss. Drawer 80 Case #1014

John J. Fisher, Admr. Est. William Fisher, Dec'd

vs

John B. Thrasher, R. H. Bagley and S. F. R. Abbey

Sureties: Hugh Wall, Richardson Parkinson. Heirs not named.

****

1873 Lincoln Co. Miss. Drawer 80 Case #1016

Lucinda Gwin and M. M. Gwin, her husband, of the State of Texas

vs

Ross A. Ellzey

****

1843 Copiah Co. Miss. Drawer 80 Case #1018

William R. Gresham and Sarah Andrews

vs

Jesse W. Griffin and Caroline Roberts, Admrs. Est. John A. Roberts, Dec'd

****

1831 Adams Co. Miss. Drawer 80 Case #1021

William Foster, Exec. Ests. of Mary Gilbert, Nancy Gilbert and William Gilbert

vs

Samuel King, Gdn. for Albert Milton Gilbert, Emily Ann Minerva, Laura Jane Amelia and Olivia Mary Elizabeth King.
See Wills.

****

1831 Western Dist. of Miss. Drawer 80 Case #1029

Bank of Mississippi

vs

Felicita Gireandeau, sole devisee, and Peter M. Lapice, Exec. Est. of Gabriel Gireandeau, Dec'd.

****

1826 Amite Co. Miss. Drawer 80 Case #1039

Re: Estate of Joseph Williams, Sr., Dec'd — David Lee, Admr. and Gdn. for infant heir, Isabella Williams. Inventory.
Sureties: David Lee, Thos. McDowell and William Stewart, Jr.

****

1826 Amite Co. Miss. Drawer 80 Case #1039

Re: Inventory and final account in Est of Isabella Williams, infant heir of Joseph Williams, Dec'd, by David Lee, Gdn.

****

1838 Adams Co. Miss. Drawer 81 Case #1049

Maxwell W. Bland, by next friend, Richard Bland

vs

Hardy Hendren, David B. Scarbrough and wife, Jane, Dempsey Jackson, John Watt and Glendy Burke

****

1843 Yazoo Co. Miss. Drawer 81 Case #1062

E. C. Wilkinson

vs

Sarah R. Grayson, Admx. Est. Spencer Grayson, Dec'd

****

1839 Hinds Co. Miss. Drawer 81 Case #1065

James Sanders, Admr. Est. William Sanders, Dec'd

vs

Ethelwin Sadler

****

1871 Holmes Co. Miss. Drawer 81 Case #1072

M. C. Howard by next friend, W. A. Drennan

vs

O. T. Stephens, Isaiah Howard and James S. Weathersby

****

1838 Warren Co. Miss. Drawer 81 Case #1097

Harriet L. Moore by next friend and uncle, Edward W. Moore

vs

William G. Livingston and William G. Hamm

Harriet L. Moore was daughter of William and Margaret Martin Moore and niece of William Martin of Perquimans Co. North Carolina.

****

1842 Holmes Co. Miss. Drawer 81 Case #1109

Phillip B. Pope

vs

Mary Davis, Admx. and David Davis, Admr. Est. Wiley Davis, Dec'd.

****

1839 Hinds Co. Miss. Drawer 81 Case #1118

Michael Jones Dickson, David Dickson, Martha Ann Dickson, all heirs of James Dickson, Dec'd

vs

Lonzo Latham

****

1838 Copiah Co. Miss. Drawer 81 Case #1134

Sarah Andrews, widow of Jamason Andrews

vs

William Gresham, Admr. Est. Jamason Andrews

The petition refers to: Sarah Andrews, daughter of Richard Head of Chester Dist. S. C., Frances Lucinda Head, daughter of Richard Head and Sarah Head, wife of Richard Head.

****

1843 Wilkinson Co. Miss. Drawer 81 Case #1146

William C., Benj. L., Amy J., and Charles Coon by Benj. Killgore, their Gdn.

vs

John L. Jones, Admr. de bonis non David F. Coon, Dec'd

****

1843 Claiborne Co. Miss. Drawer 81 Case #1154

Commercial Bank of Rodney, Miss.

vs

James M. Smith, James Payne, Daniel Frisby

****

1839 Rankin Co. Miss. Drawer 81 Case #1156

Mary Janet Thompson by Frederick Johns, Gdn.

vs

Collins S. Tarpley, Rufus F. Flack, James M. Marr, Wadlington Mills and wife, Charlotte A. Mills

****

1843 Yazoo Co. Miss. Drawer 81 Case #1163

Thos. E. Hardaway and John T. Boykin

vs

James Biles, Admr. Est. Willie Biles, Dec'd.

Nancy Biles only named heir of Willie Biles, Dec'd

****

1843 Holmes Co. Miss. Drawer 81 Case #1165

William A. Land

vs

Gustavus J. Elliott, Admr. Est. William Merryman, Dec'd

Heirs of Merryman not named.

****

1839 Hinds Co. Miss. Drawer 81 Case #1187

Joseph A. McRaven

vs

Harriet A. Baird, Tazwell Baird, Isabella Baird, Felix Baird and Margaret Baird, all heirs at law of Felix W. Baird, Dec'd

****

1843 Madison Co. Miss. Drawer 81 Case #1188

Arnold Russell and Co. for use of H. R. W. Hill

vs

John H. Cheatham, Exec. Est. Sarah W. Cheatham, Dec'd

John H. Cheatham only heir named. Joseph Vannoy, bondsman.

****

1839 Yazoo Co. Miss. Drawer 81 Case #1188-a

Dauphin Knighten

vs

Henry L. Ratliff, a minor—William White, Gdn.

****

1839 Adams Co. Miss. Drawer 81 Case #1194

Eleanor Percy Ware (Daughter)

vs

Nathaniel A. Ware (Father), William B. P. Gaines, Thos. G. Percy, Elisha Warfield, Catherine Ann Warfield and Thomas B. Warfield.

Litigation involving substantial inheritance of Eleanor Percy Ware from her deceased mother who was Sarah Ellis. Sarah Ellis Ware had two children: Eleanor Percy Ware and Catherine Ware Warfield, wife of Elisha Warfield of the State of Kentucky. Eleanor Percy Ware married William Henry Lee.

****

1838 Hinds Co. Miss. Drawer 81 Case #1196

James Harper and John M. Carpenter

vs

Joseph A. Ferguson, Admr. Est. Jesse Alford, Dec'd and J. Brewer Munger, Nancy Munger (wife of J. Brewer) Isaac Heath and wife, Phoebe, Thomas Asbury and wife, Caroline, Isaac Alford, William Alford, Ferrell Alford, Martha Alford, John D. Vaughn, David C. Vaughn, Susan Vaughn and Mary Jane Vaughn, all heirs at law of Jesse Alford, Dec'd.

****

1845 Claiborne Co. Miss. Drawer 81 Case #1201

John B. Conger

vs

J. H. Robertson, Admr. Est. R. M. Livingston, Dec'd Heirs of Livingston not named.

****

1874 Washington Co. Miss. Drawer 81 Case #1215

A. B. Carson, Admr. Est. John L. Fisher, Dec'd

vs

Stevenson Archer, Trustee for E. Richardson and A. H. May

****

1840 Rankin Co. Miss. Drawer 82 Case #1221

Jacob Magee, Nehemiah Magee, Huriah Ginn, Rice Wells, Charles S. Smith, Allen Franklin, Orin C. Dow—Signers on bond of $24,000.00 to Sheriff W. P. Coleman as security for slaves.

****

1839 Rankin Co. Miss. Drawer 82 Case #1221-a

James R. Harris, John B. Byrne, Lewis F. Herman, Charles Biggs and Charles A. Lacasto

vs

Nehemiah Magee, Jacob Magee, Sanford M. Garvin and Thomas Ross

Litigation involves sale of slaves in the possession of Nehemiah Magee and Jacob Magee.

****

1839 Hinds Co. Miss. Drawer 82 Case #1253

Virginia Sims by next friend, Cowles Mead

vs

B. G. Sims, Thomas Hundley, Henry I. Shackleford, William S. Wells and William M. Rivers

Litigation involving prenuptial contract between Benjamin G. Sims and Virginia Catlett, nee Winter, daughter of William H. Winter and Catherine Winter, both Dec'd., late of Franklin Co. Ala.

****

1844 Yalobusha Co. Miss. Drawer 82 Case #1281

Samuel Foster

vs

James W. Summer and Mary Summer, Execs. Est. J. M. McKennee

****

1839 Holmes Co. Miss. Drawer 82 Case #1286

Wade H. Turner, A. B. Saunders and John M. Hollingsworth

vs

Samuel Swisher, Ellen Stark, Samuel Sample, Thos O. Marr, Edward C. Wilkinson, Robert Steele, Hugh F. Young and I. W. Dickens

Injunction restraining sale of slaves. Bond fixed at $12,000.

****

1839 Adams Co. Miss. Drawer 82 Case #1287

H. G. Runnels, A. D. Davis and R. A. Patrick

vs

David Davis, Admr. de bonis non Est. Wiley Davis, Dec'd

The widow, Mary G. Davis, was removed as Admx. in the insolvent estate of Wiley Davis, Dec'd.

****

1839 Yazoo Co. Miss. Drawer 82 Case #1295

Aaron Grigg, Ruth Harmon, John Lee and wife, Sarah, All Citizens of State of Kentucky; George Grigg, Elizabeth Williamson, Aaron Harlan and wife, Elizabeth, All Citizens of State of Ohio; David Colglazer and John Grigg, Citizens of State of Indiana; all heirs of John Colglazer, Dec'd, late of Yazoo Co. Miss.

vs

Milton Pyles, Spence M. Grayson, William Finney, Execs. of purported will of John Colglazer, Dec'd.

****

1844 Madison Co. Miss. Drawer 82 Case #1309

Louisa J. Fitzhugh, late Louisa J. Lathem, widow of Lorenzo Lathem

vs

Hervey Lathem, Exec. Est. Lorenzo Lathem, Dec'd

See Will of Lorenzo Lathem. Suit involves Dowry rights of Louisa.

****

1839 Yazoo Co. Miss. Drawer 82 Case #1311

Nicholas W. Ford, Edward Ford, William F. Markham, W. G. Freeland

vs

Henry H. Pease, and John B. Pease, Admrs. Est. Louis L. Pease, Dec'd, and William Pease, Dec'd; Henry H. Pease, John Harmon Pease, Jamerell Pease and Charles E. Pease, all heirs at law of Louis J. Pease and William Pease.

****

1839 Hinds Co. Miss. Drawer 82 Case #1312

Homer Ramsdale, Edwin J. Brown, Marshall B. Blake

vs

Wm. M. Cook and Geo. S. Dameron, Admrs. Est. Samuel Gwin, Dec'd

Samuel Gwin died intestate in 1838.

****

1839 Marshall Co. Miss. Drawer 82 Case #1319

Samuel McGowen, Gdn. for John E. Hill and Thomas Hill

vs

William Downing, Richard Loftis and James F. Trotter

****

1836 Hinds Co. Miss. Drawer 82 Case #1329

Eveline S. Wilson, Admx. Est. Isabel M. Wilson, Dec'd

vs

Ezra Marble and Peter C. Calhoun

****

1839 Claiborne Co. Miss. Drawer 82 Case #1344

Kittura Brian (Bryan), now Kittura Hollis

vs

Heirs of A. Whiting, Dec'd; Charles Patterson, John W. S. Moore and wife, Mary B. Moore, Charles P. McReynolds, Henry D. Patterson, Charles P. Bacon, Charles Mills, Martha Patterson, S. Thomson, Margaret P. Thomson, William Fletcher, Francis Gray, William F. Gray, Elizabeth Fletcher, James Watt, Margaret Watt, George M. Dortch, Elizabeth Dortch, Rebecca Gaines, Caleb Worley, Martha A. Worley, James P. Fletcher, Charles P. Fletcher, all non residents of State of Mississippi; Thomas Holliday, Copiah Co. Miss.; William Whiting, Claiborne Co. Miss.; Jeremiah M. Rhodes and wife, Maria Louisa Rhodes of Claiborne Co. Miss.; Ephraim G. Peyton of Copiah Co. Miss.; Kinchen A. Marttis, Hinds Co. Miss.; John Whiteman, Philamon H. Petty, Harvey T. Palmer, George Lake, Geo. W. Summers, Thomas Brian, Sarah Spalding, John B. Thrasher, and wife, Eliza, Eden Brashears, Christian Scheak, James Harper, John M. Carpenter, William Smythe, all of Claiborne Co. Miss. Also James A. McAllister, Corilla M. Parker a minor, Geo. G. Steen, James Murphy, Israel Barrett, Edward R. Christie, Geo. Cochran, Dan Ames and William Holt.

****

1835 Hinds Co. Miss. Drawer 82 Case #1347

Last Will and Testament of Major David Smith of Hinds Co. Miss.
See Will.

****

1822 Adams Co. Miss. Drawer 82 Case #1396

Mary Curry, James Curry, by next friend, Claiborne Steele

vs

James Duke

Mary and James Curry were heirs of Jacob Curry. Litigation involves slaves.

****

1838 Attala Co. Miss. Drawer 82 Case #1402

William McAllister, Admr. Est. John McAllister, Dec'd

vs

Bennett Smith

****

1839 Attala Co. Miss. Drawer 82 Case #1402-a

John W. Bozlin, Admr. Est. Joseph Gibson, Dec'd and Gdn. for Sarah Gibson (widow), a minor.

vs

Bennett Smith

****

1844 Marshall Co. Miss. Drawer 82 Case #1412

Ebenezer Kilpatrick

vs

Thos. J. Dye, Walter J. Dye, Robt. J. Dye, Jeremiah Walker and wife, Amanda, Wm. P. Coates and Richardson S. Coates (children of Sophia R. Coates, nee Dye), Wm. F. Farrar and Sarah Ann Farrar (children of Mary Ann Farrar, nee Dye), all heirs of William Dye, Dec'd.

****

1839 Marshall Co. Miss. Drawer 82 Case #1433

John Lehr, Admr. Est. J. S. Goodwin, late of Holmes Co. Miss.

vs

George G (or Gray) Skipworth

****

1845 Adams Co. Miss. Drawer 83 Case #1447

James H. McCoy

vs

Zachariah Rhodes and Eli Montgomery, Admrs. Est. Mary Montgomery, Dec'd

****

1839 Warren Co. Miss. Drawer 83 Case #1450

Edwin G. Cook

vs

Robt. Turnbull and wife, M. Jane, Robt. L. French and Joseph Littlejohn.

****

1850 Co. not shown. Drawer 83 Case #1452

William Barnes, Admr. Est. Mason Reynolds, Dec'd; Arthur Scott and Sarah Scott

vs

Buckner Harris, Admr. Est. Edward D. Learned, Dec'd.

****

1839 Holmes Co. and Yazoo Co. Miss.

Drawer 83 Case #1465

Joseph W. Deloach

vs

Mary Ann Deloach, minor heir of Wm. C. Deloach, Dec'd; John L. Bugg and wife, Sarah Ann Bugg.

Wm. C. Deloach, Dec'd was son of Melbry Deloach, Dec'd.

****

1845 Claiborne Co. Miss. Drawer 83 Case #1510

Bank of Port Gibson

vs

Thos. W. Baugh and wife, Martha, Execs. Est. Horace Carpenter, Dec'd
See Will of Horace Carpenter.

****

1839 Hinds Co. Miss. Drawer 83 Case #1518

Anderson Young

vs

Margaret E. Young

Divorce Petition

Married: Jan. 13, 1828 in Clark Co. Ky. Summons served in Livingston Co. Ky.

****

1839 Hinds Co. Miss. Drawer 83 Case #1532

Joseph Ray, Exec. and James Collins, M. D. Kimbrough and Isaac Askew, Sureties of Est. of Wm. Goodson, Dec'd.

vs

Fort Alford

Goodson heirs: Martha D. Goodson, Rachael Fort and Sarah Fort, daughters of Hanna Goodson Fort, Dec'd.

****

1812 Claiborne Co. Miss. Tr. Drawer 83 Case #1536

Richard and Prosper King, Admrs. Est. John Eldergill

vs

John Cummins, Admr. Est. Arthur Carney, Dec'd

****

1845 Copiah Co. Miss. Drawer 83 Case #1545

Washington Clements, Admr. and Leona Clements, Admx. Est. Stephen Clements, Dec'd.

vs

Thomas R. Reed, Joseph A. Ferguson, James I. Cottingham, Wm. M. Haley

****

1845 Madison Co. Miss. Drawer 83 Case #1559

William McBride

vs

William B. Ross and Martha Ross, Execs. Est. William A. Fort

Case involves indebtedness of John W. Hanna and Eliza D. Hanna to Est. Wm. A. Fort, Dec'd.

****

1839 Yazoo Co. Miss. Drawer 83 Case #1560

Michael O'Conner Kennedy

vs

Alexander H. Morton, Admr. and Paulina T. Rainey, Admx. de bonis non Est. Robert A. Goddard.

Paulina T. Rainey succeeds her deceased husband James T. Rainey as Admr.

****

1839 Holmes Co. Miss. Drawer 83 Case #1562

Mahala Shaw, late Mahala Powell, widow of Samuel R. Powell, and husband Edward Shaw, Admrs. Est. Samuel R. Powell, Dec'd

vs

Simeon Thompson and William Anderson

****

1839 Holmes Co. Miss. Drawer 83 Case #1570

William A. Dickson, Admr. Est. James C. Dickson, Dec'd.

vs

I. S. Goodwin

James C. Dickson died April 8, 1835

****

1839 Yazoo Co. Miss. Drawer 83 Case #1574

Hiram Selcer, Exec. Est. Pierre B. Tutt, Dec'd

vs

Richardson Bowman

****

1845 Madison Co. Miss. Drawer 83 Case #1574-a

John Stone and wife, Anna Eliza Stone, late widow of Thos. Collins, Dec'd

vs

Joseph Collins, Admr. de bonis non Est. Thomas Collins, Dec'd.

Heirs: Ann Eliza Stone (widow), Margaret Sophia Collins and Mary Jane Collins, infant children of Thomas Collins, Dec'd.

****

1845 Hinds Co. Miss. Drawer 83 Case #1576

Robert Clark, Admr. de bonis non Est. Edwin Perry, Dec'd

vs

Peter Murphy

****

1839 Madison Co. Miss. Drawer 83 Case #1584

Elizabeth McCarroll, Admr. Est. Charles M. McCarroll, Dec'd.

vs

William J. Brown and wife, Elizabeth Brown.

Heirs: Alexander and Ansley McCarroll

****

1839 Warren Co. Miss. Drawer 83 Case #1612

Phoebe Kenley, formerly Phoebe Sims

vs

David Kenley, a resident of the Republic of Texas, late of Claiborne Co. Miss.

Petition for separate maintenance. Marriage contract dated December 19, 1832.

Phoebe Kenley was widow of Arthur B. Sims, Dec'd.

****

1877 Monroe Co. Miss. Drawer 84 Case #1620

Harvey Murphy, Marks Weiler, Samuel Haas, Abraham Krauss, all of Aberdeen, Miss.

vs

William Hodges and wife, Sarah, Jacob Gattman, Isaac Randle, James G. Randle, Mrs. Anna L. Watkins, William W. Watkins and Mason M. Cummings

****

1845 Holmes Co. Miss. Drawer 84 Case #1624

Nicholas O'Rielly, surviving partner of Edmund and Phillip O'Rielly

vs

Hezekiah Harrington

Edward Wadlington and William M. Sparks, Sureties.

****

1840 Lowndes Co. Miss. Drawer 84 Case #1625

Elizabeth Powell by next friend, Paschal B. Wade

vs

Cornelius Powell and Geo. W. Smith, Trustee

Elizabeth Whitwell of Lowndes Co. married Cornelius Powell of Franklin Co. Ala. in 1829. Litigation involves marriage contract made in Franklin Co. Ala. A copy of this contract in file.

****

1842 Lowndes Co. Miss. Drawer 84 Case #1629

Margaret Allen by next friend, Soloman Clark of Pontotoc Co. Miss.

vs

John L. Allen (husband of Comp't), Edwin F. Watkins,

Daniel McNeil, James A. Murray, James E. Matthews, Willis W. Cherry, Daniel Baldwin, Agnes T. Morse, William H. Harrison, William Harrod.

Chickasaw Nation lands subject of litigation.

****

1824 Franklin Co. Miss. Drawer 84 Case #1629-a

Robert Allan and wife Sealey

and

Thomas K. Pickett and Micajah Pickett

Contract. Witnesses: James Calcote and Gabriel Pickering

****

1840 Scott Co. Miss. Drawer 84 Case #1635

Alfred Garner, Gidean Garner, Susanna Garner, Ebenezer Jones and wife, Ivena, James A. Jones and wife, Drucilla, all of the State of Tennessee, and all heirs of Lewis Garner, Dec'd.

vs

Willis Garner, Scott Co. Miss. Exec. Est. Thomas Garner, Dec'd.

Thomas Garner was the father of Lewis Garner who died in Tennessee in 1812. Thomas Garner died in Warren Co. Tennessee in 1814.

****

1840 Warren Co. Miss. Drawer 84 Case #1639

Thomas L. Walker and wife, Ellen (Eleanor) Walker

vs

George Bunyard, William R. Lewis and John F. Walker

****

1840 Claiborne Co. Miss. Drawer 84 Case #1650

Samuel Q. Middleton, with Sureties: James Glass, Isaac Rolls and John B. Gibson

vs

Ruth Middleton

Bill recites that Samuel Q. Middleton, Stephen Middleton and Samuel Miller were children of Martha Miller who died in 1838. They were also grandchildren of Ann Gibson.

****

1840 Yazoo Co. Miss. Drawer 84 Case #1657

Edward C. Wilkinson, Admr. de bonis non Est. Richard F. Floyd, Dec'd

vs

Elizabeth M. McMorrough, Admx. Est. John M. McMorrough, succeeding John McKinstry, resigned.

****

1840 Yazoo Co. Miss. Drawer 84 Case #1658

John B. Hall of Yazoo Co.

vs

Nancy T. Hall, nee Nancy T. Cook

Divorce Petition.
Married: April 2, 1816 in Davidson Co. Tenn.

****

1845 Claiborne Co. Miss. Drawer 84 Case #1658-a

Robt. J. R. Swearingen, Admr. Est. George W. Swearingen, Dec'd

vs

John B. Conger

****

1876 Madison Co. Miss. Drawer 84 Case #1668

R. J. Ross, Admr. (Est. not named)

vs

Thomas McMahon and Henry O'Hara

****

1845 Jefferson Co. Miss. Drawer 84 Case #1670

American Colonization Scy

vs

Isaac R. Wade, Exec. Est. Isaac Ross, Dec'd

****

1826 Franklin Co. Miss. Drawer 84 Case #1675

John Quincy Adams, President of the United States

to

Joseph Winn and William Thompson

Land Patent, 640 20/100 acres Sec. 4 T6 R3E Franklin Co. Miss. August 1, 1826. Original patent in file.

****

1842 Adams Co. Miss. Drawer 84 Case #1676

Samuel Davis, Agt. for Ann E. Hill

vs

Frances A. Newcomb and wife, Eliza L., Levin M. Patterson and Zebulon E. Pendleton

****

1841 Madison Co. Miss. Drawer 84 Case #1686

William Bennett, James P. Clark, Robert Riddle

vs

C. T. Smith, Exec. Est. J. M. Smith, Dec'd
See Will of J. M. Smith

****

1852 Co. not shown. Drawer 84 Case #1687

Colin S. Tarpley

vs

Mary Jane Thompson, Admx. Est. M. T. Anderson, Dec'd

****

1843 Simpson Co. Miss. Drawer 84 Case #1694

Patsy Myrick, Admrx. Est. Dennis Myrick

vs

Briant Barlow, Admr. Est. John Barlow, late of Perry Co.

Heirs: Henry Barlow of Copiah Co.; Southall Myrick and wife, Missouri Myrick, nee Barlow, daughter of John Barlow, Dec'd of Clark Co. Ala.

****

1840 Rankin Co. Miss. Drawer 84 Case #1695

Murrell J. Smith

vs

Thompson Berry, Admr. Est. Nathaniel Touchstone, Dec'd.

****

1840 Rankin Co. Miss. Drawer 84 Case #1695-a

Murrell J. Smith and William Steen

vs

Hezekiah Holcomb and Richard R. Richardson, Admrs. Est. Richard Richardson, Dec'd

****

1840 Warren Co. Miss. Drawer 84 Case #1704

Daniel W. Gantley

vs

Walter R. Puckett, James Campbell, Thos. L. Arnold

****

1848 Warren Co. Miss. Drawer 84 Case #1707

James W. Mitchell

vs

Benj. J. Hicks, Admr. de bonis non, with will attached, of John L. Irwin, Dec'd

Hicks succeeded John W. Vick as Admr. Est. John L. Irwin, Dec'd

****

1875 Prentiss Co. Miss. Drawer 84 Case #______

A. E. and J. J. Reynolds

vs

John Taylor, Gdn. for Ellen J. Key

****

1840 Hinds Co. Miss. Drawer 84 Case #1739

Benj. H. Powell, a citizen of Virginia, Admr. with will attached, Est. Milenor L. Stratton, Dec'd, late of State of Virginia

vs

John D. King and Samuel M. Puckett both of Rankin Co. Miss.

Heirs: Ann Elizabeth Stratton (widow), Mary Frances, Ann Eliza, Sarah Eleanor (infant children), all of Powhatan Co. Virginia.

See Will of Milenor L. Stratton.

****

1839 Adams Co. Miss. Drawer 84 Case #1743

S. T. McAllister, Admr. and Ann P. Gemmell, Admx., with will annexed, of Peter Gemmell, Dec'd

vs

Thomas Vonner, Robt. W. Wood, David H. Pentecost, Covington H. Cropper

****

1846 Wilkinson Co. Miss.. Drawer 84 Case #1744

James Hill, Admr. Est. George Brister, Dec'd

vs

James Sullivan

Heirs: Gilbert Holly and wife, Margaret, Rebecca Brister, Adeline Brister, Charles Tenny and wife, Jane, William Brister, John Annis and wife, Sarah and Ann Brister (widow of George).

****

1840 Adams Co. Miss. Drawer 84 Case #1750

Samuel K. Montgomery and wife, Mary Ann

vs

Charles N. Rowley of Concordia Parish, La.

****

1840 Adams Co. Miss. Drawer 84 Case #1750-a

Nathaniel L. Carpenter, Samuel Carpenter, Charles R. Rowley

vs

Samuel K. Montgomery

****

1840 Warren Co. Miss. Drawer 84 Case #1757

Joseph Miller, Admr. de bonis non Est. James C. Dickson, Dec'd

vs

James B. Robinson, Admr. de bonis non, Est. Isaac Caldwell, Dec'd

****

1847 Warren Co. Miss. Drawer 84 Case #1757-a

Joseph W. Miller, Admr. Est. James C. Dickson

vs

Thomas Kearny and Elizabeth Kearny, Exec. Est. Isaac Caldwell, Dec'd

See Will of Isaac Caldwell

****

1842 Madison Co. Miss. Drawer 85 Case #1770

William Denson and Leroy D. Sharp, Execs. Est. Thos. W. Camp, Dec'd

Magness Teague and Albert G. Forney

****

1846 Adams Co. Miss. Drawer 85 Case #1799

William Rucker, Johnathon Rucker, Daniel Rucker, brothers and sole heirs of Peter Rucker, Dec'd

vs

William Bisland, Samuel H. Lambdin and Daniel Smith, Execs. Est. Peter Rucker, Dec'd.

****

1846 Amite Co. Miss. Drawer 85 Case #1801

William O. Lee by next friend, James D. Lowry

vs

E. T. McLean, guardian for William O. Lee, infant.

File mentions Rebecca C. Carroll, Admx. Est. Edward Carroll, Dec'd as having married James M. Smiley. James

F. Lowry, William McKewen and James M. Smiley named as bondsmen.

****

1845 Copiah Co. Miss. Drawer 85 Case #1845

Ala F. Bridges, Admr. Est. James Bridges, Dec'd

vs

Shelton H. Heard, Samuel S. Heard and Charles W. Harris.

****

1840 Jefferson Co. Miss. Drawer 85 Case #1846

Janson W. Holmes, Exec. Est. King H. Holmes; Wm. G. Holmes; Robert T. Dunbar and wife, Elizabeth, nee Holmes; Elizabeth D. Holmes and Lydia Ann Holmes, infant heirs of Simpson H. Holmes, Dec'd by Janson W. Holmes next friend; John H. Martin and Howard Martin, infant heirs of Mary Martin, Dec'd late Mary Holmes, by next friend, Janson W. Holmes—All heirs of King H. Holmes, Dec'd.

vs

Thomas C. Vaughan and wife, Harriet L. Vaughan.

****

1840 Warren Co. Miss. Drawer 85 Case #1854

Lititia Longcape

vs

Thomas B. Longcape

Divorce Petition.
Married: 1823 in State of Ohio.

****

1840 Yazoo Co. Miss. Drawer 85 Case #1856

Rebecca Carradine

vs

William R. Carradine

Divorce Petition.
Married: Dec. 1836. Decree for Comp't 1841.

****

1840 Warren Co. Miss.. Drawer 85 Case #1901

John Henderson, Exec. Est. Valentine C. Ray, Dec'd

vs

Francis Illsey

****

1843 Wilkinson Co. Miss. Drawer 85 Case #1903

Nancy Quin, relict of Robert Quin, Dec'd

vs

James Quin (brother of Robert and Henry Quin)

Robert Quin died 1815. His brother, Henry Quin died Nov. 1838.

Heirs at law of Henry Quin: James Quin, Elizabeth McIntosh, Margaret Cole, James B. Bullock and wife, Sevina, Benj. Rogers and wife, Nancy, Mary Quin, Margaret Quin, Martha Ann Terrell, nee Quin, wife of Joseph Terrell, Robert P. Stewart and wife, Mary.

****

1841 Madison Co. Miss. Drawer 85 Case #1920

James S. Ewing, George Pollard, Branham Merrill, Survivors of Leigh Maddox, Dec'd

vs

Thos. H. Ragan and wife, Cecilia Cargill Ragan and Phineas M. Garrett, Admrs. Est. William Cargill, Dec'd.

****

1846 Warren Co. Miss.. Drawer 85 Case #1924

Margaret Smith

vs

John Babb, Admr. Est. Peter Mintzer, Dec'd

****

1840 Co. not shown Drawer 85 Case #1925

Sarah Neibert and Absolum Speilman, Admrs. Est. Joseph Neibert, Dec'd

vs

S. B. Withers

Commissioners appointed: Aylette Bucker, John P. Walworth and Jefferson Beaumont.

****

1843 Yazoo Co. Miss. Drawer 86 Case #1932

James W. Barnett, Admr. Est. James M. Pease, Dec'd; Louise M. Pease (widow) and Louise I. Pease, infant heir of James M. Pease

vs

Henry R. M. Hill, James Deck, William I. McLean, George Fisher and David G. Moore

****

1837 Madison Co. Miss. Drawer 86 Case #1970

In Re: Last Will and Testament of Abner Sholar of Madison Co. Miss.

See Wills.

****

1841 Neshoba Co. Miss. Drawer 86 Case #1993

Shem-my-ah or Ishmyah, Ohlateah, Shetah, Amistonak, Nockemantubby and Istonubba by his natural guardian, Shemmyah—all full bred Choctaws and citizens of Neshoba Co. Miss.

vs

Hugh McDonald, Alexander McKay, Neill McDonald and James McDonald all of Neshoba Co.

Shemmyah was the mother and grandmother of all Comp'ts. She married Cushonah.

****

1841 Neshoba Co. Miss. Drawer 86 Case #1994

Ah-ta-tamba, a full blood Choctaw and Citizen of Leake Co. Miss.

vs

Daniel McDonald

Injunction re: Choctaw lands. See will of Mary McDonald, widow of Daniel McDonald.

****

1850 Hinds Co. Miss. Drawer 86 Case #2059

Thomas Stubblefield

vs

Polly Stubblefield

Divorce Petition.

****

1847 Adams Co. Miss. Drawer 86 Case #2059-a

John Glenn

vs

Doxey H. Thistle, Exec. Est. Israel Leonard, Dec'd

****

1841 Madison Co. Miss. Drawer 86 Case #2071

Richard A. Cheek and wife, Jane, formerly Jane Davis, and Margaret Ann Davis by next friend, Richard A. Cheek, all of Madison Co.

vs

William Bennett and wife, Elizabeth; Thos. Davis, Admr. Est. David Davis, Sr., Dec'd and Wilson Dillon

David Davis died 1831. Elizabeth Davis later married William Bennett.

****

1851 Hinds Co. Miss. Drawer 86 Case #2088

Catherine B. Jones, Admx. Est. Edward Jones, Dec'd

vs

James Bond, Robt. H. Buckner, David P. Harrison and William H. Harrison, Admrs. Est. Vernon C. Hicks, Dec'd.

****

1841 Yazoo Co. Miss.. Drawer 87 Case #2093

Levi B. Thompson, Admr. Est. Felix Thompson, Dec'd

vs

Henry Powell, Wm. H. Nightengale and Wm. T. Jones

****

1853 Yazoo Co. Miss. Drawer 87 Case #2103

Preston S. Thompson, Admr. de bonis non Est. Felix Thompson, Dec'd

vs

Henry Rowett

****

1834 Amite Co. Miss. Drawer 87 Case #2125

James Eubanks and wife Eliza, formerly Eliza Lowry, relict of Robert Lowry, Dec'd

vs

Other heirs of Robert Lowry, Dec'd.

Heirs: Edward Carroll and wife, Rebecca Caroline, nee Lowry, Harriet Maria Lowry, James Francis Lowry, Robert Hinds Lowry and Eliza Lowry (widow).

Eliza Lowry and James Eubanks were married Nov. 8, 1831.

****

1847 Madison Co. Miss. Drawer 87 Case #2127

James R. Young, Comm. for State of Miss.

vs

John Dear and J. J. Thompson, Exec. Est. Burris Haley, Dec'd.

****

1847 Hancock Co. Miss. Drawer 87 Case #2169

Elias Wallis (Wallace), John B. Wallace, William M. Wallace and Dicey Gurman, nee Wallace and husband Prestly Gurman, all heirs of Jourdan Morgan, Dec'd, late of Hancock Co. Miss.

vs

David R. Wingate, Admr. Est. Jourdan Morgan, Dec'd.

Comp'ts were children of Lucy Morgan Wallace who was sister of Jourdan Morgan.

****

1841 Warren Co. Miss. Drawer 87 Case #2180

Jacob Cardwell and Robert Bull, residents of Shelby Co. Ky. Execs. Est. Robt. Bull, Dec'd

vs

John C. Bull and Robert Y. Black

****

1847 Oktibbeha Co. Miss. Drawer 87 Case #2181

The State of North Carolina for use of John H. Vick, Gdn. for Louisa C. Vick and Josiah Vick, infants

vs

John C. Hines, Admr. Est. Green W. Drake, Dec'd

****

1846 Marion Co. Miss. Drawer 87 Case #2253

Azel Backus Bacon, Admr. Est. Owen Richardson, Dec'd

vs

John Tynes

John Tynes and a sister Sarah Tynes were children of Pearce Tynes of the Orangeburgh Dist. of S. C. Sarah Tynes married Owen Richardson.

****

1842 Hinds Co. Miss. Drawer 87 Case #2280

Thomas H. Green

vs

Daniel P. Mann and Mary M. B. Perkins, Admrs. Est. Daniel P. Perkins, Dec'd

****

1842 Adams Co. Miss. Drawer 87 Case #2290

Alex Montgomery, Admr. Est. Joseph Bonnell, Dec'd; Ferdinand L. Claiborne, Tr. for Ann Eliza Phillips

vs

Michael Barrett and wife, Frances.

Ann Eliza Phillips was daughter of William Brooks and relict of Joseph Bonnell, Dec'd

****

1841 Yazoo Co. Miss. Drawer 88 Case #2306

James Loggins, Admr. Est. John Emerson, Dec'd

vs

Ezekiel Jones and William Russell

****

1841 Co. not shown. Drawer 88 Case #2310

Charles Miles

vs

Sarah R. Grayson, Admr. Est. Spence M. Grayson, Dec'd.

****

1848 Pontotoc Co. Miss. Drawer 88 Case #2317

Benj. D. Anderson, Admr. Est. Aaron Root, Dec'd

vs

John Carruth, James Gool, Chas. T. Smith, William Smith, Richard Orme, Wm. M. Bostick, Hugh T. Love, Andrew Nichols, Wm. Cravens, Oliver P. Wright, Daniel McNeil, Abram H. Roach, George Smith, Erasmus D. Walker, Richard W. Thomas, Leroy Carpenter, Robert T. Moore, John C. Carter, Asby B. Stansel, Sterling Withers, James W. Matthews, Nathaniel Bennett, Wm. McMahon, William Hill, Charles Andrews, Andrew Forsythe, Charles Anderson, Reuben Echols and Henry A. Orme.

****

1848 Monroe Co. Miss. Drawer 88 Case #2324

Charles Boggan, Admr. Est. Cornelius Boggan, Dec'd

vs

Robert M. Walter

****

1841 Yazoo Co. Miss. Drawer 88 Case #2326

Arthur McCrackin

vs

Young Berry, Admr. Est. Roderick McDuffey, Dec'd

****

1842 Warren Co. Miss. Drawer 88 Case #2368

Joseph Templeton for use of Wm. Barton

vs

Elias Woodborn, Admr. Est. Jesse Wright, Dec'd

Jury List: Joseph E. Davis, Andrew M. Payne, Lewis Soher, John G. Parham, Elijah H. Pace, Thaddeus Steth, Reuben M. Gibson, Thos. F. Walker, Wm. Everett, Wm. R. Narcon, Samuel Lum and Clement Garrison.

****

1842 Holmes Co. Miss. Drawer 88 Case #2382

R. L. Suggs

vs

Robert B. Frayser, Benj. Frayser, John B. Frayser, Melissa Austin, nee Frayser and husband, James Austin, Nancy

Sims and husband, Reuben Sims, Julia A. Warmack and husband, Thos. Warmack, Eliza Davis and ________ Davis, her husband, all non residents of State of Miss. and all heirs of W. J. Frayser, Dec'd

****

1845 Holmes Co. Miss.. Drawer 88 Case #2383

Hugh Dickson, Admr. Est. James C. Dickson, Dec'd

vs

Thos. B. Poindexter, Page Taylor and John G. Poindexter.

James Dickson died in 1825.

****

1842 Wilkinson Co. Miss. Drawer 88 Case #2385

Daniel Williams and Charles Samuel Williams (a minor), John M. Graves and wife, Margaret, late Williams, heirs of Isaac Williams, Dec'd

vs

Nancy Pinson (relict) Daniel B. Pinson and Elizabeth Pinson (children) heirs of Daniel B. Pinson, Sr., Dec'd.

Daniel Pinson died in 1823.

****

1842 Adams Co. Miss. Drawer 88 Case #2386

Malinda M. Brice

vs

Nelson Brice

Divorce Petition.

****

1842 Adams Co. Miss. Drawer 88 Case #2398

Catherine W. Bisland

vs

James Bisland

Divorce Petition.
Married: April 21, 1836 in Adams Co. Miss.

****

1848 Hinds Co. Miss. Drawer 88 Case #2401

Daniel Yates and Obedience Yates, Admrs. Est. Ignatius Yates

vs

James Hall.

****

1842 Hinds Co. Miss. Drawer 88 Case #2403

Dulcinea Johnson by next friend, Daniel W. Johnson

vs

Perry King, Jr., Wm. King, James King, Edward King, Mary King, Harriet King, Elizabeth Thomas and husband, James Thomas, and Mary King (relict), all heirs of Perry King, Dec'd, and of William M. Robinson and wife, Rachel, both dec'd.

****

1842 Carroll Co. Miss. Drawer 88 Case #2408

Julia A. Davis

vs

David Davis

Divorce Petition.

Children: Samuel Davis, Susannah L. Davis.

Deposition of: Sophia H. Davis of Bedford Co. Virginia. S. B. Marsh of Carrollton, Miss. acted as arbiter.

****

1848 Wilkinson Co. Miss. Drawer 88 Case #2414

Thomas Hickley and wife, Sarah E. Hickley

vs

Stephen Johnson, Gdn.

Stephen Johnson, a resident of State of Louisiana, was Gdn. for Sarah E. Hickley, nee Waller and James G. Waller, children of James Waller, Sr., Dec'd. Sarah Waller married Thos. Hickley Feb. 16, 1841. Bill mentions "wife of Johnson" also as an heir of James Waller, Dec'd.

****

1845 Warren Co. Miss. Drawer 88 Case #2427

Elizabeth Dyer by next friend, Erasmus D. Downs

vs

James Patterson, Admr. Est. Richard Parker, Dec'd.

Elizabeth Dyer was wife of Absolum Dyer. They had Martha Ann Dyer.

****

1842 Warren Co. Miss. Drawer 88 Case #2431

James Simmons and wife, Martha, late Martha Ray

vs

John Henderson, Exec. Est. Valentine Ray, Dec'd; Thos. A. Nusum and wife, Margaret, nee Simmons, of Warren Co.; Aaron Day, Malinda Barbour, Elizabeth Berry, Moses Ray, Burgers Ray, Fielding G. Ray, Rebecca Ray, Susan Ray, Nancy Ray, Sarah Ray, all citizens of State of Kentucky.

Martha Simmons was widow of Valentine Ray who died Dec. 1834 in Warren Co. Miss.

****

1842 Warren Co. Miss. Drawer 88 Case #2436

Eliza Jane Scott, Admx. Est. Wm. P. Scott, Dec'd

vs

Adelia Ann Drake and Nathaniel S. Drake

****

1847 Madison Co. Miss. Drawer 89 Case #2441

Mary E. A. Shotwell

vs

Robert Shotwell, Jr.

Litigation re: Land, crops, etc. Relationship of Mary E. A. and Robert Shotwell, Jr. not given. Bill shows Mary E. A. Shotwell married Andrew Lawson after original bill was filed. See Case #2611.

****

1842 Claiborne Co. Miss. Drawer 89 Case #2452

Fletcher Creighton, Admr. de bonis non Est. Amos Whiting, Dec'd and Alexander Baker, Richard Bigelow all of Claiborne Co.

vs

Jeremiah Callahan and William Buckley.

Amos Whiting died August 1837. Maria Louisa Whiting, widow of Amos and George Lake were original adminstrators.

****

1848 Harrison Co. Miss. Drawer 89 Case #2457

Joshua A. Talbert, Admr. Est. Isaac B. Currie, Dec'd

vs

Jacob A. Norager

Jurymen listed: Thos. W. Evans, Andrew Baggett, Phillip Saucier, Lama Dubison, Joseph Fazard, W. H. Brunston, D. Goss, Evan Williams, John Schearrer, Stephen Lafore, W. H. House and W. I. Evans.

****

1842 Jefferson Co. Miss. Drawer 89 Case #2464

Martha G. Smith, widow and heir of Peter W. Smith, Dec'd

vs

William B. Smith of Jefferson Co.

Peter W. Smith died July 1839 in Iberville Parish, La. and left will. William B. and Peter W. Smith were brothers.

****

1842 Holmes Co. Miss. Drawer 89 Case #2467

Sarah Land (widow), Rutherford Land, Martha Land (minor by Gdn. Sarah Land), all heirs of Charles Land Dec'd of Holmes Co.

vs

Margaret Land of Hinds Co., widow of Wm. Land; Silas Land, a minor (Margaret and Silas heirs of Thos. Land, Dec'd), William Johnson, Admr. Est. Thos. Land, Dec'd; Thos. Sims and wife, Margaret of Holmes Co. and John B. Forrester of Leake Co.

Litigation involves land purchased from Istauchi or Betsy Beams, Choctaw Indian woman, after the Treaty of Dancing Rabbit Creek. Bill recites Istauchi—alias Betsy Beams—had one child, Ann, who married Thomas Sims. Sarah Land was widow of Charles Land.

****

1838 Adams Co. Miss. Drawer 89 Case #2472

Rachel Rapp, Elizabeth Rapp and Ellen Rapp, free persons of color

vs

John Fletcher

****

1842 Adams Co. Miss. Drawer 89 Case #2490

Stephen Duncan, Admr. Est. Timothy Bradish, Dec'd

vs

Grafton Baker and Samuel Chamberlain

****

1842 Adams Co. Miss. Drawer 89 Case #2496

Christian Stephen

vs

Helena Rulon, Caroline Stith and John Bruss and wife, Charlotte

****

1842 Claiborne Co. Miss. Drawer 89 Case #2506

James W. Bradshaw

vs

Martha A. Bradshaw

Divorce Petition.

Married: Sept. 20, 1838 in Claiborne Co. Def't removed to Louisiana.

****

1848 Adams Co. Miss. Drawer 89 Case #2514

Chas. L. Dubuisson, Judge of Probate of Adams Co. for use of Chas. Jones and wife, Sally (freed slaves)

vs

Walter Irvine, Jr. and Mary Irvine, Surv. Execs. Est. Walter Irvine, Dec'd

Sally Jones was granted freedom under the will of George McCracken of Adams Co. of which will Thos. Munce was Exec. Munce died May 11, 1830.

****

1848 Simpson Co. Miss. Drawer 89 Case #2523

Henry Bright and William Ledgard

vs

Tristram Stubbs and William Stubbs, Admrs. Est. Peter Stubbs, Dec'd

****

1842 Wayne Co. Miss. Drawer 89 Case #2525

Oliver E. Dease, Elizabeth Dease, Rachel Fatheree, Mary Fatheree (wife of John D. Fatheree), Nancy Hopkins, all children and heirs of Micajah Wall, Dec'd.

vs

Ransom J. Jones, Admr. Est. James Depriest, Dec'd.

Micajah Wall died in 1813 or 1814. His widow, Mary Wall, married James Depriest in 1816. Heirs of Micajah Wall other than named: Micajah, Arthur and John Wall.

****

1879 Adams Co. Miss. Drawer 89 Case #2529

Henrietta Harrison

vs

Margaret Harrison, Laura Forbes, W. H. Forbes, Percy Calvit, Isaac Calvit, Elizabeth Calvit, Minnie Lum, Isaac Lum and Eugene Garvely.

****

1842 Copiah Co. Miss. Drawer 89 Case #2532

William Mullins, James Mullins, Seth Granberry, Elijah Rogers and D. Shoemaker

vs

John W. Scott and wife, Aurora V. Scott

****

1845 Jasper Co. Miss. Drawer 89 Case #2534

Charles, Elias, John and William Newell (all brothers and sons of William Newell and Fereby Newell O'Sullivant of Orangeburgh Dist. South Carolina

vs

Charles Newell and Thomas Newell.

Thos. Newell was brother of Comp'ts and father of Charles Newell. Fereby Newell O'Sullivant died in S. C. in April 1813 (will on file in Orangeburgh Dist. S. C.) William Newell, husband of Fereby, died in S. C. in 1789. They also had a daughter, Mary Newell, whose will was proven in Jasper Co. Miss. Jan. 7, 1839. The heirs of John Newell were Elizabeth, wife of William Smith, and Mary, wife of John Matthews, all of Copiah Co. Miss.

****

1842 Wilkinson Co. Miss. Drawer 89 Case #2538

Robert Norwood

vs

Mary S. Ogden, widow of Daniel Ogden, Dec'd.

Geo. P. Ogden, Algenut M. T. Hoggatt, nee Ogden, Sarah L. Whitehead, nee Ogden wife of Wm. Whitehead,

Anna N. Hubbard, nee Ogden wife of Benj. M. Hubbard, all children and heirs of Daniel and Mary Ogden and of William Ogden, father of Daniel Ogden.

****

1842 Warren Co. Miss. Drawer 89 Case #2540

Martha Parks and Samuel M. Woods, Admrs. Est. Garner Parks, Dec'd

vs

John G. Deminds and John Cowan

****

1848 Adams Co. Miss. Drawer 89 Case #2548

Osborne K. Field and wife, Sarah

vs

Joseph A. Hawley

****

1847 Madison Co. Miss. Drawer 89 Case #2552

Geo. S. Douglass

vs

John Munn of Madison Co. Admr. de bonis non Est. Joseph Munn, Dec'd; Thos. Hudnell of Nashville, Tenn.; James B. Slade of New Orleans, La.; James Dick, Henry R. W. Hill and Wm. J. McLean surviving partners of N. & J. Dick Co. of N. O.

****

1842 Adams Co. Miss. Drawer 89 Case #2562

John F. Hardy

vs

Nancy W. Perkins, Admx. and widow of James R. Perkins, Dec'd.

****

1842 Amite Co. Miss. Drawer 89 Case #2574

James M. Norwood

vs

Elizabeth Chandler, Van Camp Crawford and Dr. Edward Carroll, Execs. Est. Robt. Montgomery, Dec'd., late of Amite Co.

Robt. Montgomery was a native of Amhurst Co. Virginia and one of the first settlers of Amite Co. His will mentions a sister, Abigail Files, wife of John Files of Ala. and sister Mary Bradshaw, wife of Joel Bradshaw of Tennessee. Bequests to Elizabeth Chandler (nurse), his two sisters, and a legacy to each of his slaves.

Witnesses to will: John Everett, Wm. D. Smith and O. W. Caulfield.

****

1842 Yazoo Co. Miss. Drawer 89 Case #2575

Edward C. Wilkinson

vs

Thos. J. Jennings, Exec. Est. John Williams, Dec'd.

John Williams Died Dec. 1836.

****

1849 Claiborne Co. Miss. Drawer 89 Case #2579

Adeline P. McIntyre and T. G. McIntyre, Admrs. Est. Duncan McIntyre, Dec'd

vs

Samuel Corbin, John F. Thrasher, James J. Pearson and James F. Magee, Trustees of the late Bank of Port Gibson.

****

1842 Yazoo Co. Miss. Drawer 89 Case #2595

Nancy Ann Brown, George Fisher, Beverly Grayson and Jane Brown, Admx. Est. Jesse Brown, Dec'd

vs

Alexander McGahy, a non resident of Miss. and John M. Hendricks.

****

1848 Lowndes Co. Miss. Drawer 89 Case #2611

George R. Clayton, Admr. Est. John Oliver, Dec'd late of Lowndes Co.

vs

Ager T. Morse, David Baldwin, Elihu B. Gaston, Pascal B. Wade, John K. Ottley, Madison Watkins, John D. Montgomery, Admr. Est. of ________ Bell, Dec'd and Benj. Covington, all of Lowndes Co., Samuel F. Butterworth of New Orleans and Mary E. H. Shotwell of State of Texas.

****

1829 Adams and Franklin Cos. Miss. Drawer 89 Case #2636

Adeliza Quays of Adams Co. by next friend, Robert Anderson of La.

vs

Cornelius Byrd of Franklin Co.

Adeliza Quays was wife of Phillip D. Quays

****

1849 Yazoo Co. Miss. Drawer 90 Case #2640

James R. Burris, Judge of Probate for use of Robert Mitchell

vs

Peter Fisher, Admr. Est. of Geo. Fisher, Dec'd.

****

1849 Choctaw Co. Miss. Drawer 90 Case #2653

Catherine Muirhead (mother) and Barbara, Ethan Allen, Nicholas B., Lucretia, James and Catherine Muirhead (children)

vs

Richard, Spencer, William Green and Henry Muirhead infant heirs of Henry Muirhead, Dec'd; Levina McAdams, Nancy Heberd and husband, Joseph Heberd, Christiana David and James Hitt, Admr. Est. Charles Muirhead, Dec'd

Other heirs of Henry Muirhead: Pleasant C. and Cortez Muirhead.

****

1849 Tippah Co. Miss. Drawer 90 Case #2656

Elizabeth Guillard by next friend, Theodore Guillard (their son)

vs

Theodore Guillard (husband)

Divorce Petition.

Bill recites Elizabeth and Theodore Guillard, Sr. were married in South Carolina in 1820 and moved to Tennessee, then back to South Carolina and thence to Tippah Co. Mississippi in 1840.

****

1849 Yazoo Co. Miss. Drawer 90 Case #2649

James Hewitt

vs

Michael Langan and wife, Trahicia H. Langan, Admx. and John McFarland, Admr. Est. Phillip O'Reilly, Dec'd

Bill names Nicholas and Edmond O'Reilly as brothers of Phillip

****

1842 Hinds Co. Miss. Drawer 90 Case #2692

Mary Woodward Calcock of State of S. C. (widow of Charles J. Calcock) and Elihu W. T. Slogan

vs

Margaret E. Saunders, Mary A. Mayson, Charles C. Mayson, Alexander H. Mayson, Sarah Mayson, John H. Mallory, Francis S. Heard, Thos. B. J. Hadley, Henry K. Moss, Thos. J. Coffee, Richard N. Goode.

Charles J. Calcock was a resident of Charleston Dist. S. C. Died Feb. 1, 1839. See Will.

****

1842 Adams Co. Miss. Drawer 90 Case #2718

Wm. H. Brown and wife, Martha D. Brown

vs

James Stockman, Samuel H. Lamdin and William W. Wilkins

****

1842 Washington Co. Miss. Drawer 90 Case #2721

Mary C. Bell, Elizabeth Bell and Richard H. Bell

vs

Jacob S. Yerger, William M. Gwin and Mary E. H. Gwin

****

1849 Hinds Co. Miss. Drawer 90 Case #2721-a

Jacob Magee, Daniel Thomas and William F. Davis

vs

Augustus Jennings and Richard S. Drane as Jennings and Drane

****

1849 Washington Co. Miss. Drawer 90 Case #2730

Rice C. Ballard, Exec. Est. William Cotton, Dec'd

vs

John S. Chapman and Manlius V. Thomson

****

1842 Hinds Co. Miss. Drawer 90 Case #2731

Fidelia S. Hunt

vs

Sarah Phillips, Exec. Est. James Phillips, Dec'd and other heirs of James Phillips.

James Phillips died Aug. 1838. Heirs: Sarah (widow), Lucinda Hall, nee Phillips, Louisa Young, nee Phillips, wife of Wm. H. Young, T. R. Dixon, nee Phillips, wife of R. L. Dixon, Moses S. Phillips, William, Andrew and Hadley B. Phillips.

****

1845 Hinds Co. Miss. Drawer 90 Case #2749

Sarah Armfield

vs

Isaac Armfield

Litigation involving a marriage contract made in 1834.

****

1849 Hinds Co. Miss. Drawer 90 Case #2750

John E. Fitzgerald, Exec. Est. Ann L. Fitzgerald, Dec'd and C. S. Tarpley

vs

Janius Amis

****

1842 Yazoo Co. Miss. Drawer 90 Case #2655

Joel Stevens, Admr. Est. James Stevens

vs

Elihu Boaz and Emily Boaz

Joel and James were brothers and Emily Boaz was daughter of James Stevens.

****

1849 Madison Co. Miss. Drawer 90 Case #2656

John D. Scott, Admr. de bonis non Est. Johnson Silverberg, Dec'd

vs

Jesse Heard and Samuel D. Livingston, Admrs. Est. John F. Dearing, Dec'd.

* * * *

1844 Madison Co. Miss. Drawer 90 Case #2662

Lucinda A. Moore

vs

William H. Moore

Divorce Petition.
Married: 1819.

* * * *

1843 Carroll Co. Miss. Drawer 90 Case #2671

John McNairy

vs

John Baldwin, Admr. Est. William L. Bobbitt, Dec'd.

Heirs of Wm. L. Bobbitt: Harriet (widow) who later married Bransom Latham and Eliza Ann Bobbitt only child of Wm. and Harriet

* * * *

1849 Adams Co. Miss. Drawer 90 Case #2732

Wm. Robertson, Tr. for Commercial Bank, Natchez

vs

Richard Sanders, Robt. M. Davis and wife, Maria, Admrx. Est. Absolum Leggett, Dec'd.

* * * *

1849 Rankin Co. Miss. Drawer 90 Case #2740

Silas L. Steen, Archibald Stratton and wife, Edna, Vincent Harrison and wife, Lucretia, Thos. H. Dean and wife, Dorcas, Wiley P. Pearce and wife, Sarah, Isaac H.

Steen, Wm. H. Lane and wife, Mary J. and Serena E. Steen, a minor, all children and heirs of Robert Steen, Dec'd.

Robert Steen died Jan. 30, 1837, leaving no widow but six daughters and two sons.

****

1849 Hinds Co. Miss. Drawer 90 Case #2747

Rachel Robinson, Exec. Est. William M. Robertson

vs

Garrett Lane

****

1843 Hinds Co. Miss. Drawer 91 Case #2780

Ann Coor, Admx. and Geo. W. Barnes, Admr. Est. John Coor, Dec'd

vs

John A. Pass

****

1843 Yazoo Co. Miss. Drawer 91 Case #2796

John J. Wilson

vs

James Vose, James Shirley and wife, Adaline, Samuel B. Marsh and David O. Shadduck

A deposition of Walton Watkins states his father, Isham Watkins was agent for Adeline Shirley.

****

1848 Copiah Co. Miss. Drawer 91 Case #2799

Elizabeth Pritchard, Gdn. for minor heirs of John Pritchard, Dec'd

vs

Green Millsaps

Heirs not named.

****

1843 Warren Co. Miss. Drawer 91 Case #2805

William A. Martin and George Morton

vs

Tobias Gibson, of State of Kentucky; Ambrose Gibson and wife, Margaret; Wm. S. Bradley, W. C. Walker, Thos. E. Robbins, Geo. Selser, Allen N. G. Creath, Wm. W. Gibson, Joseph Templeton and W. W. George, all of Warren Co. Miss.

****

1849 Hinds Co. Miss. Drawer 91 Case #2815

William Burns, Exec. Est. George W. Smyth, Dec'd

vs

Frederick Stanton, James F. Sessions, Charles L. Dubisson and wife, Delia, Eliza A. Sessions, all of Adams Co., Phillip Sessions and Albert Sessions of Holmes Co., John Baynton and wife, Cornelia of State of Pennsylvania, Wm. C. Mylne of State of Louisiana and Chas. A. Lascosto of Adams Co. Miss.

****

1849 Amite Co. Miss. Drawer 91 Case #2819

Geo. F. Webb, Admr. Est. William Jones, Dec'd

vs

Augustus W. Forsythe

****

1843 Warren Co. Miss. Drawer 91 Case #2843

John S. Brien, James Simmons and wife, Martha

vs

John Henderson

(See Valentine Ray Estate)

****

1849 Yazoo Co. Miss. Drawer 91 Case #2843-a

John, Gabriel and Hiram Lusk, heirs of Charles Lusk, Dec'd.

vs

Ira Shepherd and wife, Margaret, lately Bridgers, daughter of John R. McNamer

John, Gabriel and Hiram Lusk were step sons of John Bridgers.

Litigation involves deed of gift from Bridgers to his step sons. John R. McNamer had been guardian for John, Gabriel and Hiram Lusk. Their mother, Margaret Hooker, late Margaret Lusk, was also widow of John Bridgers, Dec'd

****

1844 Claiborne Co. Miss. Drawer 91 Case #2858

Virginia E. Carpenter

vs

John M. Carpenter, Thos. W. Baugh and wife (not named), all heirs of Horace Carpenter, Dec'd.

See Will of G. M. Smith.

****

1848 Yazoo Co. Miss. Drawer 91 Case #2863

Carey D. Tucker, and John Tucker, Admrs. Est. Howell W. Runnells, Dec'd, Stephen Hamberlin, Archibald Coody, Philip Hilderbrand, Moses Hamberlin, Robt. M. Maben, Samuel Dilly for use of Martin Pleasant Co.

vs

William Hamberlin, Isaac Hamberlin and Stephen Hamberlin.

Stephen Hamberlin died Jan. or Feb. 1844. His widow married Samuel Peers two years later. Bill recites Stephen Hamberlin and wife were parents of four children—but they are not named.

****

1845 Claiborne Co. Miss. Drawer 91 Case #2871

John G. Neely and wife, Jane M. Neely, Admrs. Est. William King, Dec'd

vs

The Planters Bank of Mississippi

****

1848 Kemper Co. Miss. Drawer 91 Case #2880

John H. Oden, Gdn. for his minor children (not named)

vs

William W. Gardner and R. Church Jack

****

1847 Lawrence Co. Miss. Drawer 91 Case #2887

James M. Turner

vs

James M. Ellis, Admr. Est. David B. Cooper, Dec'd late of Lawrence Co.

****

1849 Copiah Co. Miss. Drawer 91 Case #2892

John Knott and wife, Elizabeth of State of Texas

vs

James M. Lyon

Melissa Speed, widow of John Speed married James M. Lyon of Copiah Co. in April 1844. She died in Texas in August 1847. She and Elizabeth Knott were sisters.

****

1849 Scott Co. Miss. Drawer 91 Case #2900

James Harper

vs

Elizabeth Harper, nee Boney

Divorce Petition.
Married: June 25, 1846 in Sumpter Co. Ala.

****

1849 Hinds Co. Miss. Drawer 92 Case #2904

John T. Hull, Admr. Est. William B. Woodley, Dec'd

vs

George Work

****

1843 Madison Co. Miss. Drawer 92 Case #2906

Richard Christmas and Thos. H. Christmas, Execs. Est. Wm. B. Norfleet, Dec'd and William B. Perkins

vs

John T. Johnson for use of William Woodrow

Richard Christmas (wife Mary E.) was a brother of Henry and Thos. H. Christmas. Litigation involves estate of David L. Horn of Warren Co. who died Aug. 6, 1840 naming "relatives" Henry and Thos. Christmas, his half sister Elizabeth Green and his "affectionate friends and relations, Mary E. Christmas wife of Richard Christmas and her son, William Hardeman Christmas" and naming Thos. Christmas, Executor. Wm. B. Norfleet died Sept. or Oct. 1840 leaving all of his property to William Hardeman in trust for Mary E. Christmas, except $1000.00 to his sister Minerva Ann Norfleet.

****

1843 Amite Co. Miss. Drawer 92 Case #2917

Edmund Smith, John Adams and wife, Harriet, nee Smith, Wm. Adams and wife, Permelia, nee Smith, Matilda Trantham, nee Smith, widow of Martin Trantham—all heirs of John Smith, Dec'd

vs

Andrew Gray

John Smith died in South Carolina in 1799. His widow, Sarah Smith, married Andrew Gray in S. C. in 1801. Sarah Gray died June 1842 in Amite Co. Miss. Named as arbiters: David Gordon, R. C. Westbrook, L. L.

Weathersby, Ephraim Marsalis, Duncan King, William Denman.

Depositions taken: Wm. Pate, Micajah Andrews, Wm. Oliver, William Denman, David Gordon, Henry Westbrook, R. C. Westbrook (grandson of Sarah Gray) John Kinnebrew, Chas. McMannus, Elizabeth McMannus, Hugh Montgomery, W. A. Obier, Wm. M. Haywood, John Montgomery, Susannah Adams Halford (sister of John and Wm. Adams), James D. Obier, Ephraim Marsalis and Joseph Adams.

****

1825 Wayne Co. Miss. Drawer 92 Case #2920

Fannie Harris by next friend, Thos. W. Burge

vs

Gowen Harris

Divorce Petition.
Married: 1801.

****

1849 Franklin Co. Miss. Drawer 92 Case #2954

Thomas A. Magee, Admr. de bonis non succeeding Owen H. Magee, Admr. Est. Phillip Magee, Dec'd of Franklin Co. Miss.

vs

James Harrington of Franklin Co.

Litigation involves entailed slaves willed by Willis Magee to his wife, Asha Scott Magee, and at her death to Phillip Magee, their son. Thomas A. Magee was a grandson of Willis Magee and a nephew of Owen H. Magee and Phillip Magee. James Harrington was a brother of John Bunyan Harrington (natives of England). John Bunyan Harrington married Penelope Magee, daughter of Willis and Asha Magee. James Harrington married Martha Magee, widow of Jonathan Magee, daughter of Manton E. S. Lee, Dec'd. See Will of Willis Magee.

****

1849 Franklin Co. Miss. Drawer 92 Case #2955

Thomas A. Magee, Admr. de bonis non Est. Phillip Magee, Dec'd

vs

Manton E. S. Lee

Manton E. S. Lee was the brother of Martha Magee who married first, Jonathan Magee in 1818, second, James Harrington in 1825. Manton E. S. Lee Married Lucy Q. Magee, widow of Dr. Hugh Magee, son of Willis and Asha Scott Magee and brother of Phillip Magee.

****

1843 Franklin Co. Miss. Drawer 92 Case #2956

Jane Parker, Admr. Est. Joel Parker, Dec'd

vs

Thomas Cotton

Jane Parker was born Jane McGahey in S. C. in 1790, married Lewis Magee, son of Willis Magee, in 1815. Lewis Magee died in 1830 and Jane married Joel Parker in 1831. Joel Parker died 1841. Litigation involves debts due the estate of John Furniss, maternal grandfather of Jane Parker. Thos. A. Magee, Admr. Est. Phillip Magee, was son of Lewis Magee and Jane (Magee) Parker.

****

1849 Franklin Co. Miss. Drawer 92 Case #2957

Thomas A. Magee, Admr. de bonis non, Est. Phillip Magee, Dec'd

vs

Dr. James Maxwell Smith

Dr. James Maxwell Smith was husband of Louisa Magee, daughter of Jonathan and Martha Lee Magee.

****

1849 Franklin Co. Miss. Drawer 92 Case #2958

Thomas A. Magee, Admr. de bonis non Est. Phillip Magee, Dec'd

vs

Needham Willis Magee

Needham Willis Magee was son of Jonathan and Martha Lee Magee and grandson of Willis and Asha Magee.

****

1843 Hinds Co. Miss. Drawer 92 Case #2963

Edwin R. Brown, Admr. Est. Benjamin Davis

vs

George Runceman, George Crockett and Edmund O'Reilly

****

1842 Madison Co. Miss. Drawer 92 Case #2986

Rebecca McDowell, Exec. Est. William McDowell, late of Madison Co. and Jesse Walton

vs

Levi Bankston, Jefferson W. Steen, Matthew G. Vernon and Samuel L. Young.

****

1846 Rankin Co. Miss. Drawer 92 Case #2990

Rufus S. Hardy, Admr. Est. Ben Bruce, Dec'd

vs

John T. Spencer, Daniel Fore and William T. Lindsey

****

1843 Holmes Co. Miss. Drawer 92 Case #2991

Margaret G. Jordan by next friend and son, Benj. O. Jordan

vs

Lemuel G. Lipsey and Alexander Jordan

Margaret G. Jordan married Alexander Jordan in 1814 or 1815. She was the daughter of Hannah Foster and litigation involves her inheritance from her mother. Depositions of: Edmund Cobb, Ephraim Davis, Cal James, James Devlin, Bartholemew Jordan, Samuel Jordan, Robt. Mealey, Mrs. Eleanor Boyd, Major Wm. Gamble, Thos. Aiken, Benj. Maley, all citizens of Abbeville Dist. S. C.

****

1843 Adams Co. Miss. Drawer 92 Case #3016

J. T. McCurran and William Brune

vs

Cornelius A. Harring, John Harring, Henry Chester Harring, Virginia Harring, by their Gdn. ad litem, Robt. Hughes, E. A. McLean and wife, Cornelia, Sarah Ross Harring, all heirs of Cornelius Harring, Dec'd.

****

1843 Adams Co. Miss. Drawer 92 Case #3022

Louisa V. Rucks by next friend, William Yerger

vs

James Rucks

Divorce Petition.

Married: 1827 in State of Tennessee. Six children, not named.

Louisa V. Rucks was daughter of Dr. Preston W. Brown who died in Kentucky in 1826. Her mother, Elizabeth Brown died in Tennessee in May 1843. Other Brown heirs mentioned: Wm. Brown and John P. W. Brown.

****

1850 Yazoo Co. Miss. Drawer 92 Case #3024

Claiborne Bowman, Admr. de bonis non Est. Nicholas O'Reilly, Dec'd

vs

Wm. Battaile, John W. Hendricks and Daniel W. Hendricks

****

1843 Co. not shown. Drawer 92 Case #3027

Wm. A. Hopkins

vs

Lucius J. Polk and Geo. W. Polk, Execs. Est. Rufus K. Polk, Dec'd, Sarah M. Polk (widow of Rufus), and Sarah M. Polk, daughter of Rufus K. Polk, Dec'd.
Rufus K. Polk died in Maury Co. Tenn.

****

1843 Warren Co. Miss. Drawer 92 Case #3029

Andrew I. Green

vs

Ann B. Green, widow and second wife of Abram Green, Dec'd.

Abram Green died in Claiborne Co. July 1826 leaving heirs: Andrew I., Jefferson, John D., Abram A. and Martha Green all children of his first marriage; Ann B. Green (widow) and Margaret I. Green, posthumous child. Mrs. Ann B. Green had children of a previous marriage: L. P., Caroline, Emma, Mary E., James A. and William Maxwell.

****

1843 Claiborne Co. Miss. Drawer 93 Case #3034

Francis Harmon by Gdn. and next friend, Samuel Walker

vs

Nancy B. Willison of State of Virginia, Joseph W. Dobbs, Joseph C. Lewis, Samuel R. Dobbs, Washington Dorsey, Charles F. Hamer, Elizabeth Howard, all of Yazoo Co. and William D. Hamer of Claiborne Co. and William V. Conder of Rankin Co.

Francis Harmon was the only child and heir of John Harmon who died in 1838.

****

1843 Warren Co. Miss. Drawer 93 Case #3045

John A. Bolling, Admr. ad colegendum of Samuel P. Bolling, Dec'd; Wm. B. Smith and wife, Mildred M. Smith

vs

Wm. Mills and John D. Cato

Samuel P. Bolling died in State of Virginia in 1840

* * * *

1850 Marshall Co. Miss. Drawer 93 Case #3048

Jemima Gurley, Admr. Est. Jesse Gurley, Dec'd.

vs

Caleb Brock, Admr. Est. Isaac Congee, Dec'd

Listed as jurymen: James McDonald, Edward Coleman, Samuel P. Ingram, Allen Dowdle, Pleasant Moseby, William Marsh, Jeremiah H. Maxwell, Alex G. Hall, Newton Holland, Hamilton Thornton, Hamilton McClalchey and Christopher Cawthorn.

* * * *

1843 Hinds Co. Miss. Drawer 93 Case #3054

John R. Jefferson

vs

Hiram D. Robertson of Hinds Co. and Nancy Sanders relict of William Sanders, Dec'd late of Madison Co. Miss.

* * * *

1843 Adams Co. Miss. Drawer 93 Case #3058

Daniel Abbott, Admr. and Elizabeth Bell, Admx. Est. Jesse Bell, Dec'd; India A. Bell, Ezekiel H. Bell, Thos. E. Bell, Chauncy K. Bell, Elizabeth P. Bell and Orlando H. Bell, infants and heirs of Jesse Bell, Dec'd by their mother and Gdn., Elizabeth Bell.

vs

John W. Weems and wife, Martha P. Weems

Jesse Bell died 1842.

* * * *

1843 Hinds Co. Miss. Drawer 93 Case #3061

Wright B. Hendricks

vs

Pricella Fort, widow, and Giraldus and Marcus L. Ford, sons of Joseph A. Ford, Dec'd; Richard Ford and wife, Frances, nee Fort, daughter, Omer D. Battle former Admr. and Wm. Clark Admr. de bonis non Est. Joseph A. Fort, Dec'd

Joseph A. Fort died in Hinds Co. in 1835.

****

1850 Monroe Co. Miss. Drawer 93 Case #3062

John T. Dych and Neumon J. Dobbs, Admrs. Est. George Wightman, Dec'd for use of Josiah D. Amis

vs

(Defendant not shown)

George Wightman died in 1846.

****

1843 Jefferson Co. Miss. Drawer 93 Case #3070

James and Robert G. Wood, Execs. Est. James G. Wood, Dec'd

vs

Elizabeth Allen, Francis J. Coleman and Thomas Allen all of Jefferson Co. Miss.

****

1844 Wilkinson Co. Miss. Drawer 93 Case #3074

Francis L. Mayes

vs

Wm. M. Helm, Exec. Est. Joseph H. Miller, Dec'd, late of Wilkinson Co.

Joseph H. Miller died 1837 leaving heirs two children: Joseph L. Miller and Ellis H. Miller.

****

1849 Madison Co. Miss. Drawer 93 Case #3081

John D. Scott, Admr. de bonis non Est. Johnson Silverberg, Dec'd

vs

Ebenezer F. Devine and Charles J. Searles, John H. Magruder and Brittain Bailey

****

1850 Yazoo Co. Miss. Drawer 93 Case #3048

Dudley S. Jennings

vs

Josephus Love, Admr. Est. Asa Love, Dec'd.

****

1850 Madison Co. Miss. Drawer 93 Case #3091

William Robertson, Tr.

vs

Abram A. McWillie, Exec. Est. Ann McWillie, Dec'd.

****

1850 Madison Co. Miss. Drawer 93 Case #3092

Wm. Roberts (colored) by George Calhoon Esq., his atty.

vs

Otho R. Singleton, Admr. with will attached Est. Richard W. Harper, Dec'd.

****

1844 Claiborne Co. Miss. Drawer 93 Case #3097

Wm. Dotson of Claiborne Co. and Stephen Harmon of Louisiana, Execs. Est. William Harmon, Dec'd

vs

Edward Dortch, George W. Scott and Robert Strong of Claiborne Co.

William Harmon died in 1838.

****

1844 Madison Co. Miss. Drawer 93 Case #3111

Elijah M. Graves and wife, Elizabeth M.

vs

Lydia Barrow of Hinds Co. and Samuel Barrow of Republic of Texas, Admrs. Est. William Barrow, Dec'd, late of Hinds Co., Ferdinand C. Barbour and wife, Permelia, nee Barrow, daughter of Wm. Barrow, Dec'd

Wm. Barrow died in 1838. Other heirs: Susan Hodges, feme sole, Wm. Barrow, Seth L. Barrow and wife, Sarah Elizabeth, nee Barrow, Francis M. Barrow.

****

1844 Claiborne Co. Miss. Drawer 93 Case #3113

Young Berry of Yazoo Co. Miss.

vs

Passmore Hoopes and Stephen Douglass, Execs. and Emeline Douglass, Exex. Est. James L. Douglass, Dec'd, all of Claiborne Co. lately of State of Louisiana.
Emeline Douglass married Maxwell Bland. See Will.

****

1844 Hinds Co. Miss. Drawer 93 Case #3116

Mary E. Ritchie (infant) by next friend, John F. Watson of Hinds Co.

vs

Edward Duncan.

Writ of Injunction.

Leonard B. Ritchie died in 1836. Mary E. Ritchie was only child of Leonard B. and Sarah M. Ritchie. Sarah later married Peter G. Johnson of Hinds Co.

****

1848 Yazoo Co. Miss. Drawer 93 Case #3118

John M. Sharp

vs

Samuel M. Ratcliff, Wm. Ratcliff, Edward L. Ratcliff, Allen Ratcliff, John I. Vandenberg and wife, Matilda E., nee

Ratcliff, ... Sapp and wife, Lois Ann, nee Ratcliff, Jackson A., Rufus K., James R. and Joseph S. Ratcliff, heirs of James Ratcliff, Dec'd.

James Ratcliff died in 1836. See Will.

****

1844 Adams Co. Miss. Drawer 93 Case #3169

Mary H. Chailer, Admx. de bonis non Est. Wm. H. Chailer, Dec'd; Alex Montgomery and Samuel S. Boyd

vs

Thos. Barnard, Elizabeth T., Mary A., Corine and Wm. Barnard, Ann Davis and Barnard Shipp.

Eliza I. Barnard, wife of Thomas, predeceased him.

****

1879 Warren Co. Miss. Drawer 93 Case #3213

Robert E. Trible, John F. Trible, Medora A. Trible, Ellen Wilkins and Drue Birdsong

vs

Thos. M. Cameron and Sureties: A. K. Hall and Richard Taylor.

****

1843 Adams Co. Miss. Drawer 93 Case #3214

Wm. C. Stokes and wife, Elizabeth, Harriet Harris, nee Stokes, Eliza R. George, nee Stokes, Sarah E. Harris, nee Stokes, Young W., Susan A., Henry, Elizabeth, Martha, Ann H. I., Priscilla and Janette Stokes

vs

William Queen and John Queen

The wife and children of William C. Stokes were heirs of Rem Rumson who died in State of Georgia Aug. 13, 1836.

****

1844 Adams Co. Miss. Drawer 93 Case #3233

Gibeon Gibson, of Warren Co. Miss. and Benj. Cochran of State of Va.

vs

Robert J. Walker and unknown heirs of John McLaughlin.

John McLaughlin died in Adams Co. and John Street was Admr. of his estate. He was a "foreigner" and "unmarried".

****

1844 Yazoo Co. Miss. Drawer 93 Case #3251

Samuel M. Boylan

vs

Paul Fisher, John Fisher, Michael Fisher, Henry Fisher, Peter Fisher, Mary Geddes, nee Fisher, Robt. McCain and wife, Susan, nee Fisher, Paul Hamil, ________ Dougherty and wife, Catherine, nee Hamil, ________ Kinsey and wife, Melinda, nee Hamil, ________ Gwin and wife, Mary, nee Hamil.

Paul, Catherine, Melinda and Mary were heirs of Elizabeth Hamil, Dec'd, nee Fisher, and all heirs of George Fisher, Dec'd

****

1844 Madison Co. Miss. Drawer 93 Case #3252

Josiah Powell, next friend for Amanda Rookling, Franklin Norman, Joseph Norman and Thomas Norman

vs

Mary, Cicero, I. D. Denman, A. M. and Samantha Denman, all heirs of Thos. Denman, Dec'd

Comp'ts are heirs of Thos. Norman who died intestate in Pike Co. Miss. March 1839 leaving his widow, Mary and children, Amanda Rookling, Franklin, Thomas and Josephus Norman and Rebecca and Sarah Moore. See will of Thomas Denman.

****

1849 Yazoo Co. Miss. Drawer 93 Case #3256

John J. Lamb

vs

Walter Smith Chew and Philemon Chew, Execs. Est. Thomas Chew, Dec'd; Francis and Frisby Chew.

* * * *

1843 Amite Co. Miss. Drawer 93 Case #3264

Victoria C. Street and husband, Henry G. Street, Thomas A. G. Batchelor and Lemuel Reams, Sureties

vs

James M. Smiley and wife, Rebecca Caroline Smiley, Admrs. Est. Edward Carroll, Dec'd

Edward Carroll died intestate in Amite Co. •Thomas Batchelor died in 1842 and James Batchelor administered his estate.

* * * *

1845 Co. not shown. Drawer 93 Case #_______

Joseph Woods

vs

Samuel I. Ridley, Admr. de bonis non Est. Henry Ridley, Dec'd.

Henry Ridley died in 1835 in State of Tennessee. His heirs: Elizabeth Ridley (widow), William A., Samuel J. and James Ridley.

* * * *

1845 Yazoo Co. Miss. Drawer 93 Case #3302

Nancy Ann Brown

vs

Richard D. Bailey, Admr. Est. Edmund Pearce, Dec'd

Depositions of: Alonzo Brown, son of Nancy Ann, Almonzine Brown, daughter of Nancy Ann, Amanda Pearce, widow of Edmund Pearce, Wm. H. Reed, F. A.

Bailey, Thos. Lyons, Milton Pyles, Talman C. Pickett, Franklin W. Brown and William Hall.

****

1844 Hinds Co. Miss. Drawer 93 Case #3312

Louisa M. Young by next friend, Leonidas Dixon

vs

William Young

Louisa Phillips, daug. of James and Sarah Phillips married Wm. H. Young in 1833. Sarah Phillips died in 1843 leaving heirs: Moses, William, Jack and Hudby Phillips, Louisa M. Young and Reese Hutcher, a child of her first marriage. This petition is for a trustee to receive Louisa Young's share of Sarah Phillips' estate.

****

1847 Yazoo Co. Miss. Drawer 93 Case #3325

Rosannah Tucker, nee Friley, dau. Caleb Friley, Dec'd; Nancy Morrison, dau. Polly Morrison, Dec'd who was dau. Caleb Friley; Martha Jane Boyd, infant dau. Jane Boyd, Dec'd who was dau. Polly Morrison, Dec'd; John Boyd, father of Martha Jane; Richard Boyd and wife, Elizabeth, nee Friley, dau. Hiram Friley, Dec'd who was son of Caleb Friley, Dec'd; Martin M. Friley and Elizabeth Friley, heirs of James Friley, Dec'd who was son of Caleb Friley, Dec'd; John, David, Nancy and Emily Friley, infant heirs of James Friley, Dec'd, who was son of Caleb Friley, Dec'd; all of Yazoo Co. Miss. John Edmondson and wife, Mary, nee Friley dau. of James Friley, Dec'd, of Madison Co. Miss.; Caleb Friley son of Hiram Friley, Dec'd, a citizen of the Republic of Texas; Solomon Friley, son of Hiram Friley, Dec'd; Andrew Jackson Friley, Samuel Lenak and wife, Hannah, nee Friley, Nancy F. Friley, heirs of Martin Friley, Dec'd, who was son of Caleb Friley, Dec'd; David W., James J., Caleb, Jr., Sarah A., Betsy Ann and Martin G. Friley, infant heirs of Martin Friley,

Dec'd; Andrew Jackson Friley, Jr., son of Gabriel Henderson Friley, Dec'd who was son of Martin Friley, Dec'd, all citizens of State of Tennessee

vs

Nancy Puckett; Elizabeth Friley, widow of Caleb Friley, Dec'd; William Pickett; Gray J. Vick and James Stuart (one of the heirs of John Alston), all of Yazoo Co.; Magniss F. Rogers, a citizen of Republic of Texas; Vincent Galloway of State of La.; David Beatty, Solomon Friley, Sr., citizens of Holmes Co.; James R. Enloe of Bolivar Co.; Thos. Maybry and wife, Lucy, nee Drumgool, James J. Drumgool and Love Drumgool all heirs of John Alston, Dec'd all of Madison Co. and the unknown heirs of Robert E. Beatty.

Caleb Friley died in the Republic of Texas in 1827 or 1828.

* * * *

1845 Rankin Co. Miss. Drawer 94 Case #3333

Samuel M. Puckett and Anthony Miller, Admrs. Est. Samuel Benthall, Dec'd

vs

James Elzey and Joseph Stephens

* * * *

1849 Monroe Co. Miss. Drawer 94 Case #3367

George W. Coopwood, Evalina Coopwood and William C. Coopwood

vs

John N. Willie

* * * *

1845 Jefferson Co. Miss. Drawer 94 Case #3396

David S. Servis, Admr. de bonis non Est. of Josiah Stone, Dec'd, late of Jefferson Co. Miss.

vs

William Beatty of Claiborne Co. and Aaron Killingsworth of Jefferson Co.

Josiah Stone died intestate Jan. 3, 1837 and Richard G. Davis was appointed Admr. of his estate.

****

1845 Madison Co. Miss. Drawer 94 Case #3425

Thos. J. Smith of Madison Co. Admr. Est. Francis Tidwell, Dec'd

vs

H. R. Hill, James Dick and William J. McLean

****

1845 Copiah Co. Miss. Drawer 94 Case #3441

John Morrison, Admr. Est. Joseph A. Miller, Dec'd

vs

William Barnes and wife, Madeline, late widow of Joseph A. Miller, Dec'd.

Joseph A. Miller died intestate Jan. 16, 1844, leaving no lineal descendants but leaving wife, Madeline; Anna C. Crenshaw (sister); James, Clinton, Andrew and Samuel Vaughn, infant heirs of Margaret C. Vaughn (sister) who were represented by Wyly B. Vaughn their half-brother and guardian; Robert Price, infant heir of Jane Price (sister) represented by Lewellen Price his father and next friend; Robert Miller (brother); Rebecca Morrison (sister); Zilpha Kennedy (sister); George R. Miller (brother).

****

1845 Co. not shown. Drawer 94 Case #3464

John M. Gregg and William Garrison and Elizabeth Garrison, his wife, formerly Elizabeth Williamson, all of State of Ohio

vs

Milton Pyles, Exec. Estate John Calglazer, Dec'd (an unmarried man).

****

1845 Hinds Co. Miss. Drawer 94 Case #3468

Margaret P. Dulaney by next friend, Joseph J. Battle

vs

William Dulaney

Margaret P. Dulaney was only child and heir of Benjamin W. Patton who died in State of Kentucky in 1825. John D. Patton was Exec. of estate. Margaret Patton married William J. Dulaney in Mississippi in 1837. This litigation involves the inheritance of William J. Dulaney from his father (not named) who died in the State of Virginia.

****

1845 Warren Co. Miss. Drawer 94 Case #3534

Thomas A. Marshall, Admr. Est. Thos. S. Thomley, Dec'd

vs

John M. Morton of State of Kentucky

Thos. S. Thomley died November 1843, intestate.

****

1845 Wilkinson Co. Miss. Drawer 94 Case #3540

Wiley M. Wood, Exec. Est. William Hazlip, Dec'd

vs

Rebecca Hazlip

William Hazlip died Feb. 17, 1845. See Will

****

1846 Co. not shown. Drawer 94 Case #3550

Job G. Selph and wife, Sarah; Henry Vaughn and wife, Eliza

vs

Robt. Hall, Admr. Est. John B. Forrester, Dec'd, and John L. McManus, Dec'd.

Sarah Selph and Eliza Vaughn were children of Arch McManus.

****

1852 Holmes Co. Miss. Drawer 94 Case #3573

John H. Morrison

vs

Milly Foster, relict of James Foster, Dec'd; Dorothy, Madison, Ellen and Ephraim Foster, infant heirs of James Foster, Dec'd

****

1853 Adams Co. Miss.. Drawer 94 Case #3580

James G. Gordon, Admr. Est. Benj. Kieningham, Dec'd

vs

William Hood and William L. Ellis

****

1847 Adams Co. Miss. Drawer 94 Case #3580-a

James G. Gordon, Admr. Est. Benj. Kieningham, Dec'd

vs

Wm. S. Ellis and Richard M. Ellis of New Orleans; William Hood and George A. Smith

****

1846 Carroll Co. Miss. Drawer 94 Case #3586

William Y. Collins of Carroll Co.; Reuben Collins of Hinds Co.

vs

Eliza Ann Collins, Sophia Collins and Mary Collins all of Madison Co.

Eliza Ann, Sophia and Mary Collins were children of Thos. Collins, Dec'd who died in 1839. Thos. Collins was a brother of William Y. and Reuben Collins, Comp'ts.

****

1846 Franklin Co. Miss. Drawer 94 Case #3593

Alexander McLeod and wife, Martha C.; Isaac L. Brown and wife, Mariah H.; Francis G. Spain

vs

James Johnson and wife, Helen; Nancy Spain; Wiley B. Burkes.

Depositions of: Daniel Grice, John Higdon, Wm. D. Ford, John B. Ducker and Archibald Baker.

****

1843 Yazoo Co. Miss. Drawer 94 Case #3599

Thos. E. Norrell of State of Tennessee

vs

William Yandell, Burton Yandell, John M. Sharp and Thos. C. Black, all of Yazoo Co.; Richard Carter and wife, Dorothy of State of Missouri; Susannah M. Norrell, Minerva E. Norrell and James Ming all of State of Missouri.

Sarah Jane Norrell, wife of Robt. Norrell and mother of Thos. E. Norrell, died in Sumner Co. Tenn. March 5, 1843. Heirs: Thos. E., Susannah M., Minerva E. Norrell, Dorothy Ann Carter, nee Norrell, James Ming son of Nancy Ming, nee Norrell, and of William Ming, Dec'd. Anthony Murray, father of Sarah Jane Norrell, Dec'd, died in 1807 in Buckingham Co. Virginia. Sarah Jane Murray and Robt. Norrell were married in State of Virginia. Litigation involves entailed slaves of Anthony Murray willed to daughter, Sarah Jane and subsequently sold by Robt. Norrell.

****

1846 Co. not shown. Drawer 94 Case #3616

Joseph Reid

vs

William R. Hill, Admr. Est. James M. Sims, Dec'd; Edwin, Sarah, Harriet, James Hamilton, David and Robert Sims, heirs of James Sims, Dec'd; James C. Caldwell and wife, Ann Caldwell.

****

1846 Rankin Co. Miss. Drawer 94 Case #3616-a

Alexander H. Lamar and wife, Mary Jane

vs

John Davis, George R. Weathersby and wife, Mary E.

Geo. R. and Mary E. Weathersby were Execs. Est. Edward A. Lucy, Dec'd. John Davis was brother of Mary E. Weathersby who married Geo. R. Weathersby Dec. 1839. Edward Lucy's will was probated in Rankin Co. Jan. 1846.

NOTE: This case in same jacket with preceding case of Reid vs Hill.

****

1846 Madison Co. Miss. Drawer 94 Case #3620

Coleman Nichols and William Joiner, Admrs. de bonis non Est. Sion Sanders, Dec'd

vs

Emily T. Walker and William F. Walker.

Letters of Admr. Est. Sion Sanders issued May 24, 1841.

****

1846 Rankin and Madison Cos. Drawer 94 Case #3624

Ann C. Royce of Madison Co. by next friend, Alexander G. Grant

vs

William F. Walker, George Robertson, R. S. Hunter and Owen Royce.

Ann C. Page and Owen Royce were married in Madison Co. in 1841.

Litigation involves pre-nuptial contract.

****

1852 Franklin Co. Miss. Drawer 94 Case #3657

Edmund W. Roberts of Monroe Co. Ala., Admr. de bonis non Est. William G. Godbold, Dec'd

vs

Ananias Godbold and James Andrews of Monroe Co. Ala., Admrs. Est. William G. Godbold, Dec'd.

Defendants in this case were appointed as Admrs. Sept. 1843. James Andrews moved to Republic of Texas and

Ananias Godbold moved to State of Ark. in 1845. At Aug. 1845 term of Orphan's Court Edmund Roberts was appointed Admr. de bonis non. In 1845 Ananias Godbold moved to Franklin Co. Miss. where his brother Levi Godbold and nephew, James R. Godbold lived.

****

1846 Warren Co. Miss. Drawer 94 Case #3661

Tillman Whatley, Admr. de bonis non Est. Alex Sevier, Dec'd

vs

John R. Keenan

Alex Sevier died in Warren Co. in 1846. Julia Anne Powell, wife of George W. Powell was a sister and heir of Alex Sevier. Other heirs: Lafayette Sevier, Jacob Harrison and wife, Cornelia, Virginia Shaw, Sexton H. and Louisiana Shaw.

****

1846 Hinds Co. Miss. Drawer 94 Case #3678

William W. Rives, Admr. Est. John W. Jones, Dec'd

vs

Tidence Lane, Burr Garland, James Scott, Thos. Bibb, Arthur M. Hopkins, John Martin, James D. Pleasants, James Bradley and Hugh Wilson

****

1848 Claiborne Co. Miss. Drawer 94 Case #3683

Mary L. Clark, infant, by her father Chas. B. Clark

vs

William McCreary and James Neill

****

1846 Wilkinson Co. Miss. Drawer 94 Case #3688

Jesse Sanders (son)

vs

Martha E. Newman (mother)

Heirs of Lewis Sanders: Jesse, Thomas, Eliza Sanders, Martha Sanders Ratliff (children) and widow Martha E. Sanders, of Clarke Co. Ala.

Litigation involves deed of gift from Lewis Sanders to son, Jesse Sanders in 1824. In 1825 Jesse Sanders conveyed the property to his mother Martha E. Sanders who later married ________ Newman.

****

1854 Yazoo Co. Miss. Drawer 94 Case #3692

A. W. Washburn, Admr. Est. Leonard Washburn, Dec'd. and Wm. E. Pugh (Surety)

vs

William Phillips

****

1846 Yazoo Co. Miss. Drawer 95 Case #3708

William W. Livermore, Exec. Est. Richard F. Floyd, Dec'd and Alma Post, Charles Floyd, Allison Post and wife, Elizabeth, nee Floyd, heirs of Richard Floyd, Dec'd

vs

John Johnson of Yazoo Co.

****

1846 Claiborne Co. Miss. Drawer 95 Case #3709

William Clarke, Sarah S., Mary B., Joseph and George S. Clarke, Jr. by next friend, George S. Clarke

vs

Samuel Corbin.

****

1847 Hinds Co. Miss. Drawer 95 Case #3713

Joseph Cooper and William A. Stone, Admrs. Est. John Martin, Dec'd (late of Macon, Bibb Co. Georgia), Eliza J. Martin, William A. Jarrott, Eliza M. Jarrott, Martha D., Robert, John, Rebecca T. and Lena A. Martin

vs

Pryor Lee and Thos. F. Collins

****

1846 Madison Co. Miss. Drawer 95 Case #3764

John D. Freeman, Receiver, Miss. R. R. and Banking Co.
vs
William B. Ross and wife, Martha B. Ross, Admrs. Est. William A. Fort, Dec'd.

****

1881 Sunflower Co. Miss. Drawer 95 Case #3793

F. Belden
vs
Sallie A. Lowry, Admx. Est. W. L. Lowry

****

1846 Yazoo Co. Miss. Drawer 95 Case #3894

Asahel W. Washburn and wife, Leonora; William E. Pugh, Admr. Est. Rhoda Martin
vs
William Phillips and Susan E. Martin.

Moultbrie Martin died intestate in Yazoo Co. in 1837, leaving his widow, Susan E. Martin, Rhoda Martin, Leona Martin who married Asahel Washburn, Joseph Martin and Adeline Martin, his brothers and sisters, heirs at law. Rhoda Martin died leaving as heirs at law: Leonora, Joseph and Adeline. William Phillips was Admr. Est. John Martin, Dec'd, father of Moultbrie Martin, Susan E. Martin was sole Admx. Est Moultbrie Martin. Susan E. Martin married David Barner in 1838 and thereafter left the State of Mississippi.

****

1848 Madison Co. Miss. Drawer 95 Case #3920

Bythell Haynes and William M. Quin, Exec. Est. William McCay, Dec d
vs
Agnes E. Collins (widow), William A., and Mary Collins (infant children) of Robert J. Collins, Dec'd by their Gdn. L. V. Dixon.

Robert Collins died in April 1846.

****

1847 Hinds Co. Miss. Drawer 95 Case #3930

Gov. Albert Gallatin Brown

vs

Joseph A. McRaven, Exec. Est. Samuel Smith, Dec'd

Heirs of Samuel and wife, Mary O. Smith: William D., Catherine E., Susan E., and Martha D. Smith of Hinds Co. Miss. John Hume and wife, Margaret I. Hume formerly Margaret I. Smith a citizen of the State of Texas.

Samuel Smith died 1834.
Mary O. Smith died 1843.

****

1846 Hinds Co. Miss. Drawer 995 Case #3946

Thomas Robertson and wife, Caroline M.

vs

Mary G. DeMoss, Admr. Est. Wm. C. DeMoss, Dec'd; David C. Dancy and wife, Elizabeth, nee DeMoss; Catherine Kercheval, nee DeMoss, of C. G. Kercheval; Annerson DeMoss, Alice DeMoss, David DeMoss, heirs of Wm. C. DeMoss, Dec'd.

Mary DeMoss was widow of Wm. C. DeMoss and other Comp'ts were their children. Caroline M. Robertson was late widow of William Melton who died prior to 1835. They had two sons, Thomas and William Melton.

****

1847 Adams Co. Miss. Drawer 95 Case #3965

Alexander Semington and Thos. Robbins

vs

T. B. Brabston, Admr. Est. B. F. Newman, Dec'd and William Vick

****

1847 Hinds Co. Miss. Drawer 95 Case #3976

Hiram G. Runnells and wife, Obedience of State of Texas

vs

Esther McGowan, Gdn. ad litem of James E. McGowan, Elijah E. McGowan, Sarah Adeline McGowan, A. Blanton McGowan, Gabriella McGowan, John T. McGowan, Rupel McGowan, Wm. A. McGowan, Mary E. McGowan and Octavius McGowan, all heirs of W. A. McGowan, Dec'd.

First five named heirs were minors, Esther being mother of all heirs.

****

1847 Yazoo Co. Miss. Drawer 95 Case #3991

William Hardeman, Admr. Est. Thomas Hardeman, Dec'd

vs

James Thompson, Lewis and Julius Hornthall, John M. Robb, D. Sayers, E. G. Carson all of Madison Co.; Henry Douglass, residence unknown, and S. Freelander of Yazoo Co.

****

1846 Holmes Co. Miss. Drawer 95 Case #3993

Caroline J. Davis and husband, Robt. J. Davis of Holmes Co.

vs

Edward C. Wilkinson of Yazoo Co.

Caroline and Robt. J. Davis were married Jan. 1826 in West Feliciana Parish, La.

****

1847 Warren Co. Miss. Drawer 95 Case #3994

F. Norcum, Admr. Est. A. McNeil

vs

Edward A. Mielke

****

1836 Wilkinson Co. Miss. Drawer 95 Case #3994-a

Mary Ogden (widow) and Gnd. for Geo. P. Ogden, minor heir of Daniel Ogden, Dec'd
Guardian's Deed to Robert Norwood.

****

1847 Warren Co. Miss. Drawer 95 Case #3994-b

Samuel Lum, Admr. de bonis non Est. Edward Mielke, Dec'd, succeeding Archibald McLaurin and Virginia A. Mielke (widow) as Admrs. Est. Edward Mielke, Dec'd

vs

Frederick Norcum, Elibeck Mason, Armistead Burwell and Geo. S. Yerger.

NOTE: Cases 3994, 3994-a and 3994-b are all in file 3994.

****

1847 Hinds Co. Miss. Drawer 95 Case #4007

Joseph W. Miller, Admr. de bonis non, James C. Dickson, Dec'd

vs

James B. Robinson, Admr. de bonis non with will annexed of Isaac Caldwell, Dec'd; Raymond R., Jane E. and Hannah H. Caldwell, all heirs of Isaac Caldwell, Dec'd; Edward Kearney and Mary E. Kearney minors and non-residents of State of Miss., heirs of Elizabeth Kearney, late Caldwell, widow of Isaac; William F. Robinson of Claiborne Co. Miss.

Isaac Caldwell died in Jan. 1836 in Hinds Co. His widow, Elizabeth married Thos. Kearney in 1837. Elizabeth Kearney died July 1842. See Will of Isaac Caldwell.

****

1850 Madison Co. Miss. Drawer 95 Case #4007

The Commercial Bank of Natchez by Wm. Robertson, Tr.

vs

Richard E. Alford, Admr. de bonis non Est. Robt. Cooper, Dec'd

****

1848 Simpson Co. Miss. Drawer 95 Case #4014

Nancy Gowan, widow of Merideth Gowan, Dec'd, late of Copiah Co. Admr. de bonis non Est. Merideth Gowan and James, Ann, Rose, John Henry, Thomas and Ebenezer Gowan, children of Merideth Gowan, Dec'd all of Simpson Co.

vs

Joseph G. Anderson.

Merideth Gowan died March 1835.

****

1847 Warren Co. Miss. Drawer 95 Case #4015

Seripta Bass by Wm. S. Romain, next friend

vs

Joseph Bass

Divorce Petition

Seripta Bass was late widow of Hugh Russell, Dec'd.

****

1850 Madison Co. Miss. Drawer 95 Case #4017

William Robertson, Tr.

vs

Jesse Heard and Samuel B. Livingston, Admrs. Est. John T. Dearing, Dec'd.

****

1847 Holmes Co. Miss. Drawer 95 Case #4023

Peyton L. Clower and wife, Rachel F. of Madison Co.; John Clower and wife, Sarah Ann; Thos. W. Evans and wife,

Nancy E.; Wren McMillan and wife, Juliana and William F. Sherrod

vs

Joel, William, John R. and Soloman Sherrod, George A. Cox and wife, Sarah Ann Cox.

Joel Sherrod was Admr. Est. of his brother Benjamin Sherrod, Dec'd late of Lawrence Co. Miss. who died in 1835 intestate. His widow, Rachel later married Peter L. Clower. John Sherrod, Dec'd was the father of Joel Sherrod. Benjamin was n.c.m. John Sherrod's heirs were Joel, William, and John R. Sherrod, Sarah Ann Cox, Bethany Buckley wife of Albert Buckley and daughter of Soloman Sherrod, Dec'd, son of John, Dec'd.

****

1847 Attala Co. Miss. Drawer 95 Case #4030

James A. Graves and wife, Ann, formerly Ann Mitchell

vs

Purley C. Richardson and wife, Geraldine, Daniel Thomas, Elijah Watson and Henry Smith.

James A. Graves married Ann Mitchell, widow of James C. Mitchell late of Hinds Co., on January 27, 1846. Litigation involves Isaac B. Norrell, Admr. Est. of James Gordez, Dec'd late of Rankin Co. Miss.

****

1847 Warren Co. Miss. Drawer 95 Case #4033

Daniel S. Mercier and John Sears, Jr. of Warren Co.

vs

Robert Gatewood of Scott Co., Jacob Riese and Simon Frank.

****

1850 Madison Co. Miss. Drawer 95 Case #4041

William Robertson, Tr.

vs

William McBride, Admr. de bonis non Est. Sam T. Teamster, Dec'd

****

1850 Madison Co. Miss. Drawer 95 Case #4042

William Robertson, Tr. Commercial Bank of Natchez.
vs
Richard C. Sanders, Robt. M. Davis and wife, Mariah, nee Leggett, Admrs. Est. Absalom Leggett, Dec'd.

John Leggett, a brother of Absalom and Hugh Sanders were co-signers.

****

1850 Madison Co. Miss. Drawer 95 Case #4043

William Robertson, Tr.
vs
Gustin Kearney and Martha D. Andrews, Admrs. Est. John G. Andrews, Dec'd.

****

1850 Hinds Co. Miss. Drawer 95 Case #4052

Joshua Green, Jr.
vs
Michael J. Dickson, David Dickson, Joseph W. Miller and wife, Martha Ann, nee Dickson, heirs of James C. Dickson, Dec'd; James B. Robinson, Admr. Est. James C. Dickson; Raymond, Hannah H. and Jane Caldwell, Edward and Elizabeth Kearney, representatives by devise and descent of Isaac Caldwell, Dec'd.

****

1850 Desoto Co. Miss. Drawer 95 Case #4053

Mary M. Bullard and Wiley Fitzgerald, residents of Desoto Co.
vs
John C. Pryor and E. C. N. Coffey, Ann E. Pryor.

Mary M. Bullard was widow of Christopher Bullard who died in Desoto Co. in June 1848. John C. Pryor married Ann E. Bullard, daughter of Christopher and Mary Bullard. Mary Bullard was born Mary M. Herbert and had previously been married to Reddick P. Moore, Dec'd late of Tennessee.

****

1850 Lowndes Co. Miss. Drawer 95 Case #4054

Mary E. Lawson, late Mary E. Shotwell, and her husband Andrew Lawson

vs

Jefferson M. Graybill

Mary E. Lawson was daughter of Lewis B. Taliaferro. See Cases 2441 and 2611.

****

1850 Madison Co. Miss. Drawer 95 Case #4056

William Robertson, Tr.

vs

Henry R. Coulter and James Richards, Execs. Est. Joseph Collins, Dec'd.

****

1847 Yalobusha Co. Miss. Drawer 95 Case #4061

Elizabeth Ann Morrow of Yalobusha Co. by next friend, Franklin P. Plummer of Hinds Co.

vs

Orson H. Morrow of State of Alabama.

Divorce Petition.

Married in Marshall Co. Alabama Sept. 27, 1842. A child, William Henry Morrow was born November 27, 1843. Orson H. Morrow was a son of George W. Morrow and she was daughter of William Hill, all of Marshall Co. Ala.

****

1847 Leake Co. Miss. Drawer 95 Case #4063

James L. Coleman, William Coleman, Julia A. T. Coleman, William Manderville and wife, Martha, nee Coleman, heirs of Philip Coleman, Dec'd.

vs

Matthew Rowe of State of Louisiana, Samuel Ford and William Sutherland, citizens of Madison Co. Miss.

****

1850 Smith Co. Miss. Drawer 95 Case #4066

Bartlett V. Gammage, Gdn. of Mary Ann Noble (widow) and John Edward and Joseph William Noble, minor children of Ezekiel Noble, late of Smith Co.

vs

Samuel Noble, Admr. Est. of Ezekiel Noble, Dec'd.

Ezekiel Noble died about 1848. Surties on bond: Bartlett V. Gammage, Malachi Sharbrough, Hardy L. Flowers, Edmond P. Overby and R. Y. H. Lowry.

****

1850 Copiah Co. Miss. Drawer 95 Case #4067

Ann C. Smith

vs

William Ray and John Lamar of Copiah Co.

Ann C. Smith was widow of Drury Wilkins, Dec'd late of Jasper Co. Georgia, by whom she had seven children: Charles D., Martha, John, Jerusha, George, Ann and Elizabeth Wilkins. Drury Wilkins made a will in 1834 naming John McDonald and Henry Walker as Executors and Ann Wilkins (widow) Exex. Second husband Smith's given name, nor date of marriage shown.

****

1850 Lauderdale Co. Miss. Drawer 95 Case #4080

John Falls, Admr. Est. Joel McNeely, Dec'd

vs

Henry R. Wilson.

****

1847 Covington Co. Miss. Drawer 96 Case #4082

Thos. Beavers and wife, Sarah Beavers of Covington Co.

vs

Charles Slater and wife, Melinda; Rachel and Isabella R. Baskin, minors; Daniel Cook and wife, Ada; Charles and James H. Baskin, minors; John and Samuel Baskin, minors, all of Hinds Co. Mary Baskin, widow of John H. Baskin, Dec'd; Martha Baskin and three others whose names are unknown all of Carroll Co.; Major Newton of Lawrence Co.; Samuel B. Hathorn of Covington Co. and George D. Patterson of Jasper Co.

In this case Sarah and Eliza Lewis, minor heirs of Elisha Lewis ask that William Baskin be appointed Gdn. in place of their mother, Ann Lewis, who renounced guardianship. Sarah Lewis married Thos. Beavers. Melinda Slater, wife of Charles Slater was widow of William C. Baskin, Dec'd former guardian for Sarah and Eliza Lewis. Ada Cook, wife of Daniel Cook, was widow of James Baskin, Dec'd. Major Newton was Admr. Est. Samuel Baskin Sr. who died in Lawrence Co. Miss. Samuel B. Hathorn was Admr. de bonis non Est. James C. Baskin, late of Covington Co. Miss.

****

1850 Hinds Co. Miss. Drawer 96 Case #4086

William Thomas (brother of Stephen), Mary Pearce, wife of Redwine Pearce, Eliza Cook, wife of Alvin Cook, Sarah Smith, wife of Preston Smith, Elizabeth Holcomb, wife of Josiah Holcomb, all sisters of Stephen Thomas, Dec'd, and all of Rankin Co.

vs

Rebecca Thomas, widow of Stephen Thomas, Dec'd.

Stephen Thomas died January 10, 1850. Litigation involves nun cupative will of Stephen Thomas which was witnessed by R. M. McGowan and John Byram.

****

1847 Adams Co. Miss. Drawer 96 Case #4088

Levi Harrison of Natchez

vs

Alfred R. Wynne and Benjamin Simpson of State of Tennessee and Nathaniel Harrison of Natchez.

Bill recites Wynne as a "relation" of Levi Harrison.

****

1850 Rankin Co. Miss. Drawer 96 Case #4089

Laughlin McLaurin
vs
John G. Parker, Gdn. for Amanda and Mary Jayne, minor heirs of Anslem H. Jayne, Dec'd late of Covington Co.; Joseph M. Jayne of Rankin Co.; William M. Jayne of Holmes Co.

Elizabeth Jayne was Admx. and Joseph McAffee, Archibald Anderson and Brewster H. Jayne Admrs. Est. Anslem H. Jayne, Dec'd.

****

1850 Kemper Co. Miss. Drawer 96 Case #4097

Elisha Mosely, Admr. Est. Wiley Mosely, Dec'd late of Kemper Co.
vs
Augustus H. Harris

Bondsmen: Martin F. Jones, W. S. Jones. Jurymen: Cornelius Key, John Corrothers, Thos. W. Adams, Martin Johnson, Jesse Reed, James B. Diggs, William Stewart, James H. Morse, W. C. Meeks, W. J. M. Chisholm, B. B. Winohand and Needham Holyfield.

****

1847 Warren Co. Miss. Drawer 96 Case #4105

Nathaniel T. Williams of Warren Co. Miss.; Nathaniel Francis and William H. Nicholson of State of Virginia
vs
George Powell and wife, Mary and James C. Wright, Trustee.

****

1848 Claiborne Co. Miss. Drawer 96 Case #4126

Stephen B. Curry of Claiborne Co. and Shadrack E. Nzo, Admr. ad colligendum Est. Isaiah Watson, Dec'd
vs
Nathaniel Royster of Yazoo Co.

****

1847 Rankin Co. Miss. Drawer 96 Case #4132

William F. Beresford and wife, Margaret C. Beresford

vs

Isaac Alexander of Rankin Co.

****

1848 Hinds Co. Miss. Drawer 96 Case #4151

Joseph W. Miller

vs

Abner A. G. Beazley, Admr. Est. James F. Beazley, Dec'd; Samuel C. Beazley, Admr. de bonis non Est. James F. Beazley, Dec'd

****

1848 Smith Co. Miss. Drawer 96 Case #4170

Mahala Flowers and Richard Flowers (hus. and wife), Admrs. Est. James L. McCaughan, Dec'd

vs

James L. Weems

Heirs of James L. McCaughan: Thos. I., John D., James J., David H. and Christopher McCaughan.

****

1848 Yazoo Co. Miss. Drawer 96 Case #4178

Claiborne Bowman, Gdn. Phillip and Mary O'Reilly, minor heirs of Edmund O'Reilly, Dec'd and of Nicholas O'Reilly, Dec'd; Sarah O'Reilly, widow of Edmund O'Reilly

vs

M. Langon and wife, Tralucia H. Langon

Edmund, Phillip and Nicholas O'Reilly were brothers. Edmund and Nicholas both died in 1845. Children of Phillip O'Reilly, Dec'd: James P., John E. and Frederick O'Reilly, all non residents of State of Miss. and Marcella and Dolly Ann O'Reilly of Yazoo Co. Michael and Tralucia H. Langon were guardians of Marcella and Dolly Ann O'Reilly.

****

1848 Hinds Co. Miss. Drawer 96 Case #4190

Walter A. Grisham

vs

.... Battle, widow of Elisha Battle, Dec'd; Josiah Wilson and wife, Eliza, nee Battle; Henry J. G. Battle; William W. George and wife, Mary F., nee Battle, Washington Jenkins and wife, Olivia, nee Battle, and Augustus D. Battle, all heirs of Elisha Battle, Dec'd and all non residents of State of Miss.

Elisha Battle was a resident of Hempstead Co. Arkansas in January 1842.

* * * *

1842 Carroll Co. Miss. Drawer 96 Case #4194

N. B. Hooker and wife, Martha, nee Goodson

vs

Nathan Hooker, Gdn. Martha Goodson Hooker

Martha Dorman Goodson Hooker was daughter of William Goodson, Dec'd and Elizabeth Goodson.

* * * *

1836 Hinds Co. Miss. Drawer 96 Case #4199

Joseph Regan of Claiborne Co. Miss. Admr. Est. Eleazer W. Herring, Dec'd

vs

Nicholas S. Gray of Warren Co., David Barron of Louisiana and John I. Guion of Hinds Co.

* * * *

1846 Rankin Co. Miss. Drawer 96 Case #4204

John W. Webb, Admr. Est. Stephen W. Webb, Dec'd

vs

Francis S. Smith of Scott Co.; Thompson V. Berry of Rankin Co. and Daniel D. Webb of Rankin Co.

* * * *

1850 Claiborne Co. Miss.. Drawer 96 Case #4205

David Craighead of State of Ark.

vs

Zelegman Andrews, sole survivor of firm Andrews and Brother.

Litigation involves debts due Andrews and Bro. by Est. Thomas H. Stewart in Jefferson Co. and Est. Isaac Conger in Claiborne Co. William Sillers was Exec. Est. Thos. H. Stewart and Martha Conger Admr. Est. Isaac Conger.

****

1850 Claiborne Co. Miss. Drawer 96 Case #4206

James B. Craighead of State of Ala.

vs

Richard Valentine, Admr. Est. Zelegman Andrews.

Eleazer L. Andrews, brother of Zelegman, committed suicide by drowning on April 21, 1848 in Mobile, Ala. and on April 22, 1848 Zelegman departed from Port of New Orleans for parts unknown.

****

1848 Madison Co. Miss. Drawer 96 Case #4216

Elizabeth Hall (wife of Dixon H. Hall) by Jesse Hickman as next friend; Dixon H. Hall; William T. Hall; Frances A. B. Hall; Bowling C. Hall; Robt. R. Hall; Mary E. Hall; Benj. H. Hall and Wilmot H. Hall, infant children of Elizabeth Hall and Dixon H. Hall.

vs

William Burt of Lowndes Co. Miss.

Dixon Hall was son of Dixon Hall Sr. of Autauga Co. Ala. who died about 1839. William T. Hall was also a son of Dixon Sr.

****

1849 Claiborne Co. Miss. Drawer 96 Case #4222

Robt. W. Harper, Admr. Est. Catharine C. Harper, Dec'd James Person, Volney Stamps, James S. Mason, Robert F. Moore and William Sayer, all of Claiborne Co.

vs

Stephen Edward Archer by next friend, Richard T. Harper, Admr. Est. Stephen Archer, Dec'd.

Catharine C. Harper was widow of Edward F. Barnes who died intestate in 1827. He left a minor child, Eliza F. Barnes. Catharine Barnes married Stephen C. Archer in 1839 and Stephen Edward Archer was only issue of this marriage. Eliza F. Barnes died in 1835, unmarried, and intestate. Stephen C. Archer died in 1837. Catharine Barnes Archer married Robert W. Harper in 1840 and she died in 1844.

****

1848 Claiborne Co. Miss. Drawer 96 Case #4224

Harrison Cooper of Claiborne Co. Admr. Est. Maborn Cooper, Dec'd

vs

David Bush Sr., Richard M. Harrison, Robert W. Harper, Eli C. Briscoe, George W. Elmer, James A. Mason and Passmore Hoopes.

****

1848 Carroll Co. Miss. Drawer 96 Case #4228

William Dawson of Carroll Co.

vs

Margaret Hargrove, Amanda, Benj., John, William Hargrove and Christopher and Robert Gunnaway, infants; Robert Hargrove, Eli Etheridge and wife, Elizabeth, all of Sunflower Co. Miss., James Earl and wife, Letitia, residents of State of Texas.

Robert Hargrove, Elizabeth Etheridge, Margaret, Amanda, Benj., John and William Hargrove, James Earl,

Letitia Earl, Christopher and Robert Garraway were all heirs of H. B. Hargrove, Dec'd. Letitia Hargrove was the mother of the H. G. Hargrove heirs.

****

1848 Warren Co. Miss. Drawer 96 Case #4231

Elizabeth Carradine of Warren Co. formerly of Isaquena Co. by next friend, James Felks

vs

H. G. Heart and George R. Carradine of New Orleans.

Henry F. Carradine was brother of George R. and was his business partner. Elizabeth Carradine was wife of George R. and litigation involves the replevin of slaves.

****

1848 Warren Co. Miss. Drawer 96 Case #4242

Joseph H. Johnson

vs

Isaac H. Hay, Admr. Est. John H. Martin, Dec'd

John H. Martin died Sept. 1841 leaving widow, Emily Martin, who died in 1844 and the following children: William T., Ellen, Emily M., Adolphus K., John and Harriet Martin, all minors except William T.

****

1848 Warren Co. Miss. Drawer 96 Case #4276

John Bacon, Alexander Simington and Thos. Robins of Philadelphia, Pa. and Joseph L. Roberts of State of Miss.

vs

Thomas A. Marshall, Admr. Est. Thomas S. Thornly, Dec'd and William T. and James E. Thornly, heirs of Thos. S. Thornly, Dec'd; William H. Edrington of State of Louisiana.

****

1848 Bolivar Co. Miss. Drawer 96 Case #4282

Thos. I. Coffee

vs

William Morris and Mary Simpson, heirs of Jacob J. H. Morris, Dec'd non residents of State of Miss.

****

1849 Hinds Co. Miss. Drawer 96 Case #4298

Almarine Lacey

vs

William A. Gatewood of Scott Co. Miss.

Litigation involves the estate of John Clowers, Dec'd, late of Washington Parish, La. who died in 1837 intestate leaving heirs: his widow, Cyrena Clowers who later married William F. Sibley and children, Elbert Clowers; Cynthia wife of Sherwood C. Statham; Symantha, wife of Isaac A. Myles, but formerly wife of Thos. A. Bickham; William P. Clowers; Matilda, wife of Thos. Donaho, all adults and Jackson, Peyton L., John, Thomas and Frances Jane Clowers all infants.

Frances Jane Clowers married Almarine Lacey Dec. 24, 1846 and died childless April 22, 1848.

****

1849 Yazoo Co. Miss. Drawer 96 Case #4305

John M. Hendricks

vs

Nathaniel G. Nye and wife, Lucy Ann Nye

****

1849 Yazoo Co. Miss. Drawer 96 Case #4308

Robt. S. Holt and Frederick W. Wheelis, Exec. Est. Washington Dorsey, Dec'd

vs

William E. Pugh of Yazoo Co.

****

1848 Claiborne Co. Miss. Drawer 96 Case #4309

Albigense W. Putman of State of Tenn. and Stephen B. Curry of Claiborne Co.

vs

James Watson

****

1850 Hinds Co. Miss. Drawer 96 Case #4320

Felix J. Funchess, Martin Ford and wife, Sarah A. E. Ford

vs

John M. Davis

Edmund Funchess died leaving wife, Sarah A. Funchess and two children: Felix J. and Sarah A. E. Funchess, wife of Martin Ford. Letters of Admr. Est. Edmund Funchess granted widow, Sarah A. on Nov. 26, 1838, who later married John M. Davis. Sarah A. Funchess Davis died in 1843 and Sarah A. E. Funchess married Martin Ford in Jan. 1848.

****

1870 Pontotoc Co. Miss. Drawer 96 Case #4351

Chas. G. Mitchell, Admr. de bonis non Est. William M. Duncan, Dec'd

vs

Joseph M. Heard, Martha L. Ware, Execs. Est. J. A. Ware, Dec'd; John C. James, Margaret S. James, Execs. Est. W. Z. Ware, Dec'd.

William M. Duncan and Josephine Duncan were heirs of James W. Duncan. Andrew Duncan was Admr. Est. James W. Duncan.

****

1849 Warren Co. Miss. Drawer 96 Case #4416

Claiborne Steel, Admr. Est. Robt. Thompson, Dec'd

vs

D. W. Connelly, Wm. R. Campbell and William H. Robards, residents of Washington Co. Miss.

Letters of Adm. Est. Robert Thompson issued to Claiborne Steele March 26, 1849.

****

1849 Washington Co. Miss. Drawer 96 Case #4424

Geo. A. Adams, John Tuttle and wife, Adeline, Susannah J. Perrie, Hobart Berrien, Catharine M. Berrien, Mary Ellen Adams and Ann Adams, heirs of John Adams, Dec'd

vs

John S. Courtney of Washington Co. Miss.

Samuel Adams, son of John Adams died intestate in 1848. George Adams was citizen of State of Missouri. John and Adeline Tuttle citizens of State of Maryland, Susannah J. Perrie (widow), citizen State of Maryland and Catharine M. Berrien and Hobart Berrien citizens State of New York.

****

1849 Warren Co. Miss. Drawer 96 Case #4428

Daniel Dyer

vs

Martin L. Ranney, Jr. and William Ranney heirs of Martin L. Ranney, Dec'd

****

1849 Yazoo Co. Miss. Drawer 96 Case #4462

Benj. R. Bookout of Washington Co. Miss.

vs

Adaline Whitehead, infant dau. Urban J. Whitehead, Dec'd of State of Louisiana and Gibson Barnes of Yazoo Co. Miss.

****

1849 Winston Co. Miss. Drawer 96 Case #4471

Absalom Reed and Evelina Reed, infants, of Winston Co. Miss.

vs

William J. Denson, Exec. Est. William Denson, Dec'd.

Heirs of William Reed, Dec'd: Jemima Reed (widow), Martha A. Holmes, wife of John C. Holmes, Absalom and Evelina Reed. William Reed died "prior to 1838" and widow, Jemima married Thomas Holmes in 1840. William Denson died in 1846 leaving will naming William J. Denson, Exec. Absalom Reed was 21 on July 21, 1849.

****

1856 Hinds Co. Miss. Drawer 96 Case #4517

Robt. W. James, Admr. Est. Thos. Barrett, Dec'd late of New Orleans

vs

Colin S. Tarpley

Will of Thos. Barrett probated 2nd Dist. City of New Orleans, June 10, 1846

****

1850 Madison Co. Miss. Drawer 96 Case #4565

Helen S. Johnstone, infant, by Lewis W. Thompson next friend

vs

William J. Brittan and wife, Fanny A. Johnstone Brittan and Margaret L. Johnstone

Helen S. Johnstone was daughter of John T. and Margaret L. Johnstone. John T. Johnstone died in 1848. Helen S. Johnstone and Fanny A. J. Brittan were the only children of John T. Johnstone and wife, Margaret L. of Annandale, Madison Co. Miss.

****

1852 Madison Co. Miss. Drawer 97 Case #4573

Joseph Woods, surviving partner of Yeatman Woods and Co. and Fidelia S. Hunt

vs

Samuel J. Ridley, Admr. Est. Henry Ridley, Dec'd; Elizabeth Ridley, William A. Ridley and Moses Ridley, heirs of Henry Ridley, Dec'd.

Henry Ridley died in 1835 in State of Tennessee.

****

1850 Yazoo Co. Miss. Drawer 97 Case #4578

Henry Hagan, Gdn. for Sarah A., William H., George S., James I. and Eugenia Hagan

vs

William Battaile

****

1850 Madison Co. Miss. Drawer 97 Case #4583

Josiah Newman

vs

John Munn of Hyde Park, N. Y. Admr. de bonis non Est. Joseph Meek, succeeding Jesse Meek.

****

1856 Yazoo Co. Miss. Drawer 97 Case #4598

Simeon T. Johnston, Admr. Est. William Johnston, Dec'd

vs

Sarah Johnston, widow, and Rebecca Hall, wife of David Hall, Sophronia Ann Johnston and Mary Johnston, daughters of James Johnston, Dec'd.

****

1850 Madison Co. Miss. Drawer 97 Case #4624

Nancy A. Ridley by Samuel J. Ridley, next friend

vs

John C. Ridley

Divorce Petition

Married: March 9, 1841 in State of Tennessee

****

1851 Washington Co. Miss. Drawer 97 Case #4637

Elizabeth Carson

vs

Andrew Carson.

Divorce Petition.

Married: 1831 at Point Chicot, Arkansas.

****

1852 Hinds Co. Miss. Drawer 97 Case #4638

Preston Cooper and wife, Lucretia F. Cooper

vs

Inman Williams.

Litigation involves Cooper's Wells property—an early and famous Mississippi Health Resort.

****

1850 Bolivar Co. Miss. Drawer 97 Case #4641

William B. Cook of Bolivar Co.

vs

Sizinka Brown, widow of James P. Brown, Dec'd, George Campbell, Percy and Harriet Brown, infant children of James P. Brown, Dec'd, by their Gdn. George W. Campbell—all residents of State of Tennessee and Christopher Field, Exec. Est. James P. Brown, Dec'd. James P. Brown died in 1844.

****

1850 Warren Co. Miss. Drawer 97 Case #4656

Cynthia Kent by next friend, Jesse Granberry

vs

Elias D. Kent (husband of Cynthia), Admr. Est. Saban Kent, Dec'd

****

1854 Copiah Co. Miss. Drawer 97 Case #4672

Alfred Ingraham and George Read of Claiborne Co.

vs

Thomas Millsaps, Reuben Millsaps, W. W. Millsaps, Green Millsaps and John Wheat, all of Copiah Co.

****

1850 Coahoma Co. Miss. Drawer 97 Case #4692

Valentine S. Cook of Coahoma Co.

vs

Thos. F. Cook, late of Madison Co. now of State of Texas.

****

1850 Claiborne Co. Miss. Drawer 97 Case #4695

Lewis Williams, Mary Williams and Stephen B. Williams of Claiborne Co.

vs

Josiah Newman, Admr. de bonis non Est. Reuben Newman, Dec'd, succeeding Marmaduke D. Kimbrough of Carroll Co.

****

1851 Jefferson Co. Miss. Drawer 97 Case #4711

William B. Minor and wife, Elizabeth and Jacob Vough and wife, Priscilla

vs

Robert Cox, Exec. Est. Mildred Dixon, Dec'd.

Roger Dixon and Mildred Dixon were parents of Elizabeth Minor and Priscilla Vough. Roger Dixon died in 1833 and Mildred Dixon died Dec. 20, 1849.

****

1851 Yazoo Co. Miss. Drawer 97 Case #4727

Edward C. Wilkinson

vs

Thomas J. Jennings, Exec. Est. John Willison, Dec'd

John Willison died Dec. 12, 1836 in Yazoo Co. leaving heirs: James D. and Mary E. Willison and Frances L. Bowers of Licking, Ohio, widow of late William H. Bowers of the State of Virginia.

****

1851 Rankin Co. Miss. Drawer 97 Case #4813

Joseph W. Miller and wife, Martha Ann; Michael J. Dickson and David Dickson, heirs of James C. Dickson, Dec'd

vs

Joseph Hudnell Presidene, Allen Moore, David Thomas, William G. Kersh and Charles M. Williams, all members of Board of Police of Rankin Co. Heirs of Daniel Fore: Marz White, Isaac White and wife, Joyce, Daniel Fore, Martha Fore, Jane Fore, ________________ Geer, daughter of Adeline Geer, Dec'd.

****

1851 Claiborne Co. Miss. Drawer 97 Case #4834

Alfred Ingraham and George Read of Claiborne Co.

vs

Elijah Right, Kendall Right, Thos. J. Wheat, John Wheat and Thomas Millsaps of Copiah Co.

****

1851 Adams Co. Miss. Drawer 97 Case #4876

William N. Mercer and Henry Vaughn

vs

Mary Ann Ellis, Elias Ogden and John Routh, Admrs. Est. Thomas G. Gillis, Dec'd.

Bill mentions William Ferriday and wife, Helen of Yazoo Co., George Gerrard and wife, Elizabeth C. and Albert F. Kibble and wife, Sarah of Yazoo Co. Miss.

****

1851 Warren Co. Miss. Drawer 97 Case #4901

William M. W. Cochran, Admr. Est. Robert Cochran, Dec'd

vs

William Biggs and wife, Susan.

Robert Cochran died August 1849.

****

1851 Hinds Co. Miss. Drawer 97 Case #4914

D. C. Glenn and wife, Patricia B. Glenn

vs

Benj. G. Weir and wife, Elizabeth C. Weir, late of Hinds Co. and now of State of California.

****

1848 Warren Co. Miss. Drawer 97 Case #4921

Margaret Moore, widow of Wm. Moore and Lloyd R. Coleman of Warren Co.

vs

Alexander Alexander, Benj. Albertson of Hinds Co. and Aaron Alexander a non resident of State of Miss.

File mentions Edward W. Moore and wife, Mary A. O. Moore, William Connell Walker and William C. Black

****

1851 Claiborne Co. Miss. Drawer 97 Case #4922

Thos. Alfred Barnes and James C. Bertron, infants, by next friend Samuel R. Bertron; Samuel B. Crane and Francis R. Crane, infants by next friend, Robert E. Crane, all of Claiborne Co.

vs

Henry W. Allen and James McBride.

Wm. Crane died intestate and left as heirs sisters and brothers: Catharine Barnes, Salome Ann Crane, Robt. E. Crane, Samuel B. Crane and Francis R. Crane. Catharine M. Crane married Alfred T. Barnes in April 1840. Alfred T. Barnes died 1847 and Catharine subsequently married Samuel R. Bertron. Catharine Barnes Bertron died June 25, 1849. Salome Ann Crane married Henry W. Allen on July 2, 1844 and she died Jan. 25, 1851.

****

1851 Madison Co. Miss. Drawer 97 Case #4938

James M. Walker

vs

Eliza McCool, widow of John L. McCool.

John L. McCool died in 1851.

****

1851 Warren Co. Miss. Drawer 97 Case #4945

James Shirley and wife, Adeline, James J. Shirley, Frederick Shirley, Alice Shirley and Robert Quincy Shirley, children of J. and A. Shirley of Warren Co.

vs

George Fearn of Hinds Co.

****

1851 Madison Co. Miss. Drawer 97 Case #4953

Rempson S. Dillon and wife, Elizabeth, nee McAffrey, James McAffrey and wife, Mary Ann, all of Pike Co. and heirs of Michael McAffrey, Dec'd

vs

William J. Denson and James H. Denson.

Michael McAffrey died in Madison Co. Aug. 27, 1832. William J. and James H. Denson were sons of William Denson, Dec'd.

****

1851 Hinds Co. Miss. Drawer 97 Case #4954

Nancy Sanders of Hinds Co.

vs

J. W. Welborne, William Sanders, Jr. and Hiram D. Robertson.

Nancy Sanders was widow of William Sanders who died in Hinds Co. July 3, 1835. James Sanders, son of Nancy and William, was made Admr. of William's estate but he died on May 25, 1839.

****

1851 Hinds Co. Miss. Drawer 97 Case #4959

Elizabeth Bass by next friend, George Amos, R. Hatcher and wife, Eliza, all of Hinds Co.

vs

Samuel H. Smith.

Elizabeth Bass and Eliza Hatcher were children of Jesse Bass and granddaughters of Council Bass, Dec'd.

****

1855 Hinds Co. Miss. Drawer 98 Case #4980

John W. Rives and wife, Lucy B.; Lucy B. Moss of Graves Co. Kentucky; Daniel Collins and wife, Henrietta; James H. Moss; John D. Moss and wife, Sarah E. all of Montgomery Co. Tenn.

vs

George Fearn of Jackson, Hinds Co. Miss.

Litigation involves land in Rankin Co. which had been claimed by James L. Moss, Dec'd.

****

1851 Marion Co. Miss. Drawer 98 Case #4984

George J. Hulme and wife, Jemima

vs

William J. Denson, Exec. Est. William Denson

Jemima Hulme was widow of James H. Denson, Dec'd, son of Wm. Denson, Dec'd.

Bill refers to three minor children of Jemima and James H. Denson but does not name them.

****

1851 Hinds Co. Miss. Drawer 98 Case #4985

George W. Matthews and wife, Anne

vs

William H. Fondren, William Frisby and Joseph W. Cooper.

Anne Matthews was daughter of Samuel Pepper of Lawrence Co. Miss. Samuel Pepper died November 1845. George W. Matthews married Anne Pepper in 1838 or 1939. Depositions of her brothers Gwin and John Pepper.

****

1851 Warren Co. Miss. Drawer 98 Case #4986

Thos. C. Clark

vs

Clara E. J. Clark

Divorce Petition.

Thos. C. Clark and Clara E. J. Edson were married in White Oak Springs, Wisconsin July 19, 1848.

****

1852 Yazoo Co. Miss. Drawer 98 Case #4994

Richard M. Johnson, Admr. ad colligendum Est. Benj. Johnson, Dec'd

vs

Alexander M. Morton and wife, Eleanor Morton of Yazoo Co.

Benj. Johnson died 1834 and William Ward appointed Admr.

****

1850 Hinds Co. Miss. Drawer 98 Case #5009

Maburn Barfield, Admr. Est. Needham Barfield, Dec'd

vs

Thos. Nixon, Jr. and Wade Harvey.

Letters of Admr. on Est. Needham Barfield granted Nov. 25, 1835. Rarity Barfield was widow of Needham. She later married Sessums Dunn.

****

1852 Warren Co. Miss. Drawer 98 Case #5010

Minerva D. Gett

vs

William A. Gett.

Divorce Petition.

Married in Warren Co. (date not given). William Gett left Miss. May 20, 1849 and went to State of California.

****

1855 Lawrence Co. Miss. Drawer 98 Case #5014

Nathan Morris and wife, Louisa of Holmes Co.

vs

Donaldson F. N. Turner and John Sharp.

Louisa Morris was widow of Meshack King who died in Holmes Co. in 1838. Commissioners named: William Weathersby, J. F. Mobley, Samuel Evans, I. M. Ellis and John Gartman.

****

1853 Hinds Co. Miss. Drawer 98 Case #5016

Wilson Hemmingway

vs

Robt. A. Clark, Admr. Est. William R. Gist, M. D. late of Hinds Co. and Alfred B. Cabiness, M. D

John J. Whitesides, a witness, was a brother-in-law of Dr. Gist (Dr. Gist married his sister—not named). Dr. Gist and Dr. Cabiness were professional partners.

****

1854 Warren Co. Miss. Drawer 98 Case #5020

William S. Jones

vs

John G. Kellogg, Exec. Est. Moses Hall, Dec'd.
See Will of Moses Hall.

****

1850 Warren Co. Miss. Drawer 98 Case #5033

Samuel Lum, Administrator Est. with Will attached, Robt. Bull, Dec'd of Warren Co.

vs

John C. Bull of State of Kentucky and Robert Y. Black of Louisiana.

Letters of Admr. Est. Robert Bull granted March 27, 1845 in Warren Co.

****

1850 Smith Co. Miss. Drawer 98 Case #5052

Mahala Flowers, Admx. Est. James L. McCaughan, Dec'd
vs
James S. Weems, Samuel O. Goode and John Rawls

Mahala Flowers, wife of Richard Flowers, was late widow of James L. McCaughan.

****

1850 Claiborne Co. Miss. Drawer 98 Case #5055

Hugh M. Coffey of Claiborne Co.
vs
Mary D. Horner, Admr. Est. Alexander Horner, Dec'd.

Alexander Horner died in 1849.

****

1852 Kemper Co. Miss. Drawer 98 Case #5057

Elizabeth Webster
vs
James Campbell and wife, Elizabeth Susannah Campbell.

Elizabeth Susannah Campbell was daughter and only child of James and Mary Jane Puckett. James Puckett died about 1844 leaving his estate equally divided between his wife and daughter. Mary Jane Puckett died about 1849 and left half her estate to her sister, Elizabeth Webster, and appointed Elizabeth Webster Gdn. of Elizabeth Susannah Puckett, minor. Elizabeth Susannah Puckett married James Campbell Nov. 27, 1850.

****

1850 Wilkinson Co. Miss. Drawer 98 Case #5058

Henry B. Pettibone and sister, Sarah Pettibone and Gerald C. Brandon, their uncle and guardian of Wilkinson Co.
vs
Noah James, Admr. Est. James Eby, Dec'd.

****

1852 Madison Co. Miss. Drawer 98 Case #5058-a

Jesse S. Miller and wife, Eunice J. C. Miller

vs

William A. Baldwin, Exec. Est. Jeremiah Griffin, Dec'd and Lawrence L. Griffin, Admr. Est. Isaac W. Jones, Dec'd.

Eunice J. C. Miller was widow of Isaac W. Jones, Dec'd.

****

1850 Wilkinson Co. Miss. Drawer 98 Case #5070

John Bacon, Alexander Lymington and Thos. Robbins

vs

Amos B. Thompson, Exec. Est. Little Berry Thompson, Fielding Davis and J. L. Wall.

Will of Little Berry Thompson filed for probate August 14, 1839.

****

1852 Hinds Co. Miss. Drawer 98 Case #5078

David G. Tinnin, Benj. F. Tinnin and Martha Tinnin, minor children of Nancy Price, late Nancy Tinnin, by next friend, J. W. McRaven.

vs

Robert S. Price.

Nancy Price, mother of Tinnin heirs, died Sept. 10, 1852. Bill shows Nancy Tinnin married Robert S. Price "a short time before her death".

****

1850 Hinds Co. Miss. Drawer 98 Case #5085

Cecilia Reagan, Admr. Est. William Cargill, Dec'd

vs

Phineas M. Garrett and wife, Emily, Arnold Ingold, William M. Wilbourn, Wm. S. Bodley, George M. Reese,

Harrison H. Hart, Oscar J. Stewart and William Mitchell.

Wm. Cargill, Dec'd was first husband of Cecilia Reagan and Thos. J. Reagan, Dec'd was her second husband.

****

1853 Lawrence Co. Miss. Drawer 98 Case #5086

Wiley Z. Grimstead of Holmes Co.

vs

Jacob F. Foster of Hinds Co. and J. H. Hilliard of Lawrence Co., Execs. Est. of Thomas J. Grimstead, Dec'd.

Heirs of Thos. J. Grimstead: Children of John Grimstead of Wilkinson Co. (not named), a brother; Wiley J. Grimstead, a nephew, Neil Norsworthy; nephew, Nicholas Norsworthy and brother John Grimstead. Will filed for probate in Lawrence Co. Miss. July 27, 1847.

****

1850 Lawrence Co. Miss. Drawer 98 Case #5087

John Bacon et al

vs

Daniel Magee, Benj. Gresham, Wm. H. Davis, Barnabus Allen and William Massey, all citizens of Lawrence Co. Miss.

****

1852 Madison Co. Miss. Drawer 98 Case #5089

William Robertson, Trustee

vs

William S. Bailey, Admr. Est. John R. Grisby, Dec'd and Joseph H. Vannoy.

****

1850 Adams Co. Miss. Drawer 98 Case #5095

David S. Stacy, Admr. Est. Charles L. Lee, Dec'd of Concordia Parish, La.

vs

Samuel Barker

Charles L. Lee died in Mississippi in 1836 leaving large estate in Miss. and in Concordia Parish, La.

****

1852 Warren Co. Miss. Drawer 98 Case #5115

Harriet Friley

vs

Soloman Friley

Divorce Petition. Married: July 1829 in Yazoo Co. Miss.

****

1834 Claiborne Co. Miss. Drawer 98 Case #5133

David Kenly, Admr. Est. Arthur B. Sims, in right of wife, Phoebe Kenly

vs

John B. Conger, Gdn. for Alison Wade Sims, infant.

Arthur B. Sims died in 1831, leaving as widow, Phoebe Sims and infant son, Alison Sims. Phoebe subsequently married David Kenly.

****

1834 Warren Co. Miss. Drawer 98 Case #5139

Minerva Wrenn, Admr. Est. Belfield Wrenn, Dec'd

vs

Chas. Spann and Susan Spann, Admrs. Est. Robert M. Spann, Dec'd.

Minerva Wrenn succeeded Jacob Hyland and Jones Wrenn as Admrs. Est. Belfield Wrenn, Dec'd.

****

1854 Hinds Co. Miss. Drawer 98 Case #5143

Wm. P. Morris, Joseph Henry Morris, Mary E. Morris, Flora Morris and Bettie Morris, minor heirs of William

Morris, Dec'd, by their Mother and Gdn., Martha A. Morris, widow of William Morris, Dec'd

vs

John Morris and Hyman Hilzheim.

William Morris died March 6, 1851.

****

1853 Warren Co. Miss. Drawer 98 Case #5144

Jacob Oates and William G. Nolan, Rose Ann Nolan and Frances Mason Nolan, infants by next friend and father, N. G. Nolan—

Ex Parte Petition.

William G. Nolan married Eliza Mason, daughter of Samuel Mason of Warren Co. in 1844. Samuel later lived in Front Bend, Texas. Eliza Mason Nolan died in State of Texas in 1850. This petition is for division of lands on Deer Creek in Issaquena Co. Miss.

****

1853 Hinds Co. Miss. Drawer 98 Case #5151

John Thatcher

vs

Margaret Campbell, Exex. Est. William P. Campbell, Dec'd.

Heirs: Margaret Campbell (widow) and children: Leila S., Caroline N., William R., Martha G., Stella, Joseph H. and Margaret Campbell.

****

1853 Hinds Co. Miss. Drawer 98 Case #5159

Robert B. Miller

vs

Ann M. Miller

Divorce Petition.

Ann M. Lahan married Robert B. Miller Feb. 22, 1847.

****

1856 Hinds Co. Miss. Drawer 98 Case #5180

William D. Crane

vs

Joseph A. Crane, Admr. Est. Samuel Crane, Dec'd of Madison Co.; Elizabeth Downing and husband, Thomas Downing of Hinds Co.; Jane Ashley of Attala Co.; Emily Thompson and husband, Edward Thompson of Madison Co.; Malinda Price and husband, R. D. Price of State of Texas; Edward O. Chaffee and Leroy P. Thompson, Madison Co.; Benjamin T. and Ann Yates, minors, by their Gnd. Emily Yates of Leake Co.; Hester Ann Crane of Madison Co.

Benj. T. and Ann Yates were children of John M. and Emily Yates, Joseph A. Crane, Elizabeth Downing, Jane Ashley, Emily Thompson and Malinda Price were brothers and sisters of Samuel Crane, Dec'd.

****

1853 Yazoo Co. Miss. Drawer 98 Case #5189

Seaborn M. Phillips and James J. Phillips of Yazoo Co.

vs

Mary W. Nicholas of Hinds Co. Exex. Est. Hymerick Nicholas, Dec'd.

****

1853 Warren Co. Miss. Drawer 98 Case #5202

Eliza A. Shackleford

vs

John Keenan Shackleford

Divorce Petition.

Eliza A. Shackleford and Henry J. Shackleford were married May 23, 1832 in State of Virginia. Henry J. Shackleford died August 15, 1852.

****

1853 Madison Co. Miss. Drawer 98 Case #5217

Harvey Latham

vs

Benj. B. Frizell, Admr. Est. of Mary A. J. Frizell, Dec'd and Sarah E. Frizell, Thomas A. Frizell and Frances P. Frizell.

Benj. B. Frizell was widower of Mary A. J. Frizell and other defendants were her children. Mary A. J. Frizell died 1837.

****

1853 Hinds Co. Miss. Drawer 98 Case #5222

Maria Farabin by John Lynch, next friend

vs

Joseph Farabin

Maria Finley married Joseph Farabin in Hinds Co. Miss. in 1851.

****

1853 Jefferson Co. Miss. Drawer 98 Case #5223

Maria Louisa Elam

vs

Edgar G. Wood, Admr. Est. James Payne, Dec'd; Thos. F. Baker and wife, Martha, Robert W. Payne, Maria L. Payne, Linton Payne, Laura J. Payne, Virginia Payne and Alice Payne, all of Jefferson Co.
James Payne died in Jefferson Co. Dec. 24, 1846.

****

1853 Hinds Co. Miss. Drawer 98 Case #5225

Charles C. McGehee, Admr. Est Archibald McGehee, Dec'd

vs

Sebastian Richmond and Samuel M. Phelps.

****

1854 Hinds Co. Miss. Drawer 98 Case #5246

Hubert Spengler, Admr. Est. Joseph Spengler, Dec'd
vs
Alexander G. Grant

****

1854 Kemper Co. Miss. Drawer 98 Case #5248

James J. Corbin of Kemper Co.
vs
Bolus Cannon, Admr. Est. Benj. Cannon, Dec'd.
Benj. Cannon died in Kemper Co. in 1850.

****

1854 Claiborne Co. Miss. Drawer 98 Case #5263

Alexander Montgomery
vs
Jane P. O'Bannon (infant) of Saline Co. Mo.; Sarah Fry (infant) of State of Kentucky; Caleb B. Richardson and Adelaide Richardson (infants) of Claiborne Co. Miss.

John C. Richardson Sr. died August 1845 leaving heirs: Jane P. O'Bannon, child of Jane Richardson O'Bannon, Dec'd, John C. Richardson Jr., Sarah Fry, child of Sarah Richardson Fry, Dec'd; Mary Elizabeth Alexander, wife of Dr. John B. Alexander and Robert P., Caleb B. and Adelaide Richardson of Claiborne Co.

****

1854 Hinds Co. Miss. Drawer 98 Case #5274

Susan P. Hill (daughter) and Sarah Shields (widow), heirs of John Shields, Edwin Moody, all of Hinds Co.
vs
William C. Harper of Rankin Co.
John Shields died in Copiah Co. in 1839.

****

1854 Hinds Co. Miss. Drawer 98 Case #5279

William P. Garland

vs

Pembroke Garland, William Rice Bryant and Laura A. Bryant, infant heirs of John H. Bryant and Paulina Garland Bryant, Dec'd.

William P. and Pembroke Garland were children of William and Nancy Garland, Dec'd. Laura A. and William R. Bryant, grandchildren.

****

1854 Washington Co. Miss. Drawer 98 Case #5289

Robert W. Johnson and wife, Sarah, of Pine Bluff, Ark.

vs

Irene Smith, Alexander C. Bullitt and wife, Frances E., late Frances E. Smith, Benj. S., Robert W., Frank S. and Sally Johnson, the last four named being minor children of Comp'ts, Robert W. and Sarah Johnson.

See will of Benjamin Smith

****

1854 Warren Co. Miss. Drawer 98 Case #5295

Harriet, Elliott, James Fisher and Ann W. Smith, infants, by Gdn. Richard E. Bolling.

vs

Robert T. Brown

Comp'ts were children of Dr. William B. Smith and wife, Mildred M. Smith. He died April 1845 and Mildred married Christopher C. Preston of Madison Parish, La. in 1848.

****

1857 Hinds Co. Miss. Drawer 98 Case #5305

Rosina Spengler

vs

Hubert Spengler

Joseph Spengler died intestate on Oct. 17, 1852 leaving Rosina Spengler, widow, and children: Rosina, Mariana, Joseph, Albert C., George A., Theresa and Adelia Spengler.

****

1855 Warren Co. Miss. Drawer 98 Case #5307

Matilda Cotton

vs

James Cotton

Divorce Petition. Marriage date: 1824.

****

1854 Newton Co. Miss. Drawer 98 Case #5327

Clorinda E. Johnson

vs

Benjamin Johnson

Clorinda E. Johnson was daughter of James Fowler who died in 1844. She married Benjamin Johnson in 1846. In 1845 her grandfather, Joseph Sharp, died. Litigation involves Clorinda's inheritance from father and grandfather.

****

1854 Co. not shown. Drawer 98 Case #5334

Ex Parte—Elisha Warfield, Nathaniel A. Ware, Catharine Ann Warfield and Thomas B. Warfield.

Nathaniel A. Ware was father of Catharine Ann Warfield and she was the wife of Elisha. On Dec. 20, 1838 Nathaniel A. Ware conveyed to Thomas Warfield of Lexington, Ky., in trust for Catharine Ann and her children, certain lands in Washington Co. Miss. and Chicot Co. Ark. Children of Elisha and Catharine Ann Warfield: Nathaniel W., Eleanor P., Thos. G. Percy, Mary R., Catharine J. and Lloyd E. Warfield, all citizens of State of Kentucky.

****

1855 Washington Co. Miss. Drawer 98 Case #5382

Frances A. Lawson, widow of William H. Lawson, Dec'd and Samuel B., Frances, Wilhelmina Lawson, minor children of Wm. H. Lawson

vs

John L. Failey, Admr. with Will attached, Est. of W. H. Lawson, Dec'd and William Hunt.

****

1855 Warren Co. Miss. Drawer 98 Case #5384

James C. Tanner and wife, Margaret, Minerva McCord, Martha McCord, Mary McCord, Charles Detterly and Louise McCord

vs

David Conn

Margaret Tanner, Minerva, Mary, Martha and Louisa McCord were heirs of Maria L. and William McCord. Maria L. McCord died 1844. James C. Tanner married Margaret McCord Oct. 14, 1851.

****

1855 Hinds Co. Miss. Drawer 98 Case #5391

Fannie McRaven, by brother and next friend, Presley C. Richardson

vs

Stewart McRaven

Divorce Petition. Married in State of Tennessee in 1832.

****

1855 Hinds Co. Miss. Drawer 98 Case #5407

Elizabeth Downing

vs

Thomas and Edmond Whaley

Elizabeth Downing was wife of Reuben Downing.

****

1855 Holmes Co. Miss. Drawer 98 Case #5426

James N. McLean

vs

William T., Georgiana and Edward W. Wade, heirs of William H. Wade, Dec'd

****

1853 Hinds Co. Miss. Drawer 98 Case #5432

Ann Farr, by next friend, William Wilkinson

vs

Charles K. Farr

Divorce Petition. Married in Hinds Co. March 11, 1847.

****

1856 Washington Co. Miss. Drawer 98 Case #5436

John F. Courtney

vs

William M. W. Cochran, Admr. Est. Robert Cochran

****

1830 Amite Co. Miss. Drawer 98 Case #5467

John P. McNeill

vs

John Burton and William King.

William King died September 1819. File mentions "Dr. Gerald who lived eighteen miles from Liberty Court house". Witnesses: Samuel B. Marsh, Edmund Jenkins, Charles Davis, Gabriel Felder and Harbuth Frith.

****

1846 Hinds Co. Miss. Drawer 98 Case #5925

Charles D. Learned

vs

Samuel White, Admr. Est. P. Rutilius R. Pray, Louis Daniel and wife, Maria L. (late widow of P. R. R.

Pray), Rufus Otis Pray, Cornelia N., George W. and Theodocia Maria Pray, children of P. R. R. Pray, all of Hancock Co. Miss.

Charles Learned and Maria L. P. Daniel were two of the children of the late General David Learned and his wife, Mary. Maria Learned married P. R. R. Pray in Maine in 1820.

****

1850 Warren Co. Miss. Drawer 99 Case #6022

Redding B. Herring

vs

Anthony V. Winans, Thomas M. Green and Harry T. McKay

****

1850 Claiborne Co. Miss. Drawer 99 Case #6025

Henry G. J. Powers and wife, Maria Louisa Powers

vs

Sarah Calvit, Exec. Est. John Calvit, Dec'd, and John Cowden, Admr. Est. Joseph Calvit, Dec'd

Maria Louisa Powers, born July 28, 1814, was daughter of Joseph Calvit.

****

1850 Hinds Co. Miss. Drawer 99 Case #6029

Joseph Dennis of Hinds Co. and Moses Granberry, Admrs. Est. Stephen Granberry, Dec'd

vs

Mark A. Gillespie, Richard A. Kent and Elias Kent.

Stephen Granberry died Aug. 28, 1840 and Letters of Adm. on his estate granted Oct. 28, 1840.

****

1850 Choctaw Co. Miss. Drawer 99 Case #6032

Benjamin Grimes, Admr. ad Colligendum, Est. Nicholas O'Riley, Dec'd

vs

Charles Calhoun and Edward Johnson

****

1852 Adams Co. Miss. Drawer 99 Case #6044

John Bacon, Tr. etc

vs

Richard P. Winslow and Sarah Englehard, Admrs. Est. Edward Englehard, Dec'd.

****

1853 Franklin Co. Miss. Drawer 99 Case #6046

Willis Byrd, Admr. de bonis non Est. Lee Byrd, Dec'd

vs

Sutton Byrd, Admr. Est. Asha Byrd, Dec'd

Heirs of Asha Byrd: Mary Byrd, wife of Sutton Byrd, Sr., George I. Byrd and Susan Ford, wife of John S. Ford.

Wiley Wells, Exec. Est. Lee Byrd died April 1, 1844.

****

1850 Covington Co. Miss. Drawer 99 Case #6047

Archibald D. Graham, Admr., with will attached, Est. of Alexander Graham, Dec'd.

vs

Cornelius McLaurin and Robert Magee.

Jurymen: G. F. Robertson, N. R. Robertson, Hinton Powell, J. M. Speed, Seaborn Lee, D. G. Bullock, Daniel McInnis, Middleton Graves, Neil McInnis, Frederick Smith, Wade Goodson, M. J. S. Coulter.

****

1850 Carroll Co. Miss. Drawer 99 Case #6048

James R. Lowrie and wife, Arabella
vs
James H. Hubert, Admr. Est. A. W. King, Dec'd

Arabella Lowrie was late widow of A. W. King who died in 1847. Bill states "he died intestate leaving widow and several children." Children not named.

****

1850 Carroll Co. Miss. Drawer 99 Case #6049

Mary T. Govan, Exex. Est. Mary A. Pugh, Dec'd
vs
John A. Binford.

****

1850 Kemper Co. Miss. Drawer 99 Case #6060

Benj. Tarbutton for use of James B. Payne
vs
Margaret Harden and Irvin Adams (her surety).
Margaret was widow of John B. Harden, Dec'd.

****

1851 Carroll Co. Miss. Drawer 99 Case #6074

Richard W. Crowson of Carroll Co.
vs
Joseph W. Ferguson, Aaron, John and Thomas Ferguson, Eliza Collins, wife of Felix B. Collins, Jennetta, Martha Jane and Rohannan Collins, Pleasant D. Robinson and wife, Ann, John W. Lewis and wife, Matilda, David B. Bain and wife, Elizabeth, Margaret Emmons (a feme sole), all of Carroll Co. Miss. James H. Ferguson of State of Louisiana and Elizabeth Ferguson widow of Elijah Ferguson of Carroll Co., all heirs of Elijah Ferguson, Dec'd.

****

1851 Wayne Co. Miss. Drawer 99 Case #6104

George W. Harris

vs

Thomas F. Hicks, Admr. Est. James Vance, Dec'd late of Clarke Co. and Clement, Willis and William Lang, Admrs. Est. William A. Lang, Dec'd.

****

1851 Warren Co. Miss. Drawer 99 Case #6109

Samuel Edwards

vs

Martha Edwards, Admr. Est. Richard Edwards, Dec'd, and Hiram and Daniel Hilderbrand (her sureties)

Martha Edwards was widow of Richard Edwards, Dec'd. Letters of Adm. on his estate issued 1849.

****

1849 Hinds Co. Miss. Drawer 99 Case #6116

John F. Slaughter

vs

William H. Garland, Admr. de bonis non Est. Samuel Garland, Dec'd succeeding Burr Garland, Dec'd.

****

1852 Pontotoc Co. Miss. Drawer 99 Case #6118

W. H. Duke

vs

B. D. Anderson, Admr. Est. Aaron Root, Dec'd.

****

1851 Itawamba Co. Miss. Drawer 99 Case #6129

Napoleon Norman and wife, Eliza Jane (late Burnett), and Edmond Manahan wife, Matilda Ann (late Burnett)

vs

Bolling Clarke Burnett

Bolling Clarke of Dunwiddie Co. Virginia died in 1809. Mary Burnett of Tennessee was granddaughter of Bolling Clarke and the grandmother of Eliza Jane Burnett, born 1822, and of Matilda Ann Burnett, born Jan. 21, 1825, the daughters of Richard Burnett, Dec'd. Bolling C. Burnett and Richard Burnett were sons of Mary Burnett. Richard died in Lawrence Co. Ala. in 1836 leaving Eliza Jane and Matilda Ann his only heirs, and Bolling C. Burnett, Admr. of his estate. Eliza Jane married Napoleon Norman in Sept. 1842 and Matilda Ann married first, Samuel Chambers June 6, 1844, who died Oct. 1844, and second, Edmond Manahan July 27, 1846. Bolling Burnett moved from Lawrence Co. Ala. to Monroe Co. Miss. in 1835. The widow of Richard and mother of Eliza Jane and Matilda Ann (not named) continued to live in Lawrence Co. Ala.

****

1851 Lawrence Co. Miss. Drawer 99 Case #6141

Matthew B. Cannon, Judge of Probate for use of Lina Newsom

vs

Pharoh Benson and Anderson Douglas, Execs. Est. Herod Benson, Dec'd; John Newsom (husband of Lina), Zaney Martin and husband, John Martin, Hiram J. Benson, Prew Benson, Mina Lowe, Parthena McMurtray and husband, M. H. McMurtray, all heirs of Henry Benson, Dec'd.

Herod Benson was Exec. Est. Henry Benson, Dec'd, prior to his death.

****

1851 Yazoo Co. Miss. Drawer 99 Case #6151

Robert S. Holt and Frederick W. Wheelis, Exec. Est. Washington Dorsey, Dec'd

vs

William E. Pugh, late of Yazoo Co.

****

1837 Jefferson Co. Miss. Drawer 99 Case #6155

William C. Donoho and wife, Frances D.
vs
James E. Mattingly

Bondsmen: Edward R. Murray, Thos. W. Garrett, James H. Blanchard and Franklin A. Montgomery.

****

1857 Amite Co. Miss. Drawer 99 Case #6156

Alexander McKowen, Admr. Est. William McKowen, Dec'd
vs
Elijah S. McCoy and Samuel B. Haygood

Jurymen: Wm. L. Huff, John H. McGehee, Dan C. Short, E. L. Westbrook, Ira Parsons, W. Z. Lea, Ephraim Marsalis, William Denman, R. F. Williams, H. G. Wall, S. Raborn and C. H. McLean. Witnesses: Wm. K. Hamilton, Dr. John V. Wren, Dr. E. R. Dunn, James M. Gallent and James M. McElwee

****

1851 Harrison Co. Miss. Drawer 99 Case #6162

John Henderson, Admr. Est. Phoebe Hunter, Dec'd succeeding Edward P. Fourniquet; John and Mary Tiberias; Mordecai, Ann and George Bryant, children and heirs of Thos. Bryant, Dec'd; Mary, Thos., Henry and Alice Laverty, children and heirs of Moses Bryant, Dec'd; Ann Walker and husband, Timothy Walker, sole heirs of Thos. Bryant. 2nd. Dec'd, a son of Moses Bryant; Ann Hazlett and husband Wm. Hazlett; Phoebe and Benj. Fletcher (Ann Hazlett, Phoebe and Benj. Fletcher, children and heirs of Phoebe and John Fletcher, Dec'd), said Phoebe being the only child and heir of Benj. Bryant, Dec'd; Ann Hall (widow), only heir of Mary Dickinson, Dec'd, formerly Mary Bryant—all being legal representatives and heirs at law of John Hare, Dec'd

vs

John C. Jenkins, Admr. Est. Dr. John F. Carmichael, Dec'd

John Hare was son of Andrew Hare who died in 1800. John Hare died in 1806. Maternal uncles and aunts of John Hare were: Thos., Moses and Benj. Bryant, Phoebe Hunter, Mary Dickinson and Deborah Starr, all of whom were dead in 1834, except Deborah Starr who died in 1830 leaving a child who died shortly thereafter. Andrew Hare's Will on file at Lexington, Fayette Co. Kentucky in which he names "My dear wife Margaret, my son John and any other children I may hereafter have". Moses Bryant died "before 1820".

****

1851 Adams Co. Miss. Drawer 99 Case #6170

William Robertson, Trustee

vs

Joseph Winchester, Admr. Est. George Winchester, Dec'd. George Winchester died Feb. 4, 1831, intestate.

****

1851 Wilkinson Co. Miss. Drawer 99 Case #6176

James G. Waller of Wilkinson Co.

vs

Maria Ogden, Admx. Est. John Ogden, Dec'd.

Heirs of John Ogden: Maria (widow), Thos. E., Luther, Daniel Ogden, Sarah Irions, William (son of Robert Ogden, Dec'd who was son of John, Dec'd), Tanner and Mary Jane Kilpatrick, (children of Martha Ogden Kilpatrick, Dec'd daughter of John, Dec'd), Jane Ogden Kilpatrick and husband, Andrew R., Sarah Jane and Mary Williams (children of Patience Ogden Williams, Dec'd).

****

1857 Adams Co. Miss. Drawer 99 Case #6178

Stephen Duncan, Admr. Est. Anna M. Linton, Dec'd

vs

Samuel W. Speer, Admr. Est. Abigail F. W. Speer, Dec'd.

****

1851 Wilkinson Co. Miss. Drawer 99 Case #6180

John McCrea and Thos. E. McCrea of Wilkinson Co.; Francis Dunham, Amanda S. Dunham and husband, Blackwell B. Dunham, James Brown and wife, Esther D., Elizabeth B. Curley and husband, ... Curley, George B. Draughn and wife, Mary, John Henry Simmons, William Simmons, Anthony Simmons, Charles Simmons (a minor), Francis Norwood, Eli Norwood, all heirs of William McCrea, Dec'd

vs

Aaron Robinson, Admr. Est. Mary McCrea, Dec'd

William McCrea late of Amite Co. died April 1836 leaving his widow, Mary McCrea, who died in August or September 1850. They had no children and Mary died intestate. William McCrea's will probated in Amite Co. Miss.

****

1851 Jefferson Co. Miss. Drawer 99 Case #6184

James Payne, James Wood and Robert G. Wood of Jefferson Co.

vs

Douglas H. Gordon, Exec. Est. Basil Gordon, Dec'd late of Virginia

****

1851 Adams Co. Miss. Drawer 99 Case #6185

Fanny Leiper, a free woman of color of Cincinnati, Ohio

vs

Malvina Huffman, O. S. Benis, Jos. Winscobb and James Walsh all of Adams Co. Miss.

****

1851 Franklin Co. Miss. Drawer 99 Case #6201

Thomas W. Robbins and wife, Margaret B. Robbins of East Feliciana Parish, La. and Christopher C. Cain and wife, Martha Cain of Amite Co.

vs

Dugold McMillan of Copiah Co., Admr. Est. Thaddeus J. Maxwell, Dec'd late of Franklin Co. Miss.

Thaddeus J. Maxwell born May 1823—died Oct. 28, 1849, leaving his widow, Mrs. Mary McMillan Maxwell of Franklin Co. but no children, and no heirs other than Margaret B. Robbins, Martha Cain, Franklin C. Maxwell and William Maxwell children of William C. and Martha Maxwell (William C. Maxwell, Dec'd was a paternal uncle of Thaddeus J. Maxwell) and Jane Parker, nee McGahey of Franklin Co. who was related to the decedent in the same degree as petitioners. Thaddeus J. Maxwell was the son of Thomas S. Maxwell and Agnes Maxwell, both Dec'd, late of Franklin Co.

****

1851 Panola Co. Miss. Drawer 99 Case #_____

Solomon Small and Elizabeth Beaty, Admrs. Est. Abel Beaty, Dec'd

vs

Edmund V. Dickens and Jesse D. Porter

****

1851 Lawrence Co. Miss. Drawer 100 Case #6217

Jesse Maxwell, Admr. Est. William Cooper, Dec'd late of Lawrence Co.

vs

James M. Turner, Admr. Est. Delilah Eldridge, Dec'd

****

1851 Jefferson Co. Miss. Drawer 100 Case #6224

Penelope McGill, James M. McGill and John A. McGill

vs

David Bone

Litigation involves estate of John Tucker of Jefferson Co. who died in 1837 intestate and Thos. A. Compton was appointed Admr. of his estate.

****

1851 Pontotoc Co. Miss. Drawer 100 Case #6229

John Lockwood and Walter Lockwood

vs

Nathaniel G., Lucy Ann and Shadrack Nye

****

1851 Hinds Co. Miss. Drawer 100 Case #6242

Green Evans of Leake Co., Cullen Evans of Hempstead Co. Ark., William J. Berry (a minor) of Winston Co., Benj. F., William I., Girard, James Lycurgus and Reuben M. Stewart by next friend, Geo. W. Stewart of Choctaw Co., all heirs of Tilford Kelly, Dec'd.

Tilford Kelly died in Feb. 1848 in the home of Wilson F. Dillon in Hinds Co., Green Cullen and John Evans were brothers of the half-blood of Tilford Kelly. William J. Berry of Winston Co. was sole issue of Green Berry and Pernecey Berry (nee Evans). Benj., William I., Girard, James Lycurgus and Reuben Stewart were children of Geo. W. Stewart and Julia Ann Stewart (nee Evans) both deceased.

****

1851 Madison Co. Miss. Drawer 100 Case #6248

Samuel J. Ridley, Admr. Est. Henry Ridley, Dec'd

vs

Moses Ridley

****

1851 Wayne Co. Miss. Drawer 100 Case #6284

Nathan Griffin, Sr., Jeremiah Walker and wife, Lucinda, Stephen Stovall and wife, Jane, James McMillan and wife, Peggie, John Calhoun and wife, Agnes, Patsy Griffin, widow of Buckner Griffin, Dec'd, Richard

Griffin Jr., Anderson B. Smith and wife, Amelia, nee Griffin, Holman, Thomas and Mitchell Griffin, Leonard McCord and wife, Margaret, nee Griffin, William Griffin, Nathan Griffin, Jr., Leonard Griffin, Sarah Griffin, Ledbetter Hughes and wife, Jane, (William, Nathan Jr., Leonard and Sarah Griffin, minors, by their brother, Richard Griffin, Jr. and William Cowan)

vs

Thomas Smith and wife, Sarah (late widow of Ralph Stovall), Walter Stovall and Sarah Stovall, minor children of Ralph Stovall, Dec'd.

Richard Griffin, Sr. married Amelia Sims, daughter of Nathan Sims, in Abbeville Dist., S. C. in 1785 and removed with her husband to Lincoln Co. Ga. Richard Griffin, Sr. died and Amelia married John Cowan in Lincoln Co. Ga. and their son, William S. Cowan was born in 1812. John and Amelia Cowan moved to Mississippi in 1820 and John died in 1822. Amelia Cowan died in Wayne Co. Miss. in 1841.

****

1851 Hinds Co. Miss. Drawer 100 Case #6290

Richard B. Spann of Sumpter Dist. S. C.

vs

Crawford L. Brown (sometimes called Lewis Brown), Alexander G. Grant, James W. Stackhouse, James W. Kirkpatrick, all of Hinds Co.; David A. Fatheree of Warren Co.; William Harris of Claiborne Co.; Hiram Harris of Jefferson Co.; Vines M. Lindsey of Choctaw Co;. Garrett Lane of State of Tennessee and James R. Cotton, address unknown.

Bill states that Richard B. Spann was only surviving trustee of deed of settlement made in 1833 to William Spann of Sumpter Dist. South Carolina and his wife, Elizabeth R. Spann, nee O'Quin, who was a granddaughter of Elizabeth Adams of Sumpter Dist. S. C. Elizabeth Adams also had sons, William and John and daughter, Catherine Adams. Elizabeth R. O'Quin married 1st, James S. Spann and 2nd, William F. Spann.

****

1851 Monroe Co. Miss. Drawer 100 Case #6291

Matthew W. Lindsay, Admr. Est. William Chambers, Dec'd

vs

Nathaniel J. Chambers

William Chambers of Orange Co. N. C. was father of Samuel Chambers. Samuel Chambers died in Monroe Co. Miss. in 1844 leaving a will, Reuben Davis and William F. Dowd serving as Admrs. Nathaniel Chambers was a son of William and brother of Samuel. Matilda Chambers, widow of Samuel subsequently married Manahan.

****

1851 Harrison Co. Miss. Drawer 100 Case #6294

Ursin Eaby, Emilie Washington Frederick, Lewis Jefferson Frederick, Auguste Hermes Frederick, Josephine and Amanda Frederick, minor children of Lewis A. Frederick, by Emilie Frederick, their mother

vs

Jacob Baptiste and wife, Eugenie, nee Krebs.

Eugenie Baptiste was sister of Augustine Krebs, daughter of Antoine Krebs and a great niece of Francisco Krebs.

****

1857 Leake Co. Miss. Drawer 100 Case #6315

Ruth Hill

vs

Mary Brown, and David McWilliams, Admrs. Est. Jacob K. Brown, Dec'd

****

1851 Tippah Co. Miss. Drawer 100 Case #6318

George Gray, Exec. Est. Samuel Rutherford, Dec'd

vs

Levi Roden and wife, Elizabeth, Admrs. Est. William O. Rutherford, Dec'd late of Tippah Co.

Elizabeth Roden was late widow of William O. Rutherford.

****

1851 Yalobusha Co. Miss. Drawer 100 Case #6320

Thomas Kirkman

vs

Thomas N. Waul, Exec. Est. Rev. Samuel Hurd, Dec'd.

Litigation involves estate of Mary Smith Hurd who died Oct. 8, 1843, leaving a child, Jane Smith. Mary Smith Hurd was wife of Rev. Samuel Hurd and a marriage contract between them was filed in Lauderdale Co. Ala.

****

1851 Hinds Co. Miss. Drawer 100 Case #6329

James Trimble

vs

Greene E. Beauchamp, Admr. Est. James Williams, Dec'd.

****

1851 DeSoto Co. Miss. Drawer 100 Case #6350

Andrew Merrill and wife, Sarah, Jane Merrill and James McCarson all heirs of William McCarson, Dec'd.

vs

Davis and Melinda J. Stafford, Execs. Est. William McCarson, Dec'd.

****

1851 Amite Co. Miss. Drawer 100 Case #6353

William B. Wall

vs

Charles F. Felder and wife, Mary Ann

Mary Ann Felder was widow of John Sibley who died in 1847. Thomas Garner was Co-Admr. of John Sibley's Estate.

****

1852 Co. not shown. Drawer 100 Case #6372

Henry Ammons

vs

James Poe and Hamilton Ammons, Admrs. de bonis non Est. Jonathan Ammons, Dec'd

Depositions of Henry Loggins and of William Caldwell both of Choctaw Co.

****

1852 Noxubee Co. Miss. Drawer 100 Case #6374

Eldred Rawlins, James W. McClung and Edmund Irby

vs

Wm. Q. Poindexter and Levi Keese, Admrs. de bonis non Est. Geo. Mason, Dec'd.

Elizabeth Mason, widow of George who died April 1, 1837, at Huntsville, Noxubee Co. was named executrix of his will.

****

1852 Claiborne Co. Miss. Drawer 100 Case #6379

John C. Calhoun and Mary H. Calhoun only surviving children of Ezekiel Calhoun, Dec'd; Amelia A. Young.

vs

Christiana Marilla Rail and Colista Julia Rail, infant heirs of John Rail, Dec'd by next friend Martin W. Hulbert.

John Rail died about 1847 leaving will in which he named William Dotson and Moses D. Shelby as Execs. Amelia A. Rail, daughter of John, married Thomas Young.

****

1852 Warren Co. Miss. Drawer 100 Case #6388

Abner G. A. Beazley, Admr. Est. James F. Beazley

vs

David Shelton, Admr. Est. Charles C. Mayson, Dec'd; Franklin Bedford, Jeremiah Richards both of Hinds Co., Robert B. Washington of Rankin Co. and Fairfax Washington of Hinds Co.

James F. Beazley died Sept. 28, 1835. Charles C. Mayson died in 1837.

****

1852 Amite Co. Miss. Drawer 100 Case #6390

Caroline L. Daniel, nee Buford and husband, William A. Daniel

vs

Justus Hurd and Isabella (Eliza) Hurd, Gdns. for Caroline Buford (Daniel). Caroline Daniel was infant heir and only child of Samuel Buford, Dec'd.

****

1852 Hinds Co. Miss. Drawer 101 Case #6395

William Burns, Admr.

vs

Daniel H. Yeizer, et al

Elizabeth Yeizer of Baker's Creek Plantation, Hinds Co. Miss. died in 1834 leaving children: Daniel H., Archibald L., George W., Charles R. and Eliza L. Yeizer, Eleanor Monks, nee Yeizer, now wife of Samuel Neill, Prudence G. Strother wife of Walter Strother, Mary L. Strother wife of Thompson Strother. Will also named Mary Ellen Monks and Eliza Monks, granddaughters and daughters of Eleanor Neill. Will on file at Raymond, Hinds Co. Miss.

****

1852 Carroll Co. Miss. Drawer 101 Case #6416

Marmaduke D. Kimbrough of Carroll Co. Admr. Est. Reuben B. Newman, Dec'd

vs

Lewis, Mary and Stephen B. Williams of Claiborne Co. Miss., George G. Torry and George W. Darden, also of Claiborne Co.

Josiah Newman succeeded M. D. Kimbrough as Admr. Est. Reuben B. Newman, Dec'd.

****

1852 Lafayette Co. Miss. Drawer 101 Case #6421

Henry Young, Gdn. for Newel C. Young (minor)

vs

George Young, Admr. Est. John Young, Dec'd

****

1852 Yalobusha Co. Miss. Drawer 101 Case #6423

A. W. Davis of Tallahatchie Co. Admr. Est. John C. Carson, Dec'd

vs

James A. Houston and Benj. Carson, Admrs. Est. William Carson, Dec'd.

John Carson, a resident of State of Ala. died in 1840 or 1841, intestate. John was the son of William Carson of Tallahatchie Co. Miss. but late of Abbeville Dist. S. C. See Will.

****

1852 Yalobusha Co. Miss. Drawer 101 Case #6437

David Holman, Admr. Est. William Pinchback, Dec'd

vs

Thos. N. Ward, Thos. Simmons and James L. Calhoun.

****

1852 Lawrence Co. Miss. Drawer 101 Case #6477

Joseph O. Frelick and wife, Virginia Frelick, nee Burge

vs

James M. Turner, Gdn. for heirs of T. W. Burge

Heirs: Virginia Burge Frelick, Edward Everhard Burge, Thos. M. Burge. File shows the mother (not named) of these heirs died in 1838 "after the death of T. W. Burge".

****

1852 Choctaw Co. Miss. Drawer 101 Case #6483

Leroy Hammond and wife, Nancy

vs

William McMullen

Nancy Hammond was daughter of John Gooch late of State of S. C. who died Oct. 8, 1840 leaving will probated in Chester Dist. S. C. Nancy Gooch married Leroy Hammond in 1822 in S. C. and removed to Miss. in 1845. See will of John Gooch.

****

1852 Carroll Co. Miss. Drawer 101 Case #6493

Samuel Standford and William Smith

vs

Richard T. Johnson and Mary A. Ward and Thos. C. Hutchins.

Litigation involves estate of Alfred W. King, late of Carroll Co. who died Jan. 17, 1848.

****

1852 Franklin Co. Miss. Drawer 101 Case #6499

Lewis M. Hollinger, Admr. Est. John David Washaw, Dec'd

vs

Jacob Stern and wife, Mary C. A. Stern

Mary C. A. Stern was Mary Catharine Angelina Reilander prior to her marriage in 1843 to John David Washaw. John David Washaw died in 1847 leaving a will. His widow, Mary, married Jacob Stern. Hamilton Witherspoon, a witness, refers to Josiah Marshall as "my brother in law".

****

1852 Madison Co. Miss. Drawer 101 Case #6504

Patrick R. Kenna and wife, Catharine (late Catharine Graves of Pulaski Co. Ark.)

vs

Thomas Graves, Exec. Est. John Graves, Dec'd.

Catharine Graves was sister of John Graves, Dec'd. See will of Graves.

****

1852 Panola Co. Miss. Drawer 101 Case #6520

R. H. Nickle, Gdn. for minor heirs of Thomas Nickle, Dec'd

vs

W. C. Rayburn, Jacob Kuykendall and D. C. Williams.

****

1852 Warren Co. Miss.. Drawer 101 Case #6521

John G. Parham, Admr. de bonis non Est. William S. Reaves, Dec'd

vs

Robert B. Scott, Richard R. Randolph, Henry Strong, Thos. A. Marshall, John Brown, Thos. P. Hardaway and wife, Susan L., Richard K. Meade (Exec. Est. Peter E. Scott), Mildred M. Smith (Admx. Est. William B. Smith, Dec'd), and William H. Wilford.

Albert G. Reaves was appointed Admr. Est. William S. Reaves Nov. 1846.

****

1852 Wilkinson Co. Miss. Drawer 101 Case #6535

Mason E. Saunders

vs

William M. Wentworth, Admr. Est. Thomas Rowan, Dec'd

William M. Wentworth qualified as Admr. Est. Thomas Rowan in Probate Court of Franklin Co. Dec. Term 1851. Mentioned: Mary and James J. Rowan.

****

1852 Choctaw Co. Miss. Drawer 101 Case #6551

Lewis Christopher and wife, Elizabeth

vs

Nancy Cox

Nancy Cox was widow of Daniel Cox who died in 1841 or 1842. See Will of Daniel Cox.

****

1852 Franklin Co. Miss. Drawer 101 Case #6559

Calvin L. Ford, Admr. de bonis non Est. Phillip Ford, Dec'd

vs

Benj. F. Gilbert, Wm. B. Gilbert and Anthony W. Faulkner

John Ford was Exec. Will of Phillip Ford in which Phillip left his property to his mother, Elizabeth Ford, and at her death to descend to his brothers and sisters (not named). John Ford died 1848 or 1849.

****

1852 DeSoto Co. Miss. Drawer 101 Case #6603

Andrew Merrill and wife, Sarah Jane, nee McCarson of DeSoto Co., Jane Merrill, nee McCarson, widow of Jacob Merrill late a citizen of Buncombe Co. North

Carolina and James McCarson a citizen of Henderson Co. North Carolina

vs

Davis Stafford and wife, Malinda Jane.

Sarah Jane Merrill and James McCarson were sister and brother of William McCarson who died in 1849 leaving a will in which his wife Malinda Jane was named executrix and principal devisee. She later married Davis Stafford of DeSoto Co. See will of William McCarson.

****

1852 Panola Co. Miss. Drawer 101 Case #6614

William G. Jolly, Amanda N. Jolly, William G. Jolly, Gdn. for Martha I., Anna E., Frances S., Robert H. and Virginia C. Jolly, minor heirs of William Jolly, Dec'd

vs

John H. Keith and Micajah J. Vaiden, Admrs. Est. William Jolly and Cynthia Jolly

William Jolly died Feb. 1847. Cynthia was widow of William Jolly.

****

1852 Carroll Co. Miss. Drawer 101 Case #6615

Jackson Langley and wife, Amanda, William Fisher and wife, Minerva, James Standley, Jr. and John Harlon, Admrs. Est. David Standley, Dec'd.

David Standley died in Carroll Co. in 1844, intestate. Amanda Langley and Minerva Fisher were his daughters. Amanda married Jackson Langley in 1848. Other heirs of David Standley were: Frances Cavender, wife of James Cavender, Martha Rogers, Dec'd late wife of John T. Rogers, Sarah Standley, Mary Jane Harrison, James M. and Samuel H. Standley all of Carroll Co. and Elizabeth Carter and T. T. Patton non residents of State of Mississippi.

****

1852 Monroe Co. Miss. Drawer 101 Case #6623

W. A. Tucker and wife, Minerva T. Tucker (late Minerva Tennessee Buckingham)

vs

Stephen Cocke

Heirs of Nathaniel B. Buckingham Sr. late of Lincoln Co. Tenn.: Nathaniel B. Jr., Maria Louisa Buckingham, Mary E. Davis, nee Buckingham, wife of John B. Davis, Rebecca Jack Moore, nee Buckingham, wife of Lucien B. Moore, Sarah Jane Anderson, nee Buckingham, wife of John H. Anderson, Adeline Frances Coopwood, nee Buckingham, wife of Benj. F. Coopwood, Sterling H. Buckingham, Martha Kendall, nee Buckingham, wife of Richard Kendall, all of Monroe Co. Miss.; Thos. E. Buckingham of Chickasaw Co.

Minerva Tennessee Buckingham married W. A. Tucker in 1830.

****

1852 Marshall Co. Miss. Drawer 101 Case #6641

Ebenezer Kilpatrick of Marshall Co.

vs

Ransom H. Byrn, Admr. Est. William Dye, Dec'd; Lucy Ann H. Alderson, widow and legatee of James C. Alderson, Dec'd, and Gardentia Waite, Exex. Est. James C. Alderson, Dec'd.

William Dye died "about 1846". James C. Alderson died "about 1848-49".

****

1852 Noxubee Co. Miss. Drawer 101 Case #6645

James H. Gilmore

vs

Willis Sanders, Exec. Est. Jeremiah Sanders, Dec'd

****

1852 Kemper Co. Miss. Drawer 101 Case #6646

Henry E. Neal
vs
James W. Hull, Admr. Est. John Neal, Dec'd

John Neal died Oct. 1845.

****

1852 Kemper Co. Miss. Drawer 101 Case #6647

Dorset White and wife, Nancy (late Nancy Harrell)
vs
Thomas Davis, Exec. Est. Dorothy Harrell, Dec'd

Nancy White was sister and heir of Dorothy Harrell late of Kemper Co. who died in 1850. Other heirs: Roxana Pollock and Isabella S. Slade (sisters), Alfred G. and Amett W. Harrell (brothers). Amett H. Jagers, Daniel L. Jagers, Harriet Jones, Paulina Spinks and Absalom P. Davis, nieces and nephews, all children of Hollen Davis, late Jagers, sister of Dorothy Harrell.

****

1852 Lowndes Co. Miss. Drawer 101 Case #6649

George Hairston Sr., Marshall Hairston, Geo. Pannell and wife, Bethenia Ruth, Robert G. Jones and wife, Elizabeth, Ruth A., Susan A., Geo. S. and Marshall Hairston (last four named were minors)
vs
Ruth Hairston, widow of Robert Hairston, Dec'd.

****

1852 Lawrence Co. Miss. Drawer 101 Case #6651

Sarah Englehard, widow of Edward Englehard, Dec'd; Rosa and Joseph A. Englehard, minors, by next friend Richard P. Winslow; Turner Wilson and wife, Elanor C., Melissa Prestridge, Wm. D. Steen, William Mullen and wife, Sarah A., Daniel D. Cummings and wife

Cynthia, John A. Steen, Nancy J. Steen and Permelia Maxwell, all heirs of James Steen, Dec'd.

vs

Benjamin Buckley

Edward Englehard died Feb. 13, 1836.

****

1852 Jefferson Co. Miss. Drawer 101 Case #6659

Prosper K. Montgomery and John H. Chambliss, Execs. Est. Hiram Baldwin, Dec'd

vs

Martha Williamson, William H., George C., Hiram M. and Sarah Baldwin, Jacob S. Young and Henry Newton Young, all of Chicago, Ill., Sarah Dodd, wife of Richard Dodd of Chicago, Frances Collins, Bloomfield, N. J., Webster Collins of Newark, N. J., Wilson Collins of Connecticut, Thos. Collins (address unknown), Mark Collins, Bloomfield, N. J., Mary Valivia and Sarah Elizabeth Jewell and Thomas Wilcox of Bloomfield, N. J., Daniel P. Pearson, Forked River, N. J., Bilsey Exley, wife of Thos. Exley, Jonathan Smock, Deborah Nevins, wife of Martin Nevins, Mary Vanarsdale, wife of Isaac Vanarsdale all of Bloomingham, N. J., and all heirs of Hiram Baldwin, Dec'd.

Hiram Baldwin died in Jefferson Co. Miss. September 15, 1851.

****

1856 Lawrence Co. Miss. Drawer 102 Case #6641

Mary Powers widow of Joseph P. Powers, Robert Underwood and wife, Mercy, Samuel Powers, William Powers, Alfred Sartin and wife, Theresa, Daniel Powers all adult heirs of Joseph Powers, Dec'd

vs

Eliza A. Pendleton widow of J. W. Pendleton, Joseph Parkman and wife, Nancy, of Lawrence Co., Charles

Pendleton, Frederick Pendleton and James Page of State of New York, Charles Fulsom and Lewis Fulsom of Hancock Co. Miss., all heirs of Zebulon E. Pendleton, Dec'd, and Henry Sones.

Joseph Powers died July 1838. Zebulon Pendleton died March 14, 1842. Samuel A. Powers and Z. E. Pendleton were appointed Admrs. Est. Joseph Powers, Dec'd. John Gartman and Eliza A. Pendleton (relict) were appointed Admrs. Est. Z. E. Pendleton.

****

1852 Pontotoc Co. Miss. Drawer 102 Case #6677

James I. Pickens and wife, Eleanor Frances, James I. Pickens next friend for Sarah A., Peter, K., Ann I., John Wesley and William Fletcher Pickens the minor heirs of James I. and Eleanor Frances Pickens

vs

James Thompson, Jr. and Andrew Miller

Litigation involves a trust from Sarah Liddell of Abbeville Dist. S. C. to James Thompson Jr. for use of her daughter Eleanor Frances Perkins and her children.

****

1852 Marshall Co. Miss. Drawer 102 Case #6681

Eliza White of Washington Co. Va., Admx. Est. James White, Dec'd

vs

Silas F. Trotter, J. M. Pearsall, Mrs. P. D. Mayers and Joseph Trotter.

****

1852 Claiborne Co. Miss. Drawer 102 Case #6684

Robert W. Harper and wife, Catharine E. Harper

vs

Richard T. Archer and wife, Ann B. and William Eggleston

Catharine E. Voss married Edward F. Barnes late of Claiborne Co. on Nov. 17, 1825. He died intestate April 12, 1827. Their daughter, Eliza F. Barnes was born March 15, 1827 and Abram Barnes was appointed guardian for both mother and daughter, both being minors. Abram Barnes died Nov. 1, 1830 leaving a will in which he named John A. Barnes and Thos. Freeland his executors. Richard Archer married Ann B. Barnes daughter of Abram Barnes. Catharine Barnes (widow of Edward F). married Stephen C. Archer May 6, 1834 and Stephen Archer was appointed Gdn. for Eliza F. Barnes. Eliza died July 9, 1835. Stephen Edward Archer, son of Stephen C. and Catharine Archer, was born Aug. 21, 1837. Stephen C. Archer died intestate in Claiborne Co. and on Sept. 5, 1841 Catharine Voss Barnes Archer married Robert W. Harper.

****

1853 Yazoo Co. Miss. Drawer 102 Case #6689

David Friley and Emily Friley by next friend John Friley; Nancy, Elizabeth, John and Martin M. Friley, John Edmondson and wife Mary, nee Friley, all heirs of James Friley, Dec'd.

vs

Daniel W. Hendricks

****

1853 Claiborne Co. Miss. Drawer 102 Case #6698

Stephen Duncan

vs

Lewis C. Watson, Admr. de bonis non Est. Benjamin Blanton, Dec'd.

****

1853 Monroe Co. Miss. Drawer 102 Case #6703

William Moncrief and wife, Susannah, of Monroe Co. Miss.

vs

Joseph Wardlaw, Admr. Est. Jacob Nicewanger, Dec'd.

Jacob Nicewanger died in Tipton Co. Tenn. in 1834 leaving heirs: Susannah Moncrief, wife of William, Mary Ann Wardlaw, wife of Joseph (the def't), Permelia Watson, wife of Elihu, Sarah Watson, wife of Berry Suritta Nicewanger, all the children of Margaret Sims, late Nicewanger.

****

1853 Panola Co. Miss. Drawer 102 Case #6710

Samuel Kerr, Admr. Est. Andrew Kerr

vs

Henry Laird

****

1853 Yalobusha Co. Miss. Drawer 102 Case #6713

Benj. B. Smith, Weston R. Gales, William R. Poole, John B. Buffalo and John Griffies all of North Carolina

vs

Thomas Carlzy, Daniel Robinson, Merritt Dillard and James Hubbert

****

1853 Marion Co. Miss. Drawer 102 Case #6729

John Foxworth for self and as Gdn. for Mary Elizabeth Foxworth (minor); Samuel G. Foxworth natural Gdn. for John P. Foxworth, Stephen A., George W., Franklin W., Job, Alexander S. E., and Samuel J., all children of Samuel Foxworth and all of Marion Co.

vs

Archibald D. Graham

Alexander Graham late of Marion Co. died in 1840. John and Samuel Foxworth married sisters of Alexander Graham. Mary Graham was widow of Alexander and Archibald D. Graham was son of Alexander Graham. See Will.

****

1853 Jefferson Co. Miss. Drawer 102 Case #6732

George Torry, Admr. Est. William Sape, Dec'd

vs

Hurnden J. McKey and Isaac A. Sims

****

1854 Wayne Co. Miss. Drawer 102 Case #6736

Jabez Roberts and wife, Elizabeth of Clarke Co.; Cincinnatus W. Matthews of Lauderdale Co. Miss.

vs

Wiley Rogers, Admr. Est. Henry F. Rogers, Dec'd

Elizabeth Roberts and Burwell Rogers were sister and brother and heirs of Henry F. Rogers, Dec'd, whose estate was first administered in Wayne Co. Jan. Term 1850.

****

1853 Covington Co. Miss. Drawer 102 Case #6744

Richard Flowers and Archibald Anderson, Admrs. Est. Bunbury Flowers, Dec'd

vs

Archibald G. Wilkinson and his sureties, Duncan Wilkinson and Allen Stewart.

****

No date shown. Co. not shown. Drawer 102 Case #6745

Benj. F. Edwards

vs

William C. McGee, Gdn. for infant heirs of James G. McGee, Dec'd.

Heirs not named.

****

1853 Madison Co. Miss. Drawer 102 Case #6748

Barnabas Herrod

vs

Henry R. Coulter and Amanda M. Henderson, Admrs. Est. George W. Henderson, Dec'd.

****

1853 Rankin Co. Miss. Drawer 102 Case #6754

John P. Moss, Lucy B. Moss and James H. Moss, minors, by next friend, Daniel Collins

vs

George Fearn of Hinds Co. and Robert F. Bibb of Rankin Co.

John, Lucy, James H. and William Moss were children of James L. Moss who died intestate in 1838. Henry Moss was a brother of James L. Moss.

****

1853 Franklin Co. Miss. Drawer 102 Case #6761

Alexander McLeod and wife, Martha, Isaac S. Brown and wife, Maria and Francis G. Spain, all children and heirs of James Spain, Dec'd late of Franklin Co.

vs

James Johnson

James Spain died in 1827 in Franklin Co. Other heirs of James Spain: Helen Johnson (dau.) wife of James Johnson, Ann Burke (dau.) wife of Wiley B. Burke and Nancy Spain (his widow).

****

1853 Adams Co. Miss. Drawer 102 Case #6765

Antonio Chavalier

vs

Elizabeth Dunbar, Robt. J. Dunbar and Henry W. Dangerfield, Execs. Est. Isaac Dunbar, Dec'd

****

1852 Adams Co. Miss. Drawer 102 Case #6767

Alexander K. Farrar, Hiram B. Cole, Thos. H. Corbun and wife, Catherine Caroline

vs

Pharaoh Carter and wife, Susan

File shows James Cole died in 1812 and his widow married Absalom Griffin in 1814. Absalom Griffin was the father in law of Pharaoh Carter. H. B. Cole was born in 1807, Clarissa Cole was born in 1809, Frederick Cole born 1811. Absalom Griffin died in 1833 in Franklin Co. and Mrs. Griffin (mother of the Coles) died in 1818 or 1819. Testimony brought out the fact that John Bradley was son of Luther Bradley, that James Cole was brother in law of Luther Bradley, having married Scytha Cole and that Cole and Griffin came to Mississippi from Kentucky.

****

1851 Warren Co. Miss. Drawer 102 Case #6783

John Babb, William Babb and William E. Kirk

vs

Isaac H. Hay, Admr. Est. John H. Martin, Dec'd, Emily Martin Jr., Harriet, Adolphus R., William T., Ellen H., John H. Martin Jr., Emily Martin (widow of John H. Martin Sr.), James J. Pleasants and Nathaniel Wilson.

****

1853 Madison Co. Miss. Drawer 102 Case #6790

David Wilson, Andrew Wilson, Hugh Vanzant and wife, Dicy, nee Wilson (sister of Charles and Miller Wilson, both Dec'd), Wilson Graham and wife, Jane (dau. of Samuel Wilson, Dec'd), William A. McIntyre and wife, Susan, John Wilson and Samuel Wilson all heirs of Samuel Wilson, Dec'd

vs

Thos. G. Melton of Madison Co. Miss.

Chas. Wilson died in Leake Co. Miller Wilson lived in Madison Co. and died in 1848.

****

1853 Lowndes Co. Miss. Drawer 102 Case #6796

Robert Hairston of Lowndes Co. and George Hairston of State of Va.

vs

Ruth Hairston, George Hairston, Sr., Marshall Hairston, George Pannell and wife, Bethenia Ruth, nee Calloway, John Calloway, Elizabeth P. Dillard and Samuel Hairston, all of Virginia.

Robert Hairston was son of Hardin Hairston and George Hairston was son of Samuel Hairston. Robert Hairston (uncle of Comp'ts) died March 6, 1852 in Lowndes Co. Ruth S. Hairston of State of Va. was widow of Robert Hairston, Dec'd. Hardin, Samuel, George and Marshall were Robert's living brothers. John A. Hairston, Dec'd late of Yalobusha Co. left four children: Elizabeth, wife of Robt. L. Jones, Ruth A., Susan A., George S. and Marshall Hairston, all minors who lived in Yalobusha Co. Ruth Hairston *sister* of Robert Hairston, Dec'd and widow of Peter Hairston Dec'd left four children: Elizabeth P., widow of Peter F. Willard, Dec'd, Samuel, George and Peter Hairston all of Virginia. America Calloway, Dec'd, a sister of Robert Hairston, Dec'd left as heirs: John Calloway (husband), Bethenia R., wife of George Pannell (dau.) and George Calloway (son), all of Virginia. Will of Robert Hairston probated in Lowndes Co. Miss.

****

1853 Warren Co. Miss. Drawer 102 Case #6803

James M. Gaskins and Elizabeth Gaskins by next friend, Dicy Slavins (Stevens?)

vs

Benson Blake

James and Elizabeth Gaskins were only children of James Gaskins, Dec'd. Dicy Slavins (Stevens?) was widow of James Gaskins who died about 1844 and widow of Henry Slavins (Stevens?) who died in 1849. She married David Garrison about 1851.

****

1854 Wilkinson Co. Miss. Drawer 102 Case #6810

Ophelia Carter

vs

David Carter, Harvey D. Smith and Ferdinand C. Ford.

Ophelia Ford married David L. Carter in Sept. 1841 "at age of 18 years". At the time of their marriage David L. Carter was a widower 37 years of age. She was a daughter of Thomas Ford, Dec'd and a sister of Ferdinand C. Ford.

****

1853 Warren Co. Miss. Drawer 102 Case #6812

Wm. B. Minor and wife, Elizabeth, Jacob Vough and wife, Priscilla G., all of Warren Co. Miss.

vs

Robert Cox, Exec. Est. Mildred Dixon, Dec'd.

Elizabeth Minor and Priscilla Vough were children of Robert Dixon, Dec'd who was a brother of Roger Dixon, Dec'd whose wife, Mildred, administered his estate in 1833. Mildred Dixon died Dec. 20, 1849, leaving a will in which she left her property to Elizabeth and Priscilla. Rachel Dixon, widow of Robert, was mother of Elizabeth and Priscilla. In 1834 an agreement was made between Mildred Dixon as Admr. Est. Roger Dixon, Dec'd and Charles Riley and wife, Lucy, Philip Dixon, W. B. Minor and wife, Elizabeth, Albert Gallatin Bennett and wife, Mary, William I. Reed and wife, Priscilla, Henry Latham and wife, Susan, Robert and Nancy Dixon, all heirs of Roger Dixon, Dec'd.

****

1853 Lowndes Co. Miss.. Drawer 102 Case #6819

James M. Wynne, Admr. Est. John Owen, Dec'd
vs
Bentley D. Arnold and Robert Jemison, Jr.

****

1858 Tishomingo Co. Miss. Drawer 102 Case #6831

Philip Tuggle and wife, Mary Louisa
vs
Ann Johnson and Wm. B. Hawkins

****

1853 Amite Co. Miss. Drawer 102 Case #6832

Cyrus Yale, Jr.
vs
Iverson G. L. McGehee and James D. Caulfield of Amite Co. Miss.

****

1855 Lawrence Co. Miss. Drawer 102 Case #6842

James M. Turner, Admr. de bonis non Est. Thomas Burge, Dec'd
vs
William C. Mackie, Gdn. for Beverly Burton Burge and Thomas Mc Burge, minors, Joseph Frelick and wife, Virginia, nee Burge.

Thomas W. Burge of Lawrence Co. died June 1834 leaving will in which Joseph Neyland and Delilah Burge (widow of Thos.) were named Execs. In 1836 Delilah Burge married Andress S. Eldridge. Delilah died June 1838. Other heirs of Thomas Burge, Dec'd: Robert Fenton Burge. Virginia Caroline Burge married Joseph Frelick in August 1847.

****

1853 Lafayette Co. Miss. Drawer 102 Case #6871

Elijah Boyd, Wiley Boyd, Green H. Scone and wife, Matilda, Solomon Kerr and wife, Adeline, Carter A. Boyd and wife, Susan and Miles H. Boyd, all heirs of John Boyd, Sr., Dec'd.

vs

Paul B. Barringer, Admr. Est. William R. Cox, Dec'd.

Wm. R. Cox was Admr. Est. of John Boyd, Jr., son of John Boyd, Sr.

****

1853 Pontotoc Co. Miss. Drawer 103 Case #6879

Mary A. Duncan by Reuben F. Mastin, next friend

vs

Thomas L. Duncan

Divorce Petition. Married Jan. 4, 1853 in Pontotoc Co. Miss.

****

1853 Noxubee Co. Miss. Drawer 103 Case #6880

James A. Burch and wife, Martha

vs

John P. Stovall et al (other heirs of Mary Henkle)

Mary Henkle of Noxubee Co. died March 5, 1853. Heirs: Martha, wife of James A. Burch, Jane, wife of John P. Stovall, Elizabeth, wife of Wm. Stroud, William James and Albert Henkle. William James was resident of S. C., Albert Henkle was resident of Madison Co. Miss.

Witnesses to nun cupative will of Mary Henkle were: Nancy Gilmore and Margaret Morgan, both of Noxubee Co.

****

1853 Holmes Co. Miss. Drawer 103 Case #6891

Jesse B. Walton for self and as Gdn. for Thomas A., Ann V., Ailsey S. and Susan W. Walton and Georgianna

Wade (infants); James N. McLean and wife, Selena H., Samuel Hoskins and wife, Sarah, Thos. Wright and wife, Mary E., William F. Cole and wife, Aurelia Q., Napoleon W. Hoskins and wife, Frances L. and James B. Walton

vs

James Olive, Admr. Est. Ailsey Olive, Dec'd.

Ailsey Olive died in 1852. Jesse B. Walton and Selena McLean were her children. Sarah Hoskins, James D. Walton, Mary E. Wright, Aurelia Q. Cole, Frances L. Hoskins, Thos. A., Ann, Ailsey S. and Susan W. Walton were children of Thos. Walton, Dec'd, a son of Ailsey Olive. Georgianna Wade was child of a daughter of Ailsey Olive (not named). Thomas, Silas, William and Mary E. Sand, children of Mary Sand a daughter of Ailsey Olive.

****

1853 Carroll Co. Miss. Drawer 103 Case #6896

Benj. Sturdivant and wife, Eliza (late Eliza Purnell)

vs

Frank Hawkins, Galbraith F. Neill and Henry M. Purnell, Execs. Est. of Micajah T. Purnell, Dec'd.

Micajah T. Purnell died in 1849. His heirs: M. T., Jr., Elizabeth A., Eliza Martin and James Purnell. Eliza Purnell married Benj. Sturdivant in 1853. Elizabeth A. Purnell married Edward Toller.

****

1853 Marshall and Tippah Cos. Miss.
Drawer 103 Case #6907

Wm. L. Jordan, Mark Thompson Jordan, Albert H. Jordan, Miles B. Watson and wife, Eleanor, John Ross and wife, Catharine, Thos. Harris and wife, Margaret, all of Marshall and Tippah Counties; Geo. F. Mahon of Louisiana, Patrick Childress of Arkansas, Geo. W.,

Mary Ann and Emerith A. Jordan, Jackson Smith, Henrietta Smith and Josephine Mahon of Louisiana

vs

John Gordon and wife, Elizabeth, Admrs. Est. Andrew C. Jordan, Dec'd., William M. Mixon, all of Tippah Co.

Andrew C. Jordan died in August 1836 leaving wife, Elizabeth and children: Eleanor, wife of Thos. Ford, Catharine, William L., Jenetta, Mark Thompson Jordan, Albert H., George W., Mary Ann, Nancy and Emerith A. Jordan and grandchildren: Jackson, Margaret and Henrietta Smith, Children of Edith Jordan and H. G. Smith. Elizabeth, widow of Andrew Jordan, married William G. Ledbetter in 1839 and after death of Ledbetter married John Gordon (def't) in 1844. Thos. Ford died and widow Eleanor married Miles B. Watson. Catharine married John Ross, Jenetta married George D. Mahon. Jenetta Mahon died in 1839 leaving Josephine, her only child. Nancy Ford married Patrick H. Childress and died leaving one child who died in infancy. Margaret Smith married Thomas Harris.

****

1853 Tippah Co. Miss. Drawer 103 Case #6912

William A. Jordon et al (see case #6907)

vs

Francis L. Leake Admr. Est. Robert R. Thomas.

****

1853 Marshall Co. Miss. Drawer 103 Case #6913

William Echols

vs

J. C. P. Hammond and wife, Permelia A.

William Echols was father of Joseph Echols who was killed in Marshall Co. in 1847 by one William Sledge. Permelia A. Hammond (def't) was widow of Joseph

Echols and subsequently married Dr. J. C. P. Hammond of Alabama.

****

1853 Copiah Co. Miss. Drawer 103 Case #6916

James Lawrence

vs

John Fatheree, Jr. and wife, Sarah Fatheree, Admx. Est. Thomas D. C. Lawrence, Dec'd.

See will of Elizabeth Lawrence. James (comp't) was son of Wm. H. Lawrence and a grandson of Elizabeth who was the mother of Thomas D. C. Lawrence, Dec'd.

****

1853 Lowndes Co. Miss. Drawer 103 Case #6917

Sarah Darden and husband, Elisha Darden, Martha Jane Hall and husband, William Hall, all of Lowndes Co. Miss.

vs

William Medley of Itawamba Co.

Comp'ts are grandchildren of William McWilliams who died in Monroe Co. July 11, 1825 leaving will. His daughter, Ritta McWilliams married Dent Millican and they were the parents of Sarah Darden who married Elisha Darden on Oct. 4, 1849 and Martha J. Hall who married William Hall "about 1847". William Medley, Admr. Est. William McWilliams, was an uncle of the Comp'ts.

****

1853 Covington Co. Miss. Drawer 103 Case #6928

Samuel M. Stewart and wife, Sarah

vs

Joshua Burkhalter, Admr. Est. Jesse Burkhalter, Dec'd.

Jesse Burkhalter died 1843 intestate. Sarah Stewart was an heir.

****

1853 Franklin Co. Miss. Drawer 103 Case #6931

Hiram T. Adams, Admr. Est. of Nathaniel Kinnison late of Claiborne Co.

vs

Abram I. Guice, Admr. Est. Mary Kinnison late of Franklin Co.

Nathaniel Kinnison died April 1848. He was son of Wm. and Mary Kinnison. Lydia Kinnison, wife of Nathaniel, was daughter of Ailsey Matthews. She was separated from Nathaniel and living in Ky. at the time of his death

****

1853 Bolivar Co. Miss. Drawer 103 Case #6941

Catharine Bolls by next friend, Thomas Kidd

vs

Thos. I. Manley and Andrew B. Dodd, Admrs. Est. David Willis, Dec'd and John W. Bolls, all of Bolivar Co.

David Willis was a bachelor. Catharine Bolls was the wife of John W. Bolls and a niece of Peter McIntyre.

****

1847 Bolivar Co. Miss. Drawer 103 Case #6943

Thomas Kidd and wife, Sarah, of Warren Co., John W. Bolls and wife, Catharine, Abraham T. Smith and wife, Emily, all of Bolivar Co.

vs

Thomas J. Manley and Andrew B. Dodd, Admrs. Est David Willis and William Cannon, Exec. Est. Thomas Barrow, Dec'd, of Adams Co.

George Willis made a deed of gift April 8, 1800 to Robert Willis who died in 1827 or 1828. The wife of Robert Willis (not named) died in 1836. Children of Robert Willis: David Willis, Catharine, wife of John Bolls, Sarah, wife of Thos. Kidd and Alexander Willis, Dec'd whose only child Emily K. Willis married Abraham T. Smith. David Willis died Feb. 1844.

****

1853 Winston Co. Miss. Drawer 103 Case #6952

James Barron, Ezekiel, Solomon and Thomas Barron, David Snow and wife, Nancy, William J. Barron and Robert T. Barron (minors) by next friend, Hannah Barron; James, Mary, Nancy and Levy M. Crawford, minor children of David T. and Mary Crawford, both deceased, by next friend, Hannah Barron, all of Winston Co.

vs

Solomon R. McClanahan and wife Rebecca of Winston Co.

Comp'ts all heirs of Joseph Barron late of Choctaw Co. who died November 1851. Mentioned: Members of Winston Co. Board of Police, Joshua Leach, Samuel Avery, David Hull, John Mathas and Nathaniel Woodward.

****

1853 Winston Co. Miss. Drawer 103 Case #6953

John F. Moore, Admr. Est. of Lindsey Shoemaker, Dec'd.

vs

Heirs of Lindsey Shoemaker: Watson, Jackson, W. P., L. F., Chas. M., James and Louisa Shoemaker, Jane Crowder, nee Shoemaker, wife of W. R. Crowder, Susan Britton, nee Shoemaker, wife of Thomas Britton and Sarah M. Moore, nee Shoemaker, wife of John F. Moore (Comp't).

****

1853 Choctaw Co. Miss. Drawer 103 Case #6965

Alexander F. Townsend, Admr. Est. William Gray, Dec'd

vs

Rebecca Campbell and husband, John B. Campbell, Alfred Moore and E. J. Bond.

****

1854 Monroe Co. Miss. Drawer 103 Case #6972

Lewis Nabors and James Owens, Admrs. Est. James Mullins, Dec'd

vs

Stephen Cocke of Lowndes Co., Sterling Buckingham and John B. Davis of Monroe Co.

Litigation involves Est. of Jesten Cocke, Dec'd and Cornelius W. Boggan and Eliza C. Cocke, Admrs. Est. Jesten Cocke, Dec'd.

****

1854 Warren Co. Miss. Drawer 103 Case #6977

Andrew Gamble

vs

Martha M. Hicks, Admx. Est. Dr. Benj. I. Hicks, Dec'd late of Vicksburg, Miss.

****

1854 Claiborne Co. Miss. Drawer 103 Case #6979

Murdock Bain, Hugh Malloy and wife, Janette (late Janette Bain) heirs of James Bain, Dec'd

vs

Anthony C. Hutchins, Admr. Est. James Bain, Dec'd.

Litigation also involves estate of Alexander Bain, late of England.

****

1853 Hinds Co. Miss. Drawer 103 Case #6980

Martha A. Morris, Widow of William Morris, Dec'd

vs

John Morris of N. Y. State, Exec. Est. William Morris, Dec'd

William Morris was a citizen of Hinds Co. Miss. but died in New York State October 16, 1850.

****

1855 Marion Co. Miss. Drawer 103 Case #7003

Jacky Magee and wife, Anna, nee Anna Tynes of Marion Co., Major O. Connelly and wife, Susan, nee Tynes of Pike Co., Michael O'Rourke and wife, Sarah, nee Tynes of Marion Co.

vs

John Warren and Jane Magee, Admrs. Est. Fleming Tynes, Dec'd.

Heirs of Fleming Tynes, Dec'd: Jane Magee, widow of Fleming Tynes, Sarah O'Rourke, Susan Connelly, Anna Magee, Martha Tynes, Tyra T. D. Tynes, Louisa Smart, wife of Nathan P. Smart, Betsy, wife of John R. Connelly of Sabine Parish, La., Emily Rankin, wife of James C. Rankin of Washington Parish, La.

Inventory of Est. of Fleming Tynes filed for probate Nov. 1830—Book B. Page 221, Marion Co. John Warren died December 1851 leaving will in Marion Co.

****

1854 Adams Co. Miss. Drawer 103 Case #7008

Eliza I. Paine, Admx. de bonis Est. Adam Bower late of Adams Co.

vs

Eliza Pendleton and Zebulon Pendleton (her husband) of Lawrence Co. and Mary Rice and husband, Charles Rice.

Eliza Pendleton was late widow of Adam Bower. Other heirs: Martha, wife of Wm. H. Phipps, Sarah, wife of David Gibson.

****

1853 Lowndes Co. Miss. Drawer 103 Case #------

Sanford O. White of Lowndes Co.

vs

Ann Bartee, Admx. Est Paschal B. Wade, Dec'd and Neal Bartee, Trustee

****

1854 Adams Co. Miss. Drawer 103 Case #7016

John McCullough, Admr. Est. Robert McCullough, Dec'd
vs
Elizabeth McCullough and Winfield S. Gibson.

Elizabeth McCullough was widow of Robert McCullough, Dec'd. Their four minor children: James, Mariah, Keziah and Nathaniel.

****

1854 Copiah Co. Miss. Drawer 103 Case #7027

Richard H. Taliaferro and Samuel J. Morehead, Execs. Est. Peachy R. Taliaferro, Dec'd
vs
George Read and wife, Susan and Peachy Taliaferro (infant) by next friend, Herman B. Mayes.

William Q. Taliaferro died in Sept. 1840 leaving a will in which he named his brother, Peachy R. Taliaferro, Exec. He left his entire estate to his wife, Susan and their child, Peachy. His brother, Peachy R. died Dec. 14, 1840 leaving a will in which he named Richard H. Taliaferro and Samuel J. Morehead as Execs. Litigation involves slaves inherited by William Q. from the estate of Mrs. Peachy Gilmer. Susan, widow of William Q. married George Read.

****

1854 Lauderdale Co. Miss. Drawer 103 Case #7040

Charity Parks
vs
Elias Edwards, Henry Buchanan and James M. Trussell

Charity Parks was widow of James R. Parks who died in State of Louisiana August 1843 leaving as heirs: Susannah, wife of James M. Trussell of Lauderdale Co., Elizabeth L., wife of Elias Edwards of Winston Co., William J. and Wayman A. Parks (infants) of Lauderdale Co. and his widow, Charity.

****

1854 Holmes Co. Miss. Drawer 103 Case #7041

Robert J. Ward and Thomas B. Land

vs

Wm. C. Harrington and wife, Martha.

Charles Land died in Holmes Co. in 1834 leaving widow, Sarah Land and three children, Thomas B., Rutherford C. and Martha Land who married W. C. Harrington in 1847.

****

1854 Clarke Co. Miss. Drawer 103 Case #7054

Roland B. Crosby, Admr. Est. Susan Crosby, Dec'd

vs

William Covington

****

1854 Madison Co. Miss. Drawer 103 Case #7064

Malcolm Cameron, Gdn. for Phillip P. Cameron (his infant son now deceased)

vs

John R. Cameron

Malcolm Cameron married Tennesse Tenquite Nov. 17, 1841. Phillip P. Cameron, their child, died July 27, 1852 leaving a half brother John R. Cameron (Def't). Phillip was born August 9, 1842. Tennessee Cameron died Jan. 24, 1844. John R. Cameron was a child of the second marriage of Malcolm Cameron (wife's name not given).

****

1855 Warren Co. Miss. Drawer 103 Case #7074

John M. Chilton

vs

A. W. Brian

Litigation involves Nathaniel Cox, Admr. Est. Samuel B. Slocumb, Dec'd.

****

1854 Kemper Co. Miss. Drawer 103 Case #7079

Jane S. Jackson and Edwin A. Jackson

vs

William R. A. Jackson

Matthew Jackson died Jan. 18, 1853 intestate, leaving widow: Jane S. and son Edwin A. Jackson, William R. A. Jackson, Albert E., James A. and Martha J. C. Jackson.

****

1854 Holmes Co. Miss.. Drawer 103 Case #7083

Leland Noel and wife, Margaret, David W. Saunders and Benj. W. Saunders, minors, by next friend, Leland Noel

vs

Jones Harvey, Samuel Sample and Benj. Griffin surviving Execs. Est. Daniel M. Dulaney, Dec'd., Mary M. Sample, Admx. de bonis non Est. Isaac Sample, Isaac S. Harvey, Mary A., Elizabeth C. and Wade Harvey, infant children of Jones Harvey and wife, Sarah, both deceased.

Daniel M. Dulaney died in Holmes Co. in 1843 leaving will in which Margaret Saunders (now Noel) and David and Benj. Saunders, the children of Sarah E. Harvey formerly Saunders, now deceased, shared. Sarah Dulaney Saunders Harvey died in 1852 or 1853.

****

1854 Franklin Co. Miss. Drawer 103 Case #7088

Josiah Marshall, Admr. de bonis non Est. John King, Dec'd.

vs

Livingston P. King, Admr. Est. Missouri Marshall, Dec'd.

Missouri Marshall was widow of John King. Their children: Livingston P., Mary E. and Sarah V. King. Douglas S. King was brother of John King, Dec'd. Missouri King married Josiah Marshall.

****

1854 Hinds Co. Miss. Drawer 103 Case #7092

John Stone and Samuel Matthews, Execs. Est. Perry Cohea, Dec'd

vs

Robert Josselyn, Commissioner

****

1854 Hinds Co. Miss. Drawer 103 Case #7093

Ethelbert Barksdale and Franklin C. Jones

vs

Julia M. Price, Admx. Est. Charles M. Price, Dec'd. and George R. Fall.

Charles M. Price died in 1850.

****

1854 Madison Co. Miss. Drawer 103 Case #7098

Robert J. Ward, George Jonas and William P. Saunders all of New Orleans

vs

Abram A. McWillie and wife, Jane S. McWillie

****

1854 Noxubee Co. Miss. Drawer 103 Case #7107

Elizabeth Neill by next friend, Andrew J. Davis

vs

Robert Neill

Elizabeth Neill was child and heir of William Neill late of Sumpter Co. Ala. Other heirs: James Neill, Andrew J. Davis and wife, Ann R., Nancy Jane and Margaret Rose Neill

****

CASES IN DRAWER 115 NOT NUMBERED

1856 Adams Co. Miss. Drawer 115

Laura C. McGill

vs

J. A. McGill

Divorce Petition. Married Oct. 18, 1855 in Jefferson Co. Miss.

****

1829 Covington Co. Miss. Drawer 115

Robert Magee and Isham Weathersby

vs

Anslem H. Jayne

****

1812 Adams Co. Miss. Tr. Drawer 115

Rebecca Magruder

vs

Dr. Walter Magruder

Divorce Petition. Married March 23, 1809 "in town of Wheeling in State of Virginia".

****

1852 Rankin Co. Miss. Drawer 115

Narcissa Ann Moss

vs

Henry C. Chambers

Narcissa Ann Moss was wife of Henry K. Moss of Rankin Co. Miss.

****

1825 Wayne and Marion Cos. Miss. Drawer 115

Christopher Collins and wife, Rachel

vs

Ann Hendricks, Jacob Collins and wife, Lucy, John H. and Collins L. Horne, Jacob Collins, Jr., Hendricks Collins,

Robert Collins, Christopher Collins, Jr., Joshua Collins, Jr., Benj., Joseph, James and Eli Collins, John McDonald and wife, Charlotte, Mary, Ann, Elizabeth, Rachel, Jr., Ruth, Louisa, Lucy, Jr., John William and Martha Collins and James Patton, all of Wayne Co. Litigation involves will of John William Hendricks.

****

1827 Jefferson Co. Miss. Drawer 115

Ferguson Hudson

vs

Parthena Hudson.

Divorce Petition. Married May 16, 1821.

****

1824 Co. not shown. Drawer 115

Margaret G. Jourden

vs.

Lemuel Lipsey

Margaret Foster, daughter of Robert and Hannah Foster of South Carolina, married Alexander Jourden in 1814 in S. C. James Foster, brother of Margaret, lived in Holmes Co. Miss, and brother, Joseph Foster, lived in Tennessee.

****

1830 Simpson Co. Miss. Drawer 115

Neil Little, Admr. Est. Alexander Little, Dec'd and Duncan Little

vs

Effie Little

Alexander Little died "before Nov. 1829". Jurymen listed: Robert Little, James Murray, Lewis Howie, Daniel Shots, Thos. J. Everett, Jesse Williamson, Edward T. Wingate, John Thompson, Hiram Walker, Richard Walker, David Hayse and Eli Regent.

****

1849 Co. not shown. Drawer 115

Samuel Lum, Admr. and Virginia A. Mielki (relict) Admr. Est. Edward C. Mielki

vs

Frederick Norcum, Ellick Mason, Armistead Burwell and George S. Yerger.

****

1843 Wilkinson Co. Miss. Drawer 115

W. C., Benj. L., Henry J. and Charles Coon, by Gdn. Benj. Kilgore

vs

John L. Jones, Admr. Est. D. F. Coon, Dec'd
Comp'ts: Heirs of D. F. Coon, Dec'd.

****

1833 Hinds Co. Miss. Drawer 115

James C. Dickson

vs

Jesse Bass and Council R. Bass, Admrs. Est. Edward P. Bass, Dec'd.

Jurymen: Perry King, Levi Spurling, F. Alford, Redwine Pierce, Wm. Bracy, Wm. Caines, John Tinnon, James Harris, Washington Pleasants, Edward T. Noble, John T. Knox and Samuel T. King.

****

1833 Warren Co. Miss. Drawer 115

John Breathitt

vs

Eugene Magee, Admr. Est Joseph C. Lewis, Dec'd.

****

1836 Washington Co. Miss. Drawer 115

Samuel Carson, Admr. Est. Daniel Slagle, Dec'd

vs

William W. Blanton and Andrew Carson.

****

1826 Adams Co. Miss. Drawer 115

Elizabeth Chaney

vs

Prosper King

Elizabeth Chaney was widow of Bailey E. Chaney who died in Louisiana Dec. 25, 1825. They were married in State of Miss. 1798.

****

1827 Jones Co. Miss. Drawer 115

Winifred Evans

vs

John Evans of Covington Co.

Winifred Evans was "Widow Williams" at time of her marriage to John Evans. Date not given.

****

1835 Hinds Co. Miss. Drawer 115

Re: Will of William Goodson, late of Hinds Co. Miss. Will names wife, Elizabeth, daughter, Martha, grandchildren, Sarah Ann Collins and Rachel Sherwood. Will on record in Raymond, Miss.

****

1849 Copiah Co. Miss. Drawer 115

George W. Grant.

To

Elizabeth W. Grant (wife)

Property settlement. Elizabeth Grant was Elizabeth Stillman prior to her marriage to George W. Grant March 17, 1838.

****

1815 Adams Co. Miss. Tr. Drawer 115

Mary W. Grant

vs

John Grant

Divorce Petition. Married: August 4, 1804 in State of Virginia.

****

CASES IN DRAWER 116 NOT NUMBERED.

1842 Covington Co. Miss. Drawer 116

John G. Parker, Gdn. for minor heirs of Anslem H. Jayne, Dec'd (Heirs not named)

vs

Laughlin McLaurin, Angus M. McLaurin and Allen Stewart, all of Covington Co.

****

1854 Wilkinson Co. Miss. Drawer 116

John A. Scott and Joseph Scott of Rapides Parish, La.

To

Susan Philbrick of Wilkinson Co. Mississippi.

Deed to lands in Wilkinson Co. Miss. Consideration $10,000. At the death of Susan Philbrick lands were to be divided between James Saunders G. Scott, Caroline Susan Scott, John Abraham Scott, Sarah Eliza Scott, Maynard Richardson Scott—all grandchildren of Susan Philbrick and children of John A. Scott.

****

1815 Adams Co. Miss. Tr. Drawer 116

George Poindexter

vs

Lydia Poindexter (his wife) and Jesse Carter (her father)

Articles of separation and separate maintenance for wife and minor son, Albert Gallatin Poindexter.

****

1850 Co. not shown. Drawer 116

Mark Prewitt

vs

William C. Coopwood, Admr. Est. John C. Cheny, Dec'd

Bill to set aside conveyance of negroes and other Chattel property. Heirs not named.

****

1823 Warren Co. Miss. Drawer 116

Abram Prim and Jordan Prim

And

John Lane, Admr. with will attached of Newit Vick, and George Wyche, Trustee.

Contract re: Lands in Vicksburg, Miss.

****

1851 Pontotoc Co. Miss. Drawer 116

N. S. Price, Admr. Est. John Goodson, Dec'd

vs

Booker Foster

****

1836 Adams Co. Miss. Drawer 116

Abram Quin, natural tutor of daughter, Mary Quin, acknowledges receipt of $3436.70 from Silas Talbert, Exec. will of John Frantom, Dec'd.

Mary Quin was granddaughter of John Frantom, late of Rapides Parish, La.

****

1836 Adams Co. Miss. Drawer 116

James T. Rowan

vs

Estate of Sarah Rowan, Dec'd.

Litigation involves the inheritance of Alfred W. Rowan and James H. Rowan, sons of James T. Rowan and Elizabeth T. Rowan and grandsons of Sarah Rowan, Dec'd.

****

1842 Wilkinson Co. Miss. Drawer 116

The West Feliciana Railroad Co.

vs

Admr. Estate of E. Stockett

****

1819 Adams Co. Miss. Drawer 116

Joseph Sessions

vs

Dinah, Thomas, Isabella, Susan, John, Nelson, Sarah and Margaret Fleming, Mary Campbell, nee Fleming, and husband Anthony Campbell, all heirs of David Fleming, Dec'd.

****

1811 Adams Co. Miss. Tr. Drawer 116

Mrs. Sarah Smith, alias Mrs. Sarah Franklin of Adams Co. Miss.

vs

Samuel R. Franklin of State of Pennsylvania (Lt. and paymaster 10th Regiment Infantry United States Army).

Divorce Petition. Married 1796.

****

1831 Copiah Co. Miss. Drawer 116

Re: Estate of John Saunders, late of State of South Carolina.

Thomas Saunders of Copiah Co. Miss. named as heir.

****

1823 Jefferson Co. Miss. Drawer 116

Laurence Scarbrough

vs

Dorce Scarbrough

Witnesses summoned: Joel Selman, Henry Wise, Robert Prater.

****

1840 Claiborne Co. Miss. Drawer 116

William S., Thomas B. and Robert M. Scott

vs

Thomas Freeland, William Briscoe and Jeremiah Watson.

****

1819 Co. not shown. Drawer 116

Fyke Armstrong, Guardian for James M. Stanfield

vs

Sarah Stanfield Allen (mother of James M. Stanfield) and James Allen (stepfather).

****

1831 Co. not shown. Drawer 116

Thomas L. Trevoss

vs

Heirs of James S. Cartetts.

Heirs not named.

****

1811 Adams Co. Miss. Tr. Drawer 116

Manuel Texada

vs

Augusta Solano Rodreguiz, heir and daughter of John Joseph Rodreguiz, Dec'd.

****

1817 Amite Co. Miss. Drawer 116

William P. Thomas and wife, Mary, nee Perkins, of Amite Co., James Cox and wife, Sarah, nee Perkins, of Adams Co., John Elmore and wife, Elizabeth, nee Perkins of Amite Co., Joseph Perkins, infant, by Guardian, Elizabeth Perkins—all heirs of Joseph Perkins, Dec'd.

vs

Estate of Sarah Perkins, Dec'd. and Charles Perkins.

Sarah Perkins was widow of Joseph Perkins.

****

1850 Marshall Co. Miss. Drawer 116

Hamilton Thornton, Admr. Est. William Crain, Dec'd. and William Bogard

vs

Richard Johnson, Admr. Est. William Johnson, Dec'd. and James F. Trotter and Wyatt Epps.

****

1814 Adams Co. Miss. Drawer 116

Robert Tremble

vs

Estate of Edward Pate

****

1867 Monroe Co. Miss. Drawer 116

Titus C. Westbrook and Moses Westbrook, Jr., heirs of Moses Westbrook, Dec'd. by next friend, Thomas Christian.

vs

Robert Adams, Admr. Est. Wyatt Moye

****

1829 Co. not shown. Drawer 116

Margaret Winston and Samuel Winston, Admrs. Est. Lewis Winston, Dec'd

vs

Mary Galbreath, Admr. Est. Robert D. Galbreath and Margaret, Jane, Mary, George and James Galbreath —all heirs of Robert Galbreath, Dec'd

****

1845 Adams Co. Miss. Drawer 116

Re: Eliza C. Wood, Trustee in Deed of marriage settlement between Dr. Charles S. Abercrombie and the late Mary C. Bowman Abercrombie made in 1833.

Minor heirs of Mary C. B. Abercrombie: Eliza, Celeste, John B. and Mary Josephine Abercrombie.

****

1827 Monroe Co. Miss. Drawer 116

Re: Consent of Sam Edmondson for his wife, Jane Edmondson, late Jane Martin, Widow of William Martin, Dec'd to act as Executrix of Estate of William Martin, Dec'd.

GERMAN BERRY'S WILL

Dated Jan. 6, 1880

The State of Texas)
County of Freestone)
January the 6th)

I German Berry of the aforesaid State and County, a farmer and stock raiser, make this my last will.

I give, devise and bequeath my estate and property real and personal, as follows, that is to say:

I give and bequeath to A. J. Berry Eleven hundred dollars, besides at a former time, I gave him a quarter of a section of land estimated to be worth Five hundred dollars one horse worth one hundred dollars and some cattle.

I give and devise to Louisa R. Hughes and her heirs Twenty Six Acres of land, being a portion of the R. B. Longbotham league and I give and bequeath to her and her heirs all of my cattle, one mule, one horse and one filly.

Having prior to this my last will and testament given, devised and bequeath to Joseph B. Berry one quarter of a section of land worth Five hundred dollars and Six hundred dollars in gold.

I also gave, devised and bequeathed to Pleasant B. Berry one quarter section of land worth Five hundred dollars.

I also gave and devised to Sarah Ann E. Cooper one hundred and Fifty Acres of land worth Five hundred dollars.

I also gave, devised and bequeathed to Mary C. B. Webb one quarter of a section of land worth Five hundred dollars, one horse, worth one hundred dollars and Ten heads of Cattle, worth one hundred dollars.

In witness whereof I have signed and sealed and published this instrument as my will at home in Freestone County Texas, on this 6th day of January A. D. 1880.

German Berry L. S.

The said German Berry at said home in said State of Texas and County of Freestone and on said 6th day of January A. D. 1880 signed and sealed this instrument, and published and declared the same as and for his last will And we, at his request, and in his presence, and in the presence of each other, have hereunto written our names as subscribing witnesses.

W. M. Seely
J. D. Carroll
J. T. Seely

No. 508
Will
German Berry
Filed Nov. 8th 1882

Admitted to Probate and ordered to record Nov. 21st, 1882.

O. C. Kirven
Co. Judge
F. C. Tex.

Recorded 137 & 138

Died Oct. 17th 1882— A. J. Berry, Applicant

WILL OF SAMUEL BROWN

I Samuel Brown of the County of Simpson State of Mississippi being in good health of body and of sound and disposing mind and memory (praise be God for the same) and being desirous to settle my worldly affairs whilst I have strength and capacity so to do make and publish this my last will and testament hereby revoking and making void all former wills, deeds of gift by me at any time heretofore made and first and principally I commit my soul into the hands of the Creator who gave it and my body to the earth to be entered in the burying ground of my land and at the same place in which James I Irby's child is buried at the discretion of my executor hereinafter named. And as to such worldly goods it hath pleased God to intrust me with I dispose of the same as follows—

I give and bequeath to my beloved daughter Cecilia Brown five dollars of my estate, to my beloved son John Brown five Dollars of my estate, to my son Hezekiah Brown five dollars of my estate, to my daughter Kireah Thomas five dollars of my estate, to my daughter Emila Copeland five dollars of my estate and to Solomon Brown five dollars of my estate, and to my daughter Elizabeth Chapman five dollars of my estate, and to my beloved son Isham Brown all of my estate of every kind whatsoever real or personal after giving the other heirs their legal dowry to wit all my lands negroes all my horses all my cattle all my hogs sheep household furniture farming utensils which I may die possessed of (except one little negro girl Evaline which negro girl I hereby give and bequeath to my nephew Samuel Carson Brown) But all of my estate aforesaid is to remain in my possession as fully and entirely as though this my will had not been published during my natural life and in case my wife Mary Brown should survive me then the same is hereby granted to her during her natural life. And I hereby appoint my beloved son Isham Brown my sole executor of this my last will and testament hereby expressly revoking all former wills by me made. In witness whereof I have hereunto set my hand and seal the twenty second day of February in the year of our Lord One thousand eight hundred and thirty seven.

his
Samuel x Brown Seal
mark

Signed Sealed and Published and delivered by the above named Samuel Brown to be his last will and testament in the presence of us who have hereunto subscribed our name as witnesses in the presence of the testator.

James I Irby
John Brown

Proven in Probate Court of Simpson Co. Miss. December Term 1837.

LAST WILL AND TESTAMENT OF RICHARD BUTLER

(State of Louisiana)

In the name of God Amen, I Richard Butler, of the State of Louisiana in perfect health and memory do make and ordain this my last will and testament in manner and form following that is to say—First I do ordain that immediately after my decease, or as soon there after as it may be convenient and reasonable all my debts due and owing by me shall be fully paid and discharged.

Item I give devise and bequeath unto my true and lawful wife Margaret Butler the one half of my estate, real and personal, movable and immovable within the State of Louisiana to have and to hold the same to her and her heirs forever provided nevertheless that it is not intended to vest in my said wife and her heirs the property and estate by me covenanted and agreed to be conveyed to my brother in law Samuel McCutcheon of the said State. So as to defeat the true meaning and intention of the said covenant and agreement and my said wife and the devisees herein after named are enjoined to carry the same into effect.

Item I give devise and bequeath unto my said wife the one third of all my real estate situated and being in the Mississippi Territory to have and to hold the same during her natural life and I give and bequeath one half of my personal property within the Mississippi Territory aforesaid to my said wife Margaret Butler to be enjoined by her forever. It is my particular request that the Executors hereinafter named are most strenuously desired to leave nothing undone to render the future days of my beloved wife happy and independent. I feel myself bound from every principle and from every inclination that this should be strictly adhered to. She has all my heart and has been to me a most faithful wife and partner and the tenderest of friends.

Item I give devise and bequeath all the rest and residue and remainder of my estate property and effects to my sisters Rebecca McCutcheon and Harriet Hooke to have and to hold the same equally divided between them for and during their natural lives.

Item Upon the death of the said Rebecca McCutcheon and the said Harriet Hooke or either of them I do give devise and bequeath the share or shares which the said decedant or decedants shall have possession as aforesaid or which is by the last above devise and bequeath intended she or they should possess to the child or children of the said Rebecca McCutcheon and Harriet Hooke or either of them to be equally divided between the said children and in case of the death of either of said children previous to marriage and without issue then his or her share to be equally divided among the surviving children as aforesaid, or in case only one child as aforesaid should survive then the share or shares above mentioned and the estate and property shall vest and remain in the said child and his or her heirs forever.

Item I give and bequeath unto the persons hereinafter named the following legacies to the payment of which the aforesaid devisees and legatees shall contribute in an equal proportion that is to say To my beloved Mother, Jane Butler, I bequeath the annual sum of One Thousand Dollars the same to be paid to her yearly and every year during the term of her natural life. To the son of my much esteemed friend, Abner L. Duncan, viz, John Nicholas Duncan, I bequeath the sum of Fifteen Hundred Dollars to be appropriated toward giving him a liberal education to be paid into the hands of his father or guardian appointed by him in three annual installments, the first to commence when the said John Nicholas Duncan shall be fourteen years old. To my faithful servant negro George I bequeath his freedom all my personal clothing and five hundred dollars to be paid to him out of the first proceeds of my estate after paying my legal debts. This I consider a debt of gratitude for his affectionate and honest conduct and I take into view the many curses I have given him often very improperly.

I give and bequeath my new pistols made by Egg of London to my worth friend, James Williams Esq. of Louisiana. To Richard Butler Price, son of Chancelor Price Esq of Philadelphia I do ordain and direct that he shall receive at the expense of my estate a complete and liberal education such a one as will qualify him for any one of the learned professions this to be done within the United States education to be chargeable to my estate from and after his twelfth year is completed. When his studies are finished and he graduated I ordain a thousand dollars to be paid him for the purchase of a library. To my brother William Butler I give and bequeath an annuity of the sum of Eight Hundred Dollars and payable quarterly. To my worthy friend Thomas Butler of Louisiana I leave my best riding horse and equipage that is a saddle bridle swords pistols and all arms belonging to me and I further give and bequeath to the said Thomas Butler all my books which my wife Margaret Butler may not desire to keep as part of her library.

To my good friend Abner L. Duncan I give and bequeath my superb Rosekell gold watch and its appendages. To my executors hereinafter named I leave and bequeath a mourning ring and a full suit of mourning to each of them.

I think it necessary to state to my brothers in law that it was originally my intention to make them my executors in conjunction with my wife but being well aware of the difficulties which generally attend any division of property and wishing to avoid and obviate all contention and strife where brotherly love and friendship ought solely to exist I have conceived it my duty and more conducive to their happiness to appoint other friends to this office wherefore I now ordain and make my wife Margaret Butler, the Honorable Thomas Butler and Abner Lawson Duncan all of the State of Louisiana Executors of this my last will and testament.

In witness whereof I have unto put my hand this eighteenth day of June, in the Year of Our Lord One thousand eight hundred and fourteen at the City of New Orleans in the State of Louisiana.

Richard Butler (Seal)

Witnesses: John Poultney, Jr.
William Henderson
F. L. Turner
John Nicholson
Richard Relf

WILL OF DAVID BAILEY

THE STATE OF MISSISSIPPI
MADISON COUNTY 21st day of January 1831

In the Name of God Amen I David Bailey of the county and State aforesaid being of sound and disposing mind and memory do make and declare this my last Will and Testament Revoking all others heretofore made in manner and form following to wit

1st I Resign my Soul into the hand of Almighty God hoping and believing in Remission of my sins by the merits of Jesus Christ and my body I commit to the earth to be buried at the direction of my Executrix or Executor hereinafter mentioned and my worldly Estate which has pleased God to bless me in accumulating I give and devise as follows

1st I give and devise to my beloved and affectionate wife Mary Bailey of the County and State aforesaid all my lands and tenements in the county and State aforesaid Also All my negroes namely Ann, Sarah, Jack, Andy, Peter, Tom, Delsey, Lucy, Jim, Sam and Nancy Also All my stock of horses cattle and sheep also All my household kitchen utensils for her the said Mary Bailey to have and to hold during her natural life and at her death to dispose of a negro girl Sarah at her will and pleasure all other property above stated to be disposed of as follows to wit, Equally divided between my beloved Sisters and Brothers namely Mary Luster, Lucy Clemmins, Milly Bailey, Jesse Bailey and James Bailey, at the same time reserving a sufficient support for my Father mother and Family during their lifetime also the increase or decrease to be as above Stated———

2nd I wish my Executrix and Executor to pay all just demands I owe in any manner whatever.

3rd I Wish and Request the Orphans court of Said County to appoint my beloved wife Mary Bailey Executrix and Augustine Kearney Executor Carry the Design of this my last Will and Testament into Effect Given under my hand and Seal This 21st January 1831 in the presence of A. Walker, Gill Herbert and Bennett Truly.

David Bailey (Seal)

Attest
Allen Walker
G. M. Herbert
B. R. Truly

WILL OF WILLIAM CARSON

State of South Carolina
Abbeville District

I William Carson of the State and District aforesaid do make this my last Will and Testament. I desire all my property both real and personal to be sold as soon as convenient after my decease by my Executors and that my just debts be paid. It is my wish that two hundred and fifty dollars be put out at interest by my Executors as soon as it can be raised out of my estate for the use and benefit of my son James which may now or hereafter be legally born to be paid out to them in equal proportions when they severally become of age or marry. It is my desire that my two youngest children, Jane Caroline and William Robert should each receive five hundred dollars to their equal proportions of my estate for their maintenance and education, and if that amount should not be expended that the ballance be paid over to them when the severally became of age or marry and I hereby appoint my son, Martin Carson, their guardian.

It is my further wish and desire that the balance of my property should be legally divided among my children (James excepted) so as to make them all equal taking into consideration what has already been advanced to some of them (viz) Tommy son John an equal proportion deducting eighty dollars already given him. To my son Martin an equal proportion deducting eight hundred dollars already given him. To my daughter, Eliza Houston an equal share after deducting six hundred dollars already given her. To my daughter Margaret Houston an equal share after deducting $600.00 already given her. To my son Benjamin I give an equal share after deducting Eighty dollars which he has already received. To my daughter Mary H. an equal share. To my daughter, Lucinda D. an equal share. To my daughter, Jane Caroline an equal share in addition to five hundred dollars for her maintenance and education. To my son, William Robert, an equal share in addition to five hundred dollars for his maintenance and education. And in case any of said children die before they become of age or marry, it is my will and desire that their proportions of my estate should go to the remainder of my children (James excepted). And I do hereby appoint my son Martin Carston and my friend John McComb executors of this my last will and testament revoking all wills heretofore made by me and declaring this only to be my last will and testament. In testimony of which I have hereunto set my hand and seal this 15th day of Sept. 1828.

William Carson (Seal)

Signed and delivered in the presence of us

Stephen Lee
John McDonald
Joshua Jones

Probated in Tallahatchie Co. Miss Jan 12, 1838.

THE LAST WILL AND TESTAMENT OF JAMES L. COLLINS, Decd

In the name of God Amen—I, James L. Collins, of perfect mind and sound memory (Blessed be God) do make and declare and establish this instrument of writing as my last Will and Testament, that is to say:

To my dearly beloved brother, John Collins I do hereby give, grant and bequeath my two negro boys, Moses and Manuel to him and his heirs forever.

To my dearly beloved brother in law, Francis Wren and his heirs, by my dearly beloved sister Mehalia Wren (once Collins) I hereby give, grant and bequeath my negro fellow, John, to him and his heirs by Mehalia Collins (now Wren).

To my dearly beloved brother in law, Francis Wren I give, grant and bequeath six negroes, that is to say, Lucy, a woman about 32 years of age and five children to wit: Miranda, a girl 9 or 10 years of age; Frank, a boy about seven years old; Sal, a girl about four years old; Emily, nearly four years of age, and Harriet, a girl nearly two years old, to have and hold in trust for the use and benefit of the lawful heirs of my dearly beloved sister, Althea Spears and her and their heirs and assigns for ever.

It is further my will and desire that my dearly beloved brother, John Collins and my dearly beloved brother in law, Francis Wren, shall within three years from the first day of January next ensuing pay or, cause to be paid to Elisabeth D. Lomy, daughter of William Lomy, Senior the sum of three hundred and thirty three and one third dollars each: and also desire and request the said Francis Wren, trustee as aforesaid for Althea Spears to pay to the said Elisabeth D. Lomy within the like period of three years the like sum of Three Hundred and Thirty Three and one third dollars, so that the three several payments to the said Elisabeth D. Lomy, when united will make the sum of One Thousand dollars.

I also wish and desire that the plantation on which I have hitherto resided, all the kitchen and household furniture and the set of blacksmith tools and all the other real and personal property which I now own, shall be sold for cash, or on credit as my executors may deem most advisable and the proceeds thereof I wish applied to the payment of my just debts and I likewise wish and desire that the interest which I have and now hold in the saddling establishment with Darling Sons, Esq (the amount which I placed in that interest was Five Hundred dollars) shall also be applied to the payment of my just debts and the surplus if any there be I wish applied to the legacy herein before bequeathed to Elisabeth D. Lomy.

Lastly I hereby make constitute and appoint John Collins and Francis Wren Executors of this my last will and testament, in witness whereof I have hereunto affixed my hand and seal, this tenth of September, Eighteen Hundred and Twenty four. The words "Francis Wren" interlined between the 10th and 11th lines of the first page and the word "Spears" interlined between the 12th and 13th lines of the second page and the words "within the like period of three years" interlined between the 13th and 14th lines of the said second page.

Signed James L. Collins (Seal)

Signed Sealed and Acknowledged in the presence of us who are present at the signing and sealed thereof in the presence of each other and in the presence of the devisor.

Signed: Thomas Torrance
Signed: W. C. Maxwell
Signed: George Hamlin

LAST WILL AND TESTAMENT OF JACOB CABLE SR.

In the name of God Amen I Jacob Cable Sr. of Jefferson County in Mississippi Territory being of sound and disposing mind and memory of an advanced age and infirm constitution taking into view the uncertainty of human existance and that it is appointed for all men once to die and to provide for the disposal of such goods and worldly effects as it has pleased heaven to Bless me with Do Make and ordain this my Last Will and Testament hereby revoking and annuling all former wills by me made or said to have been made—

First I consign my Body to the Dust from whence it came in decent Christian Burial and my soul into the hands of Almighty God who gave it—

Secondly I give and bequeath the whole of my Real and Personal Estate with the reservation herein after to be made (after the payment of my just debts and funeral expenses) to my Children to be divided and distributed by my Executors herein named in the manner following Viz the whole of my before mentioned estate to be sold by my executors on such terms as in their opinions may be most conducive to the Interest of my heirs & the net proceds thereof to be equally divided amongst my children and in case of the death of any of my children before such division or distribution the child or children of said decedant to receive the portion of his her or there parent and in case of there being no children the said portion to be equally divided amongst my surviving children.

Thirdly It is my will that my executors provide that my negro woman Hannah shall be set free and that they use such means for the procurement of her freedom as to them shall appear proper and efficatious and should it be necessary they are hereby authorized and requested to send her to the State of Louisiana or any foreign State to accomplish the same and all the expense of accomplishing the same to be paid out of my estate.

Fourthly I give and bequeath to my executors until my said negro woman shall be emancipated as aforesaid at which time the same is to be vested in said negro woman, Hannah and to be put in her possession by my said executors the following Real and personal Estate viz the dwelling House and improvements where I now live together with fifty acres of Land to be run off in such manner as may as little as possible injure the residue of the tract which said real estate was to be vested and possessed by her for and during her natural life.

Fifthly I give and bequeath to the said negro woman Hannah during her natural life the following personal Estate Viz all and singular my household and kitchen furniture and one horse and one mare of the value of Fifty Dollars eacn five cows and calves and all the hogs poultry of which I am possessed.

Sixthly and lastly I do hereby appoint my friends H. I. Balch, Armstrong Ellis and Abner Pipes executors to this my Last will and Testament In Testimony Whereof I have hereunto set my hand and affixed seal this twenty eighth day of May in the year 1814.

his
Jacob x Cable (Seal)
mark

Signed sealed and delivered in presence of

Thomas Hinds
John NewBaker
Jas. Cowdon

WILL OF RICHARD T. COLEMAN

In the Name of God Amen

I, Richard T. Coleman of Franklin County, and State of Mississippi, do make and publish this my last Will and Testament in manner and form following, (that is to say)

First- I give and bequeath unto my beloved wife, Nancy Coleman, during her life the Tract of land I now live on, with all my cattle to the amount of—all my Hogs to the amount of—Also all my Farming Utensils, Horses, Household furniture and I also bequeath to my beloved wife Nancy Coleman my crop with all my notes and accounts the amt not known- also nine negroes Names Peggy, Milly, Sophia, Chloe, Leah, Toney, Harry, Peter and Sampson. Also if I have forgot anything the residue or personal estate I do bequeath to my beloved wife Nancy Coleman, who I appoint sole executrix of this my last will and testament hereby revoking all former Wills by me made.

In witness whereof I have hereunto set my hand and seal the 11 August A. D. 1818. Signed, sealed, published and declared by the above named Richard T. Coleman, to be his last will and Testament, in the presence of us who have hereunto subscribed our names as witnesses in the presence of the testator.

Witnesses to this my Will

Joshua Hadley)
)
Thomas Hutchins)
)
Levi Wright)

Richard T. Coleman His x Mark (Seal)

CODACIL TO THIS MY WILL

I, Richard T. Coleman of the State of Mississippi and County of Franklin make and publish this codacil to be my last will and Testament in manner following (that is to say) Considering my wife Nancy Coleman to be pregnant and no provision made by deed for the yet unborn infant, as I have done for my other three children, It is my will should it please God to bring it into existance when it arrives to years of maturity that it should be put on an equal footing with my other children out of property of this my will. I do further say that my two old negroes Primas and his wife Chloe shall be free as soon as the breath is out of my body also that they shall have the house they now live in and twenty acres of land lying around it, as long as my family keeps the place or as long as they both shall live. This I do with free good will on account of the honest fidelity of these two good old negroes. This Codacil shall be an addition to this my Last Will and Testament, revoking all other writings by me made except the deeds given to my children, this I do for the affection I have for my family-and in consideration of this I do here fix my hand and seal in the presence of my wife, Nancy Coleman whom I leave sole executrix to this my Codacil, I also publish and proclaim the same in the presence of the undersigned witnesses 11 August A. D. 1818.

His
Richard T. Coleman x (Seal)
Mark

Witnesses
Joshua Hadley
Thomas Hutchins
Levi Wright

Proved in Court
B. E. Chaney C.J.Q
Sept. 28, 1818.

WILL OF DANIEL COX

Be it remembered that I, Daniel Cox of the State of Mississippi & Choctaw County being weak of body but sound of mind and perfect memory Blessed be Almighty God for the same, do make and publish this my last will and testament in manner and form following that is to say First That all my just debts shall be paid out of the monies that is now due me.

Secondly I give and bequeath unto my Beloved wife Nancy Cox one eight of the land containing eighty acres of land more or less situate in the County and State above named and being the eight of land that my residence as well as my houses and improvements is made upon also one negro woman named Rachel and her two children Eliza and George to have and to hold the above named tract of land and negroes during her life or widowhood and in either case the above named real and personal property to be divided amongst her own children Viz Daniel, Martha, Ann, Andrew A., Mary Jane, Rebecca Julia and Benjamin F. Cox at my wife's decease or marriage. It is also my will that all my property both real and personal (except the real estate I possess in Pickens Co. Alabama which shall hereafter be disposed of which I now possess shall be and remain in the hands of my beloved wife Nancy Cox until my children comes of age or marries. It is also my will that each of my children that are living with me by my present consort when they come of age or marries shall receive one thousand dollars each of the property both real and personal at its just valuation to be appraised by three disinterested persons chosen by my Executors It is also my will that my Executor shall sell my real estate lying in Pickens County, Alabama containing five hundred and thirty acres of land in two separate tracts as my title will more fully show and to be sold by my Executor on credit of five years in equal payments with good and sufficient securities for the payment of said land and I do hereby give my said Executor full power and authority for me and in my name to make unto the purchaser of said land a good and warrantee title to said land as soon as the last payment is made of said land and the proceeds arising from the sale of said lands to be laid out in educating my children and if any should be left of said monies arising from the sale of said land to be equally divided by my Executor amongst all my children whatever remainder there may be after my children now living with me shall receive in property to the amount of one thousand dollars each whatever amount of property there may be left to be sold by my Executor and the amount arising from said sale to be equally divided amoungst all my legatees And I do further appoint and authorize my well beloved son Elihu Cox my sole executor until my son Daniel Cox now living with me comes of age at which time it is my will that he shall be executor jointly with the aforesaid Elihu Cox hereby revoking all other former wills by me made.

In witness whereof I have hereunto set my hand and seal this 16th August A. D. 1841.

Daniel Cox (Seal)

Signed Sealed Published and declared by the aforesaid Daniel Cox to be his last will and testament in the presence of us who at his request & in his presence have hereunto subscribed our names as witnesses to the same.

H. Buck (Seal)
Thomas C. Covington (Seal)
Daniel Boyd (Seal)

Proved in Probate Court of Choctaw County, Mississippi March 27th 1843.

NOTE: Widow renounced inheritance and petitioned for dower. Commissioners appointed: John Pilcher, Eli Snow, Thos. Covington, James Webb and Parham Pollard.

ISAAC CALDWELL'S WILL

I Isaac Caldwell of Hinds Co. State of Mississippi being of sound and disposing memory do make and solemnly publish this as my last Will and Testament.

First, I give and bequeath unto my affectionate wife, Elizabeth H. Caldwell my whole estate, real, personal and mixed rights and credits of every kind in fee simple, to use as she may please not doubting her prudent care for our dear child Raymond.

Second, I appoint my esteemed friend, James B. Robinson and my dear wife, Elizabeth, executor and executrix of this will or either of them who may qualify and act hereby authorizing and empowering them or either of them to sell any and every article of my estate at Col. Raymond Robinson's in Hinds County, lands negroes and wherever the same may lie or be on two days public notice and to pay my just debts, fines and then apply the balance as first directed.

Thirdly, my said Executor and Executrix are not required or either of them to give bond for the Execution of the Trust here reposed. Lastly, as this Will is wholly written and subscribed and sealed by me in my handwriting, no witness. Done with solemn deliberation this 27th day of February Eighteen Hundred and Twenty Nine.

Isaac Caldwell (Seal)

Proven February Term 1836.

WILL OF THOMAS CALVIT

STATE OF MISSISSIPPI)
JEFFERSON COUNTY)

In the name of God Amen I Thomas Calvit of the State and County aforesaid being in my ordinary health of body and strength of mind knowing that it is appointed for all men to die and further knowing the uncertainty when death may happen do hereby deem it necessary to arrange my worldly affairs as well as the nature of things will permit do make and ordain the following my last will and testament.

First and principally I recommend my soul to the Almighty God and my body to the Earth to be buried in a decent though not expensive manner. Secondly all my just debts to be paid out of such estate as I may have. Thirdly I give conditionally to Mrs. Hulda Covington the annual sum of Two Hundred Dollars until her youngest child Elizabeth Covington shall arrive at the age of six years at which time the said annuity of two hundred dollars shall cease and be no longer paid.

I likewise lend to the said Mrs. Hulda Covington during her natural life a negro girl Maria with her increase to return to my estate to be disposed of as hereinafter expressed. Fourthly upon the aforesaid Elizabeth Covington (daughter of Mrs. Hulda Covington) attaining legal age I give and bequeath the sum of Ten Thousand Dollars payable at the discretion of my Executors but he or they may not be compelled to make such payment before the said Elizabeth Covington arrives at lawful age On her arriving at lawful age I further give and bequeath to the said Elizabeth the aforesaid Maria and her issue. Fifthly I further give and bequeath to the said Elizabeth Covington so much of my estate as may be necessary for the education and accomplishing her in the best manner that the Mississippi State may afford, and it is further my will and desire that my executor hereafter named take the charge of said Elizabeth Covington on her arriving at the age of six years for the purpose of her education and that he then commence and continue until completed. Sixthly I give and bequeath all the residue of my estate real and personal and mixed to my only son Samuel Calvit. Seventhly and lastly I do hereby nominate my aforesaid son Samuel Calvit my sole Executor of this my last will and Testament hereby revoking and setting aside all other wills and Testaments and acknowledging this and no other my last will and testament. In witness whereof I have hereunto set my hand and fixed my seal this second day of October in the year one thousand eight hundred and eighteen.

Thomas Calvit.

Witnesses

Philip Dixon
Saml Bullen
Elisha Breazeale

WILL OF THOMAS CALVIT

STATE OF MISSISSIPPI)
JEFFERSON COUNTY)

In the name of God Amen. I, Thomas Calvit of the County of Jefferson and State of Mississippi being at present of perfect mind and memory do make and ordain this as my Last Will and Testament.

Im primis I give and bequeath unto my beloved wife Hulda Calvit for and during her natural life the following named negro slaves that is to say Maria, and her brother Jacob and a boy called Ruben and a boy called Tony.

Item I leave in the hands of my executors here after named, to be disposed of for the use and benefit of my daughter Eliza Lucretia Calvit and the lawful heirs of her body the following property to be delivered to my said daughter whenever my said executors think proper that is to say Bill Juba and his wife Charity with their increase and Fanny the daughter of Kitty and also Maria and her brother Jacob after the decease of my said wife and also the sum of ten thousand dollars to be paid by my said executors out of my estate also it is also my will and desire that my said daughter shall live in the family of Felix Hughes until she be old enough to be sent to boarding school, or in some other family that my executors may choose and that the expenses arising from her schooling boarding and clothing shall be paid out of my estate by my executors whose I wish my daughter to be.

Item I do hereby appoint Col. James G. Wood of Jefferson Co. Joshua G. Clarke of Claiborne County, David Hunt of Jefferson County and my son Samuel Calvit the executors of this my Last Will and Testament wishing at the same time that my son would give as little trouble to the other executors as possible.

And lastly I do hereby revoke and disannul all other wills heretofore made or executed and declaring this to be my last will and testament.

In Testimony of which I have set my hand and seal this eleventh day of April in the year of our Lord Eighteen Hundred and Twenty One.

Thos. Calvit.

Signed published and acknowledged in presence of:

Thos Hinds
William Allen
Daniel James.

WILL OF CHARLES JONES COLCOCK

In the Name of God Amen

I, Charles Jones Colcock being of sound and disposing mind and memory but weak in body and mindful of the lot of man do make ordain and publish this my last will and testament hereby revoking all other and former wills heretofore at any time made by me and declare this to be my only true and last will.

I give devise and bequeath unto my beloved wife Mary Woodward Colcock all of my estate both real and personal whatsoever and wheresoever to her and her heirs forever.

And I do hereby constitute nominate and appoint my said wife and my son William Ferguson Colcock Executors of this my last will and I do hereby authorize them or either of them as such to sell convey or in any manner dispose of my Estate or any part thereof as to them or either of them shall seem meet and proper or to mortgage pledge or subject the same to any liens they or either of them may deem necessary.

In witness whereof I have hereunto set my hand and seal this twentieth day of January in the year of our Lord one thousand eight hundred and thirty nine.

C. J. Colcock (LS)

Signed sealed published and declared by the Testator as for his last Will and Testament in our presence who in his presence and in the presence of each other have subscribed our names as a witness hereto.

Elvra M. Ferguson
Thomas H. Colcock
Charles J. Colcock Jun.

Proven in the Ordinary Office Charleston District May 1, 1839.

WILL OF THOMAS DENMAN

Madison Co.
State of Mississippi

In the Name of God Amen

I, Thomas Denman of the County and State Aforesaid being of sound mind and knowing that it is appointed unto all men once to die and wishing to make a disposition of my earthly possessions do constitute and ordain this my last will and testament. First I bequeath to my beloved wife, Mary Denman, the following negro slaves viz Peter and Rhoda and their two children Elbert and Nathan, one boy named Henry, two girls named Charlotte and Louisa to hold during her lifetime and at her death they shall descend to Cicero Denman and Alexander McNutt Denman. Also one sorrel horse named Tom and one gray mare named Pris, all my stock of cattle and hogs and twenty head of sheep together with all my household and kitchen furniture, my silver Lever watch and one small shot gun, blacksmith tools and a sufficiency of farming utensils. My wife Mary shall take into her possession all of my notes and pay all my just debts, the remainder of the notes she may appropriate to her own use and benefit. I also bequeath to my wife, Mary, a pleasure carriage. Secondly, I give and bequeath to my four eldest children, James Denman, Emeline Cook, Simantha Denman and Sarintha Denman the following slaves viz Will and Nelly his wife and their children Anthony, Eliza, Caroline, Stephen, Harry and Angeline, one woman slave named Ellen and her child

Flower. All of which negroes shall be appraised by three disinterested persons whom the Court may appoint the amount of which shall be equally divided between my four eldest children, except Emeline Cook who has already received one negro named Caroline, bought for her for $575.00 which amount I desire to be deducted from her portion. I also bequeath to Samantha and Sarintha each one bed and bedstead, Samantha the Mills bedstead and Sarintha the Newman bedstead. There are also some horses and sheep not particularly specified, together with two more guns and a large shotgun and a rifle and all the other surplus articles I desire to be sold on twelve months credit and to be equally divided among my four eldest children. The negroes above mentioned to be appraised and to be divided by lotting them out to each child and not to be sold by the Executor.

Lastly I hereby nominate and appoint my Executor to this my last will and testament my beloved wife, Mary Denman and I desire that she shall not be required to give security.

Signed, Sealed and delivered by Thomas Denman as my last Will and Testament this Twenty Fifth day of November One Thousand Eight Hundred and Forty Two.

Thomas Denman (Seal)

In the presence of

D. W. Haley
William Brown
D. L. Stewart
I. R. Chambers

Proven in Probate Court of Madison Co. Miss December 13, 1842.

JAMES DOUGLASS' WILL

I, James S. Douglass, of the Parish of Concordia and State of Louisiana being feeble in body and knowing the uncertainty of this life but of sound and disposing mind and memory do make and publish this my last will and testament.

First, I direct that all my just debts be paid as soon after my decease as my Executors shall realize the same from the real and personal Estate entrusted to their care and management.

Secondly, Reposing the utmost confidence in my beloved wife Emeline Douglass I hereby constitute and appoint her Executrix and my brother Stephen Douglass and my friend Passmore Hoopes Executors of my estate real and personal lying and being in the State of Mississippi.

Thirdly, I also appoint my brother Stephen Douglass and my friend Passmore Hoopes Executors of all my estate real and personal lying and being in the State of Louisiana.

In witness whereof I have hereunto set my hand and seal this Twenty Fourth day of November One thousand eight hundred and thirty seven.

James Douglass (Seal)

Signed sealed and delivered in the presence of us who have subscribed in the presence of each other.

William Finley
Gabriel House
Rob L. Brenham
Jas Chamberlain

Proven in Probate Court Claiborne Co. Miss. December 26th, 1837.

JOHN GRAVES WILL

I, John Graves, do make this my last will and testament.

Impremis I give and devise to my brother, Thomas Graves, the following property to wit: the Tavern and property attached in the town of Brandon purchased by me in partnership with John Shields Forty acres of land in or near the town of Brandon known as the Garvin Spring tract. A lot of ground in the town of Jackson purchased by Caldwell and Miller. A tract of land containing four hundred acres more or less purchased by Col. John Blair in the County of Madison.

To have and to hold the interest which I have in Law or Equity in and to the same to my said brother Thomas Graves, his heirs and assigns forever, in trust never the less to have the same for my brother James Graves and my sister Catharine till the youngest of them shall arrive at twenty one years of age and then to convey the same to them share and share alike their heirs and assigns forever, and until and up to the time they arrive of age as aforesaid to manage and control the said property to the best advantage and out of the profits thereof to educate and support my said brother and sister.

Item I give to my said brother Thomas Graves the control and management of a lot of Irish whisky which is now on the way from Ireland to this place and which whisky belongs to myself and all others my brothers and sisters and whenever my said brother and sisters apply for their proportion of the proceeds of said whisky it is my wish and will that in the division that my said brother Thomas have my share or portion. The rest and residue of my estate, real personal and mixed I give to my said brother, Thomas Graves forever and I appoint my said brother Thomas Graves Executor of this my last will and testament.

In testimony whereof I hereunto set my hand and seal this 17th day of September 1836.

John Graves (seal)

Signed sealed published and delivered in the presence of

Rob Hughes
Wm. H. Young
John Lacy

Filed Sept. Term 1836.

WILL OF ANN GIBSON

In the Name of God Amen

I Ann Gibson of the County of Claiborne and State of Mississippi being in perfect mind and memory and far advanced in life and allowing that it is appointed for all persons once to die have therefore thought proper to make and publish this to be my last will sentiment and testament hereby revoking and dissembling all other former wills or bequeaths whatever. First after resigning my soul into the hands of him who gave it and my body to be decently buried by my Executors and consigning my worldly goods to which it has been pleasing to God to bless me I give and bequeath as follows to wit: First to my daughter Martha Miller I give and bequeath the one half of all my negro slaves (to be justly equally divided) to have and to hold during her natural life and afterwards it is my will and desire that said negroes go to and descend to the heirs of the said Martha Miller's body begotten forever. Secondly to my Granddaughter Martha Ann Gentry and to my Grandson William Fletcher Gentry jointly I give and bequeath forever the remaining half of all my negro slaves said half of my negro slaves to be equally divided between my said Granddaughter Martha Ann Gentry and my said Grandson William Gentry by my Executors and it is further my will and desire and qualifying clause to this my second devise and said second devise to my said Granddaughter Martha Ann Gentry and my said Grandson

William Fletcher Gentry is upon the following conditions and provision first that my daughter Rody B-Gentry is to have support and maintenance during her natural life out or the proceeds and profits of the negro property allotted willed and bequeathed to my said Granddaughter Martha Ann Gentry and my said Grandson William Fletcher Gentry to be allowed and paid to her by my Executor during her natural life and it is further my will and desire that my Executors have the management and control of said property above willed and bequeathed to my said Granddaughter Martha Ann Gentry and to my Grandson William Fletcher Gentry until they arrive at age. Thirdly to my grandsons Gade and Samuel Guin, Stephen and Henry Middleton I give and bequeath my negro man Garrison to be equally divided among my grandsons by my Executors after first selling said negro for that purpose said grandchildren to receive their portions of the proceeds of said negro as they become of age respectively. Fourthly to my Granddaughter and Grandson Martha Ann Gentry and William Fletcher Gentry I give and bequeath all my right and title to the land where I now live forever that is to such part or portion of said land as I hold in my own right and not as dower of my deceased husband to be held and managed by my Executors for said Granddaughter and Grandson until they become of lawful age and lastly it is my will and desire that all the rest and residue and remainder of my personal estate goods and chattels of what kind and nature soever to be sold by my Executors and out of the proceeds thereof all my just debts to be paid and the balance and remainder after the payments of my just debts I will and bequeath to my daughter Martha Miller and my Granddaughter Martha Ann Gentry and my Grandson William Fletcher to be equally divided first by my Executors and they the said Martha Miller to take one half and the said Granddaughter and Grandson the other half equally between them to be paid to them when they become of age by my Executors and I do hereby nominate and appoint Parmenas Briscoe, Claude Gibson and Erastus Lumm Executors to this my last Will sentiment and testament In testimony whereof I have hereunto set my hand and seal this the eleventh day of September Anno domini 1827.

her
Ann x Gibson (Seal)
mark

Signed sealed published and delivered by the above named Ann Gibson to be her last will and testament in the presence of us who have hereunto subscribed our names as witnesses in the presence of the testatrix.

I. B. Thrasher
Daniel Greenleaf
Thomas B. Magruder

Filed for probate in Claiborne Co. Feb. 16, 1840
William Davis, Recorder.

JOHN GOOCH'S WILL

South Carolina
Chester District

In the name of God Amen, I, John Gooch planter of the District of Chester and State aforesaid being of sound mind and memory do make and ordain this my last will and testament in the manner following viz: 1st I give and bequeath to my son William Gooch negroes Will & Jacob which negroes is now in his possession also Chloe & Rueben her husband and the future increase of the female salve from the time of the execution of this will and one thousand dollars in money to make up the inequality in his lot of slaves six hundred dollars of which sum has been paid him. 2nd I give and bequeath to my son Henry H. Gooch, Richmond & Alik already received by him also Fountain & Fanny and six hundred dollars which sum he has already received and the future increase of the female sales.

3rd I give and bequeath to my daughter Nancy R. Hammond, Moses & Ann which has been received by them and disposed of also Mariah and her increase now in her possession also Mary and Betsy and Two hundred dollars in money also the future increase of the female slaves from the execution of these presents the whole for her sole and separate use and benefit and not liable for the debts of her husband, and at her death to her child or children as may be then living the child or children of child to represent this presents. 4th I give and bequeath to my daughter Margaret S. Anderson, Sarah and her present and future increase Daniel & Jane now in her possession also Hannah and one hundred dollars in money and Peter and the future increase of the female salve from the execution of this will and foregoing divises and bequeath is for her sole and separate use and benefit and not liable for the debts of her husband and at her death to such of her children then living and in case she should die without child or children then to my Children or grandchildren that may be then living the child or children of my children to represent these presents.

5th I give and bequeath to my daughter, Martha R. Richardson Minerva & Winny Cindy & Worton and the present and future increase in her possession also Sealy and the future increase of the females from the execution of this will this bequeath is for her sole and separate use and benefit and not subject to the debts of her husband for and during her natural life and at her death to such of her children as may then be living and in case she should die without having living children then to my children or grandchildren who may survive her the children of a deceased child to represent these presents.

6th I give and bequeath to my daughter Molsey E. Rea, Pompey Little Mary with her two children Suckey with their future increase now in her possession also Stephen & Nancy and the future increase of the female slaves from the execution of this will. This bequeath is for her sole use and benefit during her life not liable for the debts of her husband and at her death to such of her children that may survive her and should she die without leaving child or children living then to such of my children and grandchildren as may be living at the time of her death the child or children of any deceased child to represent these presents.

7th I give and bequeath Jane Louisa Gooch, Richard China Louisa Margaret and William with present and future increase from the execution of this will one bedstead and suitable bed clothing for such bed at her choice and two hundred dollars in money and the present and future increase of the female sales from the execution of this will this bequest is for her sole use and benefit during her natural life at her death to her child or children who may be living and in case she should die without leaving child or children then to such of my children and grandchildren as may be living the child or children of my deceased child to represent these presents.

8th I give and bequeath to my daughter Eliza Missouri Gooch, Silla Little Reuben Amelia David and Salley and their present and future increase from the execution of this will also one choice bedstead and suitable bed clothing and bed and such articles to be furnished by my executor as I have not got also the sum of two hundred dollars in money this bequest is for her sole and separate use and benefit during her natural life and at her death to her child or children as may be living and in case she should die without leaving child or children living then the child or children of my deceased child to represent these presents.

9th. I give and bequeath to my wife Polly H. Gooch all the property I received by her on our marriage or which I may have received since that time in her right upon this express condition that she claim no part of my estate either dower in my lands or any part or parcel of my estate whatsoever real or personal which I was possessed of at the time of our marriage or which I have acquired since or which I may hereafter acquire this bequeath is in lieu and bar of dower and in case she should refuse to accept of the above provision and claim any part of my estate otherwise disposed of in this testament then the above bequeath to be void and the property so bequeathed there to fall into the residue of my estate and to pass according to a subsequent clause in this will making an equal distribution of my estate among my children.

10th I give and bequeath to my sister Martha Bennett five hundred dollars and to each of her daughters their names not reflected five hundred dollars and Franklin Bennett her son five hundred dollars to be disposed of by my executors that the above persons may receive the interest annually and not consume the principal this cause being discretionary with them hoping that they may do for the best according to the circumstances.

John Gooch

D. G. Stinson
Stephen Williams
Joseph Cortes

11th I give and bequeath to my nephew Hilliard Bud the sum of five hundred dollars on conditions he comes to possess soundness of mind if not and he should live to need the same for support to be applied for that purpose by my executors hereafter named in trust for him and if he should die without needing it or using it any part thereof then the same to be divided among my children according to a subsequent clause disposing of the residue of my estate real and personal.

12th I give and bequeath to my negro Jesse fifty dollars to be paid him in five annual installments and that each of my old slaves namely China Chloe B Reuben Dan'l

B Mary Qey Hannah Sally Nann Putham each be paid twenty dollars to be paid out of their owners except them that are to be sold to be paid by my executors.

13th I give and bequeath to my children namely William C. Gooch, Henry H. Gooch, Nancy R. Hammonds, Margaret Anderson, Martha R. Richardson, Molsey E. Rea Jane A. Louisiana Gooch, Eliza Missouri Gooch and Charlotte Melisse Gooch the remainder of my slaves to be equally divided among them and if any of my children depart this life before me then that part which any one of my children would be entitled to the same to go to the child or children of such child then that portion be equally divided among my surviving children and grand children the child or children of a child to represent these presents the different bequest mentioned to my daughters in this clause are so given and bequeathed to them that they may have the sole use and benefit of the same at the same time it is given that my executor have the sole right to retain and keep the same in trust for them according to the interest and meaning of this my will or secure the same to the best advantage.

14th I direct institute and empower my executors to sell on such terms as he may deem best all the rest of my property both real and personal.

15th I charge my debts and pecuniary legacies be paid out of the money on hand and debts due me and in case the same should not be sufficient then upon the sale of my lands.

16th I give and desire after my debts and pecuniary legacies are paid that the money remaining from debts due as sales of my personal and real estate as before directed to be sold that the same be equally divided among my children.

17th I further will and ordain that should any of my children or their husbands set up any claim either in law or equity against my estate or any account whatever such child or children are to take no part of my estate and that part hereunto bequeathed are to be held and retained by my executor in trust for the child or children of such child and in case such should die without leaving issue living then to my other children and grandchildren the child or children of the deceased child to represent these presents.

18th I give and bequeath to my son Henry H. Gooch one thousand dollars out of the residue of my estate for his services in the execution of this last will and testament.

Lastly I do hereby constitute and appoint my son Henry H. Gooch executor of this my last will and testament and I do hereby revoke all former wills made by me at any time and do declare the foregoing to be my last will and testament the same being contained in two sheets of paper having subscribed on each paper in the presence of subscribing witnesses who also subscribe their names. In testimony whereof I have hereunto set my hand and seal this 29th day of January 1840.

John Gooch (Seal)

Witnesses
D. G. Stinson
Stephen Williams
Joseph Cortes

CODICIL

Whereas I John Gooch of Chester District have made and duly executed my last will and testament in writing having date 29th day of January 1840 and thereby given and bequeathed to my wife Polly H. Gooch all the property I received by her on our marriage or which I may receive since that time in her right, now I do hereby give and bequeath Polly H. Gooch in addition to what I have already bequeathed to her my carriage and carriage horses namely Jim and Bob I do furthermore devise unto my son Henry H. Gooch one half acre of land to be laid off by him at the grave yard for a burial ground and that the same be kept by him for that purpose only and to be disposed of by him for that use as circumstances may happen or he may think advisable.

John Gooch

March 18 1840.

LAST WILL AND TESTAMENT OF NANCY GILBERT

In the Name of God Amen-I Nancy Gilbert knowing the uncertainty of life make this my last Will and Testament, first I bequeath to my son William all my real estate (except five acres around the graveyard to be used for a burying ground) and the following named negroes Cunch, Bob, Arnstreet, Len, Nat, Hester, Aggy, Milly, Flora, Liza, Indy, Vilet, Anna, Hannah and John and all my personal property except the under named. If my son William should die without a body heir then the landed property to be equally divided between Samuel King's four children under named.

Secondly I give and bequeath to Samuel King's four children to wit Albert Milton Gilbert King, Emily Ann Minerva, Laura Jane Amelia and Olivia Mary Elizabeth King the following property negroes to wit: Plato, Abram, Rachel, Easter, Christian, George, Patience, Charity, Clarenda Jemmima, Lette, Letha, Phillis, Sopha, Lucy and Selah to be equally divided between the above mentioned children when they become of age and five hundred dollars for the schooling of the above children likewise the negroes I give above to my son William if he dies without a body heir they are to be divided equally between the four children mentioned in the Will.

Thirdly I appoint William Foster and Thomas Foster Executors to this my Last Will and Testament revoking all others.

Witness my hand and seal this the 20th Sept. 1827.

Nancy Gilbert (Seal)

In the presence of
William Foster
Mary Collins
Elizabeth Foster

Filed for probate in Adams County, Mississippi Nov 27th, 1827.

WILL OF ANTHONY GLASS

In the Name of God Amen! I Anthony Glass of the County of Warren State of Mississippi being weak in body but of sound and disposing mind and knowing that it is appointed unto all men once to die and knowing also the uncertainty of the time when the event may happen and being desirous to dispose of my worldly affects while an opportunity remains I do therefore I do make publish and declare this to be my last will and testament hereby revoking all former bequests or dispositions of my property and first I recommend my soul to God who in his mercy gave it and my body I desire to be decently interred in such place as my wife Helen may select. Secondly I give and bequeath unto my dear wife Helen all manner of my property real and personal during her natural life and for that period to hold possess and enjoy the same as perfectly and entirely as the same can be had and enjoyed. Thirdly I desire and will that all and singular the property real and personal which I acquired by marriage with my wife Helen after her death shall go and belong to George Rapolge my brother in law and his heirs forever and I do hereby declare that this portion of my property shall after the death of my wife be so disposed of. Fourthly after the death of my wife I give to my brother James Glass and his heirs a house and lot in the Town of Vicksburg on the corner of Second East and Walnut Streets now occupied by Dr. Lewis, the same being a Brick Building. Fifthly I will and desire that after the death of my wife all the residue of my property except that portion already disposed of both real and personal shall be divided in the following manner to wit: Equally between my brother

James Glass and his heirs, Frances, James, Mary, and Augustus Glass, children of my uncle Andrew Glass and their heirs William and Eliza Bittner and their heirs, Mary, Jane, John and Eliza Kirkwood being the three children of my sister, Mary Kirkwood and their heirs. This disposition not to take effect until after the death of my wife and then each to take share and share alike. Sixthly I will and desire that all my just debts be paid as soon as possible out of such funds as my Executrix may be able to appropriate to that purpose. Seventhly I hereby appoint my wife Helen Executrix of this my last Will and Testament and particularly require and desire her to take care of my sister Elizabeth Whittington during her life.

Anthony Glass (Seal)

Signed and sealed in the presence of
William Richardson
Chauncy Goodrich
W. L. Sharkey

LAST WILL AND TESTAMENT OF MARY GILBERT

In the Name of God Amen—I Mary Gilbert of the County of Adams and State of Mississippi being weak in body but sound of mind and memory do make and ordain this to be my last Will and Testament in manner following to wit Item 1 I commend my soul to Almighty God that gave it and my body to be buried in a decent manner by my Executor hereinafter named.

Item 2 I give and bequeath to my nephew Albert Milton Gilbert King one negro boy named Dennis when he shall arrive at the age of twenty one years Item It is my will and desire that all of the rest and residue of my personal property consisting of cash that I may have at the time of my death debts, dues, negroes stock of every kind after my just debts and funeral expenses are paid shall be valued by three disinterested persons appointed by my executor and the amount thereof divided into three equal parts One part thereof I give and bequeath to my mother Nancy Gilbert. One part thereof I give and bequeath to my brouther William Gilbert and the other part I give to the children of Samuel King to wit, Albert Milton Gilbert King, Emily Ann Minerva King, Laura Jane Amelia King and Olivia Mary Elizabeth King. Item I give and bequeath all my negroes hereafter named to my mother Nancy Gilbert and my brother William Gilbert to wit: One negro woman named Mariah and Chito Sarah one woman named Rose and Chito Kitty Harriet Susan Milly and John provided my said mother and brother shall pay over to my executor to be laid in bank stock for the benefit of the said four children of Samuel King and for their schooling the one part of the valuation herein mentioned and bequeathed to said children and in case the same should not be paid at the time of the valuation then they shall pay interest thereon until paid which shall be applied to the schooling of said children aforesaid.

Item It is my will and desire that at the death of my mother and brother or either of them the said negroes shall go to invest in the survivor and the said children of Samuel King to be divided equally one half to said survivor and other half to said children and at the death of both my mother and brother then I give and bequeath the whole of said negroes to the said children of Samuel King and to their heirs and assigns forever. Item I have constituted and appointed my uncle William Foster Executor of this my Last Will and Testament revoking all others Hereby ratify this to be my Last Will and Testament this 26th Day of January 1826.

Mary Gilbert (Seal)

Signed Sealed Published and delivered in presence of

B. R. Grayson

A- Covington

John C. Burruss

Filed for probate in Adams County, Mississippi July 24, 1826.

LAST WILL AND TESTAMENT OF WILLIAM GILBERT

In the name of God Amen I William Gilbert of the County of Adams and State of Mississippi, Planter, and of sound mind and memory do make and ordain this to be my Last Will and Testament in manner following to wit

I give to my nephew Albert Milton Gilbert King ninety acres of land which I bought of James Bisland and after my just debts are paid I give to Albert Milton Gilbert King and three sisters to them and their heirs to be equally divided between them all of my property the property to be kept in the hands of my under named Executor and given to the children as they become of age to wit Albert Milton Gilbert King, Emily Ann Minerva, Laura Jane Amelia and Olivia Mary Elizabeth King but if I should have a body heir before my death then this will to be null and void. I have constituted and appointed my uncle William Foster my Executor of this my Last Will and Testament revoking all others hereby ratifying this to be my last Will and Testament this the 16th day of October 1829.

William Gilbert (Seal)

In presence of witnesses

A. D. Cobler
Robert Davidson
Emanuel Rogillio

Filed for probate in Adams Co. December 29th, 1829.

ABRAM GREEN'S WILL

In the name of God Amen I Abram Green of the county of Claiborne State of Mississippi being in bad health but sound in mind do constitute ordain and appoint the following as my last will and Testament, to Wit:

1st I give my son, John D. Green his executors administrators and assigns forever Negroes John, Amy and Frank.

2nd I give and bequeath unto my son Andrew I. Green in like manner negroes Tarleton, Eveline and Peyer the child of Tarleton and Eveline, Flora, and Peter the father of Eveline who is to be taken care of by my son as long as he lives.

3rd I give and bequeath to my son Abram Asbury Green in like manner Negroes Rutland, Sina, March and Minda.

4th I give and bequeath unto my daughter Martha Green Negroes, Hannah, Maria Albery and Anderson.

5th I give and bequeath unto the infant my wife is now ensient or pregnant with Negroes Lucy, Charles, Malinda and Washington to have and hold in the same manner (as well as my daughter Martha her share) as my sons afforementioned to Wit to them their Executors administrators and assigns forever.

6th I give and bequeath to my wife Ann B Green in like manner and to be disposed of at her will and pleasure in any manner she sees proper Negroes George, Mimas, Leander and Louis and also my right title or claim in any manner whatsoever that I may have in the property of my said wife belonging to her before marriage confirming the same to her in all respects. I also bequeath to her my Gig and riding horse in like manner.

7th Whereas I have heretofore given my son Jefferson Green the Tract of land on which he now resides and also a number of negroes to advance him in life and whereas I have not yet made him a deed for said land and negroes If it should happen that I die before executing proper conveyance then it is my express will that he receive the tract of land and Negroes as his full share of my Estate and that he have as good title to the same as tho I had made and executed a deed to him for the same in Fee Simple.

8th It is my will and intention that all my Real and personal property of every description shall be kept together until my just debts are paid but if my Executors should find it necessary to sell any part of my Estate or they should deem it the advantage thereof generally then my wish is that my real property or such part thereof as they shall think proper should be in preference to selling any part of my personal property and it is my further wish that such part of my real property as is not cleared out of the Land office should be paid for at as early a period as possible consistant with the interest of the whole estate.

9th I give and bequeath unto my wife, Ann B. Green all my real property and stock thereon of every description together with the appurtenances during her natural life but if the Executors should consider that the interest of my estate calls for a sale then they have full power to do so in that event. I expressly require and charge them to provide a comfortable place of residence for my said wife and after her death and the payment of my just debts the whole to be divided between my children (with the exception of Jefferson who is already provided for) if it can be done to advantage, if not then the whole to be sold and the proceeds to be equally divided among them as aforesaid.

10th In the event of any of my children particularly provided for in this will losing any part of the share of personal property devised to them (by death or otherwise) before they come to the possession of the said share, then the said share be made up to them in the division of my Real Estate when divided or if sold in money agreeable to the relative value of said slaves as they now stand and if executors deem it necessary to sell any real property rather divide the same then they are authorized to give such credits as they may think advisable.

11th It is my will that in the event of the death of any of my children herein particularly provided for that his or her share shall be equally divided among the survivors provided they have not received the share bequeathed to them and provided that said child shall die before he or she arrives at the age of twenty one but after their marriage then provided also he or she shall die without issue.

12th It is my will that when any of my children come of age or receive their share aforesaid that they receive from my estate a Bed and furniture.

13th It is my will and intention that the children of my wife by her second marriage be supported and educated in all respects as my own and my sons John D. Green, Andrew I Green and Abram Green I wish to receive the best education that circumstances will permit. So as not to sell or encumber their shares of property left them by me John and Andrew I leave in charge and under the directions of my executors and if they should deem it advisable to bring them home from school in Tennessee where they now are, my wish is that they should place them in some active employment and not permit them to remain at home in idleness. My youngest son Abram I leave in charge of and under the directions of my wife Ann B. Green in all respects both as to person and property.

14th Whereas my niece Matilda Carpenter has kindly taken into her charge my daughter Martha Green it is my wish that she should still continue to her that motherly care and attention after my death that she has heretofore done and after the payment of my just debts it is my wish that Horace Carpenter should take into his charge and manage to the best advantage the share of my estate that I have left to my said daughter until she comes of age or marries whichsoever should first happen then to be given up to her or her husband.

15th I direct my present crop now on hand to be sold as soon as advisable and the proceeds to be applied particularly to the payment of my debts due Offutt and Cronley and Horace Carpenter and also the stock of provisions now on hand shall not be taken into account in the inventory but be applied as always intended to the support of the planation.

16th I appoint as my Executor my wife, Ann B. Green, and as my Executors Cornelius Harring, Thomas Gale and Benjamin Hughes and having entire faith and confidence in their integrity it is my will that no security of any kind be exacted from them in the administering of my estate.

Lastly I hereby expressly revoke and annull all wills, parts of wills and codicils heretofore executed by me declaring this to be my only will and Testament, In testimony whereof I have hereunto set my hand and seal this the 13th day of March Eighteen Hundred and Twenty Six in the presence of the undersigned witnesses and they signing in my presence.

A. Green (Seal)

Witnesses present

Thomas Farrar
John Robertson
Richard L. Howell

WILLIAM HAZLIP'S WILL

State of Mississippi
Wilkinson County

Be it known that I, William Hazlip, of County and State above written being sound in mind do by the Grace of God make this my Last Will and Testament. viz

To my Beloved Wife, Rebecca Hazlip that my Executors secure to her all the property she was possessed of in her own right at the time of our marriage and for the love and respect I bear her, I bequeath her the sum of Five Hundred Dollars.

To John Hazlip I bequeath the sum of Fifty Dollars

To Nancy Wood One Hundred Dollars

To Charlotte Galtney One Hundred Dollars

To Mary Rabb One Hundred Dollars

To Eviline Hazlip One Hundred Dollars

Should there not be in my possession at the time of my demise money to amount willed and bequeathed as above to my beloved wife and children the above named sums are to be paid from the net proceeds of the cotton crop after deducting the currect expenses of the year or years as the same shall require. And I also bequeath all the property real and personal of which I may be in possession at the time of my death unto my youngest child Samuel Hazlip after paying the debts I may owe at the time, in case he should die in minority the property is to be divided equally between my children and wife and I do appoint Messrs Wiley M. Wood, John Hazlip and Joseph Galtney Executors of this my last will and testament. And it is also my will that the property real and personal of which I may be in possession of at the time of my death be kept together and not sold til my son Samuel W. Hazlip (should the Lord in his mercies so will arrive at the age of twenty one years) in case of his death the property is to be divided as above stated. And I do so also will that my beloved wife Rebecca Hazlip have her support from the property willed as above to my son Samuel W. Hazlip so lons as she remains unmarried, in case of her marriage she will be paid the amount as above willed, the negro boy Jack now in my possession is the property of the heirs of Thomas Holmes, Decd, he being purchased with the money belonging to them.

Signed and Sealed this 19th day of September A. D. Eighteen Hundred and Thirty Seven.

Wm Hazlip (Seal)

In presence of:

John Currier
John Alrxr Tyler
John S. Holt.

Codicil 1st

I do hereby appoint Messrs. Wiley M. Wood, and John Hazlip as Guardians of my son Samuel W. Hazlip with instructions to put him to such schools in this State or if none advantageous in a Northern State as shall afford him a good and sound education for the transaction of any business as may come before him as an unprofessional man and that the expenses necessarily accrueing thereby, be paid out of the proceeds of the property as herein bequeathed to him after acquiring his education which may be accomplished probably at the age of sixteen years, I would respectfully suggest the propriety of placing him on the farm as manager under the close supervision of his Guardians but if his natural talents and abilities and his inclination and the amount of his property should be such as to warrant giving him a professional education it is left discretionary with his guardians.

Given under my hand signed and sealed together with the body of the will this 19th day of September A. D. Eighteen Hundred and Thirty Seven.

Wm. Hazlip (Seal)

In presence of

J. M. Currier
John Alexr Tyler
John S. Holt

Filed for probate March 11th 1845.

WILL HARMON'S WILL

In the Name of God Amen, I William Harmon of the County of Claiborne and State of Mississippi being feeble and weak in body but strong and firm in mind do hereby make declare and publish this my last will and testament.

1st it is my wish that all my debts be paid then my property to be divided into two equal parts after taking out the following negroes viz Maria a woman, Winslow and Anderson her sons and Sarah Ann and Eliza her daughters and it is my will and request that my Executors or one of them take the above named woman and children to Ohio or some free State and have them made free so that they can enjoy all the rights and privileges of all free people of their color then bring them back to this State or leave the children there to receive a common English education and the boys some useful trade such as they may wish to learn and my executors approve of.

2 Onlye. It is my will and request that all of my property both real and personal be sold and divided into two equal parts or remain unsold and be divided in equal parts as my executors may think best. Then on an equal division of all my property dividing it into two equal parts I give and bequeath one half of my estate to Mary Jane Harmon, daughter of my brother Stephen Harmon to have and to hold the same forever.

3rd. I give and bequeath unto my executors the other half of my property for the sole benefit of Maria and her children, Winslow and Anderson, Sarah Ann and Eliza to be raised and educated in such manner as my executors may deem best for their good.

4th It is my will and request when the above named children become of age that the one half of my property left them and their mother be divided into five equal parts or into as many parts as there will be of them living and it is my will and request that my Executors make the same over to them to have and to hold the same they, their heirs executors, administrators or assigns forever.

5th I hereby nominate constitute and appoint my brother Stephen Harmon and William Dotson both of this

County and State my executors to this my last Will and Testament.

William Harmon

Signed, sealed and declared and published the above named William Harmon the Testator in the presence of us who at his request and in his presence have subscribed our names as Witnesses this 23rd day of August in the year of our Lord One Thousand Eight Hundred and Thirty Seven.

D. H. McIntyre
Alexr McGilvary
Wm Kinnison

Proven in Probate Court of Claiborne County, Mississippi June 25th A. D. 1838.

WILL OF MOSES HALL

Clinton, May 26, 1835

Whereas I am about to leave the State of Mi. in bad health but anticipating I may soon be called from time into eternity and being of sound mind and memory wishing to make some final arrangements of my property in case of my death I by these presents appoint William S. Jones and Catherine Hall my joint Executors in the event of my dissolution, requesting them to keep my property together till the debts be paid off and the children become of age or the daughters marry with a view to increase the amt of the estate and so to manage the whole effects as though they were their own; to borrow money on the pledge of the estate or do any act that I, myself, might do were I alive.

Furthermore in this my Last Will and Testament I direct that my Executors shall pay my aged mother for her support One Hundred dollars annually during her natural life.

Given under my hand and seal this 28th day of May 1835.

Moses Hall (Seal)

In presence of
C. Crawford
E. R. Porter

Codicil

I furthermore appoint John Kellogg my Executor in conjunction with William S. Jones and Catherine Hall to have the same powers that they have. Given under my hand and seal this 15th day of February 1836.

Moses Hall (Seal)

In Presence of
William S. Johnson
J. J. Jones

Will on file in Warren Co. Mississippi

In the name of God Amen

I Walter R. Johnson of the County of Madison, State of Mississippi do in my last Will and Testament give unto Newton L. Haxall two hundred dollars a year, provided there should be that much made clear of expenses the balance of the money be made clear by the farm clear of expenses I give unto Juliana Copeland of Virginia her lifetime and at her death to be given to her children. I do bequeath at her death my whole estate to her children in case any of the children should die I wish their estate be given to the balance of the children and not to their father. I also give to Henry, Eliza's child, his freedom. I also wish him put to the carpenter trade until he is twenty years of age. I want the tract of land which I purchased of H Billingsley and the improvements near the river sold the first of January Eighteen Hundred and Thirty One on a credit of one two and three years I also want the farm known by the name of the Prairie kept up by the whole of my estate I also which a cotton gin with an inclined wheel be built on my Paririe farm I also wish the money that I have in Virginia to go to the use of paying my debts and the balance to the use of my farm. I do leave James Cobb of Hinds County State of Mississippi and John H. Cole of Madison County State of Mississippi my Executors November 9th 1829

Signed W. R. Johnson

Attest

Jos H. Carmichale
Carney Slay
William Thompson
Anthony Byrne

LAST WILL AND TESTAMENT OF W. R. JOHNSON

Intending to leave the State of Virginia in a few days and also being in a bad state of health and believing it correct and that I have not only a legal but moral right to dispose of what property may have come into my possession by any means I now constitute this my last will and testament to wit-

First in case of my death I wish my plantation in County of Charles, City, called West Point to be sold to the highest bidder on a credit of one and two years the money for which when collected as well as all other monies due me to be paid out as fast as collected in United States Bank stock—

2nd The interest of my said monies above mentioned I will to my half brother Newton L. Haxall during his natural life but no longer.

3rd I also will to my half brother N. L. Haxall the clear profits from the hire of my negroes. I state clear profits because the profits of some will be necessary to support the others.

4th After the death of N. L. Haxall I give the property of my estate to Mrs. Juliana Copeland formerly Juliana Ruffin but in no case to be under the management of Carter Copeland or to be liable for any of his transactions but merely the income to be paid annually to Mrs. Copeland.

5th After the death of Juliana Copeland I give and bequeath the whole of my Estate to the natural heirs of the body of Juliana Copeland by her present husband but the father in no case to heir from the death of a child.

6th In case of the death of Juliana Copeland without her having a natural heir of her body by Copeland or any other person I then give my whole estate to the children of William and Jane Duprey of County

7th I appoint John B. Bland and William J. Parsons my executors to qualify without Security Given under my hand and seal the 20th day of December in the year of our Lord Jesus Christ Eighteen Hundred and Twenty Seven.

W. R. Johnson

WILL OF OBADIAH JONES

I, Obadiah Jones of the County of Limestone State of Alabama being weak of body but of sound mind and memory and knowing that it is appointed of all men to die do make and ordain this my last will and testament hereby revoking and annulling all wills heretofore made by me. In primis I constitute and appoint my beloved wife Elizabeth Sole Executrix of this my last will and testament with full power and authority to carry into execution all of my - - - in the manner hereinafter named. Secondly, it is my will that my said Executrix shall immediately after my death take possession of all of my estate both real and personal and after selling so much as shall be necessary to pay all my debts that she continue in the possession of the remainder until some one of my children shall marry or arrive at the age of twenty one years. That my said Executrix shall keep together all my slaves and that they be employed in such manner that she may think most conducive to the increase and improvement of said estate and that of the proceeds of all my property of whatever description she shall use whatever is necessary for the raising supporting and educating of my children. Also in Order that my said Executrix may have the means of increasing and improving of such property during the minority of my children I give and bequeath her full and ample power during the time to lease rent or sell any of my real estate or purchase any other tracts or parcels of land and make thereon such improvements as she may deem advisable for all which she is authorized to pay from the proceeds of said property. As it is my earnest wish that my children should be well educated I will that my said Executrix should reserve a sufficiency of the annual proceeds of said property for that purpose. It is also my will that so soon as any one of my children shall marry or become of age that a valuation shall be made of all the property then in the hands of my said Executrix except such as is herein after mentioned. And that the said child so marrying or becoming of age shall receive of my said Executrix a portion of my said property equal in value to one child part of all said property estimating in said apportionment a portion of equal value to each of my said children then living and to my wife Elizabeth. That the child marrying or becoming of age shall nominate one person who together with one to be nominated by my said Executrix shall have full power to make the valuation and lay off the portion as aforesaid. That my Executrix after paying off each portion as aforesaid shall keep together all the balance of the property for the improvement and increase thereof and for the support and education of the remaining children until all marry or become of age when such one shall receive a portion laid off in like manner and so on successively until all my children shall mary or become of age. That in case that one of my children should die before marrying or becoming of age and after a portion had been laid off for the one so dying in the manner above mentioned and those to whom portions had already allotted shall receive and equal share of the same.

I also give and bequeath the tract of land on which my family now resides together with so much more land as shall be added thereto at the land sales and the following negroes viz Lavina her children Joshua, Tom, Sally, Nancy, Davy, Hannah and Mary and their increase to my said wife Elizabeth during her natural life or widowhood and then to my children their heirs and assigns forever, provided however that my said wife shall have power by will or otherwise to designate to which of my said children said property shall belong at the death or in the event of her being married. It is further my wish in order to make the place in which I now live a comfortable home for my wife Elizabeth that the proceeds of my property be applied to the purchase of so much more land adjoining it as she may think necessary. Witness my hand and seal this 13th day of May 1825.

Obadiah Jones (Seal)

Signed sealed and delivered in the presence of

Dan Coleman
J. Y. Cummings
David R. Scott

Produced and proven in Orphans Court in Limestone Co. Alabama July 23rd 1825.

WILLIAM H. LAWSON WILL

In the Name of God Amen! I, Williams H. Lawson a citizen of Washington County, in the State of Mississippi, being temporarily at the City of Louisville in the State of Kentucky, of lawful age and of sound mind and disposing memory being in infirm and having in view the uncertainty of life do hereby make and declare my last will and testament as follows

First It is my will and desire that all of my debts and liabilities shall be paid and discharged as soon as can be conveniently done.

Second It is my will and desire that all the residue of my estate after payment of my just debts shall be divided among and held by my wife, Frances Ann Lawson, and my children Samuel, Frances and Willhelmina, in the shares and proportions provided for in the laws of Mississippi regulating the distribution of the estates of intestate decedents, at such time and in such manner as my executor hereinafter mentioned may judge best for the interest of the devisees. And it is my further wish and desire and I hereby direct that whenever partition shall be made of my estate as before mentioned the guardians who may be appointed to take charge of the respective interests of my said children shall be required to give sufficient security for the faithful performance of the duty required of them and that they invest their respective shares in a safe and secure manner so as to provide the means of supporting my said children, if possible without diminishing the principal of their several proportions of my estate.

Third It is my will and desire and I hereby invest my Executor hereinafter named or any other who may be appointed should he fail to act with ample power for that purpose that my interest in the plantation and property attached thereto jointly owned by William Hunt and myself situated in Washington County, Mississippi should be controlled and managed by my said Executor as he may judge best for the interest of my family and should it be thought best or become necessary by the terms of the contract between said Hunt and myself that the sale of my insterest therein should be made that my Executor shall have power to make said sale and to execute to the purchaser or purchasers good and sufficient deeds of conveyance for the same and to do and perform every act which may be necessary to a full execution of this power.

I hereby constitute and appoint William Tompkins of the City of Louisville in the State of Kentucky Executor of this my Last Will and Testament and it is my will and desire and I hereby request that he may be permitted to qualify without being required to give security for his acts as such.

Done at Louisville, Kentucky this 19th September 1854 Signed sealed and acknowledged in Presence of

S. C. Cox
J. A. Miller
T. Joyner

William H. Lawson (Seal)
Signed at his request
By W Tompkins

LAST WILL AND TESTAMENT OF LORENZO LATHAM

I Lorenzo Latham of the County of Madison, State of Mississippi of sound and disposing mind do make and ordain this my Last Will and Testament, first I direct that all of my just debts be paid by the collection of debts, sale of property. Next I will and direct that my negro man Joe Hudson be set free immediately after my decease and that one hundred dollars be paid to him to defray his expenses to some free State. Next I will and bequeath to me wife Louisa, my negro woman, Susan and her two children to wit Tanner and Daniel, Also give to my wife Louisa such furniture as she may select to the value of four hundred dollars, also my gold diamond ring, also one half of my silver and china ware. I give to my brother Hervey my fine diamond breast pin, and my gold head cane I give to my friend James Hunter and I direct that all my other property both real and personal be divided between my wife, Louisa and my three children, Richard, Edward and Sarah, according to the laws of the State of Mississippi and lastly I appoint my wife Louisa and my Brother Hervey Executors of this my Last Will and Testament.

Witness my hand and seal this the 24th day of April Eighteen Hundred and Forty.

Lo. Latham

Witnesses

N. Oldham
James H. Greenlee
Wm. R. Carradine

Filed for Probate Madison Co. Miss. March 25th, 1843.

WILL OF CHARLES LAND

State of Mississippi
Holmes County

June 15th 1834

This is left to my family as my last will and wish that my estate may be managed in this way but my wife and son Thomas shall have the same power that I had myself in my lifetime to sell convey the title to any part of my land on either side of the river and all of it if they think it best and the (illegible) to the payment of my just debts and all the negroes is to be kept till my son Thomas Bell comes of age or longer if they think proper and all the proceeds applied to the payment of my debts till they are settled then the balance to go to defray the expenses of the family. Rutherford and Martha is to be educated out of the estate and then the balance to be divided equally between the three children, Thomas Martha and Rutherford with the exception of Joseph, Daniel and Puss, my wife to have them her lifetime and the land which I now live on containing 160 acres at her death it is to be equally divided between the three children. My wish is that all of the property may be kept together till Rutherford becomes of age or longer if tha think proper. Now if this property can be sold without the consent of my wife before the time in this instrument set it shall be after that time she then has the (illegible) of Martha and presents till she becomes of age or marries for her benefit to be paid for the best advantage for her. In witness whereof I have hereunto affixed my hand and seal as my last will and testament with this day and year above written.

Charles Land (Seal)

Test Dr. H. Johnson

WILL OF GEORGE LAMBRIGHT

The Last Will and Testament of George Lambright of the State of Mississippi and Copiah County considering the uncertainty of this mortal life and being of sound mind and memory blessed be Almighty God for the same do make and publish this my last will and testament in manner and form following that is to say first I give and bequeath unto my beloved wife, Dorcas Lambright, the whole of my plantation with all my household and kitchen furniture, beds and bed clothes and three negroes that is to say Fany about fifty five years of age Asarish about fourteen years of age and Lida about twelve years of age and one bay mare and four cows and calves and ten heads of hogs and all the farming utensils that she will require and four yews and lams all the above bequeathed to have and to hold during her life and then to be equally divided amongst my lawful heirs and all the rest of my estate to be divided amongst my lawful heirs except the part which shall be coming to my daughter Mary Anding I bequeath to her during her lifetime and then to the lawful heirs of her body and be wholly under the control and guardianship of Martin A. Anding and I do hereby nominate and appoint my son Lewis Lambright and Martin A. Anding my Sole Executors of this my last will and testament hereby revoking all former wills by me made. In witness whereof I have hereunder set my hand and seal this 27th day of March 1835 in presence of

Test) Hugh McLaurin (J. P.))
) Neill Buie) George Lambright (Seal)
) John G. Lofton)

Proved in Probate Court of Copiah Co. Miss. April 27th, 1835.

WILLIAM McCARSON'S WILL

In the name of God Amen, I William McCarson of the County of Desoto in the State of Mississippi being in very feeble health but sound in mind and remembering it is appointed for man to die so make this my last will and testament hereby revoking all others.

First, I commend my soul and body to the God who gave me being

2nd I desire that all my just debts be promptly paid.

3rd I give and bequeath to my beloved wife Malinda J. McCarson the half section of land on which I now live to have and to hold forever with all the appurtenances thereunto belonging.

4th I give to her my said beloved wife my negroes Jane, Adeline, Anthony Alfred and George to have and to hold forever.

5th After the service of five years from my decease it is my desire that arrangements be made as well as the laws of the country will permit for Henry and Hannah to be freed from servitude.

6th I desire that my mills and the lands attached thereto being 1/4 section be sold when circumstances will permit and also any other out land I may have (with such of my stock and perishable property farming utensils and household and kitchen furniture as may not be necessary for the support and maintenance of my beloved wife) be sold and the proceeds of the same with all moneys and claims belonging to me either in notes or accounts I give unto my beloved wife Malinda Jane with the following reservations to wit I give and bequeath unto my nephew David McCarson Five Hundred Dollars. I give and bequeath to my niece Martha Merrill One Hundred Dollars. I give and bequeath unto my sister Sarah Merrill Three Hundred Dollars all to be paid out of the forementioned proceeds and funds. I also desire that Twenty Dollars be paid years to the Indian Missions belonging to or under the control of the Methodist Episcopal Church South during the natural life of my wife and lastly I constitute and appoint my beloved wife Malinda Jane McCarson Executrix of this my last will and testament.

Given under my hand and seal this 29th day of August 1849.

William McCarson (Seal)

Test: Henry K. Wilbourn
Henry Flowers
Robert H. Smith

LAST WILL AND TESTAMENT OF CHARLES McKIERNAN.

In the name of God Amen. I Charles McKiernan of Adams Co. Mississippi Territory, considering the uncertainty of this mortal life and being weak of body but of sound and perfect mind and memory --- Blessed be Almighty God for same, do make and publish this my last Will and Testament, in the manner and form following, that is to say, I do hereby appoint Loe Baker and Samuel Prostlewait of the City of Natchez Executors of this my last Will and Testament.

And I do give and bequeath unto Emeline Stephenson and Caroline Stephenson daughters of Jonothan and Elizabeth Stephenson of said county, One Thousand Dollars each, to be paid into the hands of the said Jonothan Stephenson as soon as the amount can be collected on the bonds now in my possession or in any other way. The residue and remainder of my real and personal estate, goods and chattels of every kind and nature soever, I give and bequeath for the use and support of a Hospital which may at any time hereafter be built in the City of Natchez for the relief of all sick and decrepit persons and it is my will that the whole of my property after paying the aforesaid Two Thousand Dollars and discharging my legal debts shall be let out on interest until there shall be Trustees legally appointed by the Legislature of this Territory to superintend the management of the Hospital aforesaid; then the principal and interest to be paid into the hands of the said Trustees for the sole use of said Hospital. And it is my will that all the notes on hand which are not in my possession shall remain on interest until the Hospital shall be built and Trustees legally appointed to superintend the same, then the amount of said notes with the interest shall be paid into the hands of the Trustees for the sole benefit of the Hospital, it being my will and desire that those persons whose notes on hand I now hold, shall have the use of my property until said Hospital is built and Trustees appointed as aforesaid.

And whereas I have sold unto Edmund Andrews of Adams Co. aforesaid, a certain tract of land on Fairchild's Creek payable in five yearly installments as will appear by an article of agreement between said Andrews and myself and said Andrews having paid me three installments, it is my will and I do hereby direct my Executors to execute unto Edmund Andrews a complete deed for said land and to receive said Andrews notes of hand with security for the payment of the two installments drawing interest after the said installments shall become due, said notes and interest to remain as the other notes of hand in my possession and to be appropriated in the same way. And I do hereby revoke all former wills by me made in witness whereof I have hereunto set my hand and seal this 27th of October in the year of our Lord 1810.

Charles McKiernan (Seal)

Signed, sealed and published and declared by the above named Charles McKiernan to be his last Will and Testament in the presence of us, who at his request have hereunto subscribed our names as witnesses to the same. Mississippi Territory Clerk's office, Adams Co.

The foregoing is a true transcript from Book A. Register of Wills, Folder 60 and proven 13th November 1810.

In witness whereof I have set my hand as clerk of said office--this 22nd December 1812.

--Girault, Register
I. A. Girault,

THE LAST WILL AND TESTAMENT OF WILLIAM MARTIN DECD

In the name of God Amen, This is to certify that I William Martin of Limestone County and State of Alabama being afflicted in body but of perfect mind and memory calling to mind the mortality of my body and knowing it is appointed unto all men once to die do make and ordain this my last will and testament viz first and singularly I give and commend my soul into the hands of Almighty God who gave it and my body I commit to the ground to be burried at the direction of my friends and as it respects my worldly estate I give and dispose of in the following manner I give unto my wife the one third of my property during her natural life and after her death to be equally divided amongst my children—The other two thirds to be equally divided amongst my children when the eldest becomes of age or marries. What money is owing to me and what can be realized from the crop after paying my lawful debts to be laid out in land for the use of my wife and children on the Bigby or its waters. My wife is to remove into the Mississippi state and there give security for the administration of it. She is to keep the property and children as long as she remains a widow and after as long as it is taken good care of and not liked to be wasted as the children comes of age- the use of the property is to raise and school the children - I leave my wife and Samuel A. Edmison Executors and one to be chosen by them after the property is removed to the Tombigbee-

William Martin (Seal)

Signed and sealed in the presence of
Jeffery Murrell
Nancy Murrell

Filed for Probate Monroe Co. Miss April 2, 1827

Samuel A. Edminson and Jane Edminson (formerly Jane Martin, widow and relict of said William Martin, Dec'd) Executrix and Executor.

WILL OF SAMPSON MOUNGER

In the name of God Amen, I Sampson Mounger in the County of Washington, and Mississippi Territory being desirous to settle my affairs on earth- knowing the certainty of death sooner or later being now in perfect mind and memory, first I recommend my soul to God, hoping to attain mercy through our Lord Jesus Christ and then my body to be buried in the dust in a decent manner at the directions of my executors, nothing doubting but I shall receive the same at the general resurrection and as such worldly property as it hath pleased God to indow me with, in the first place the property that I received with my wife Anny I do return to her at my death, with all the increase to will and dispose with as she see cause to whom she pleases myself having no domain against it the Balance of my property to be divided amongst my children after my just debts paid. In witness hereof I have set my hand and affixed my seal this 8th day of May in the year of our Lord 1809.

his
Sampson x Mounger
mark

Signed and sealed in the Presence of
Mathew P. Sturdevant
Luke Patrick
John Lanier

I certify the above to be a true copy from the minutes

James Mayers
Regr. O. C. W. C.

WILL OF WILLIAM McINTYRE

I William McIntyre of the County of Clark, State of Ohio and Town of Springfield being weak in body but of sound and disposing mind and memory and recollecting the uncertainty of this mortal life do make and ordain this my last will and Testament hereby revoking and disallowing former ones by me made.

First, I will that after my decease the expense of my last illness and funeral as well as all others my Just debts be paid out of my Estate by my Executor hereafter named.

Secondly It is my will that there shall not be a sale of my personal nor real estate unless the same shall become really necessary for the payment of just debts but that the whole of the estate be suffered to remain in the hands of my beloved wife Rachel for the benefit of herself and my family until my son William shall arrive at the age of twenty one years at which time there shall be given to him the said William by my executors such part or portion of my estate as they shall judge expedient and afterwards as my children either comes of lawful age or marry I will that they respectfully have such portion or portions out of my Estate as shall be Judged Expedient by my Executors.

Thirdly As I now own seven lots within the Corporation of Springfiled I will that there be given to each of my children one as far as they will go and that there be given to such one of my children as shall not receive a lot an equivalent in other property and that the farm which I now own being the South West Quarter of Section No. 25 Town No. 5 and Range No 10. M R containing one hundred and sixty acres be given and I do hereby give and devise the same to my three sons in addition to their equal proportion with my daughters of the rest of my estate.

Fourthly It is my will that when my youngest child shall arrive at lawful age if my said wife Rachel should then be dead such distributions be made of my estate as to make all my children equal except as above excepted.

But should if my said wife should at that time be living then and in that case distribution shall be made only of such part of my Estate as shall be over and above what may be Judged by my Executors to be necessary for the support and maintenance of my said wife during her natural lifetime and that after her decease so much of my estate as may yet remain shall be distributed among all my children as aforesaid.

Fifthly and lastly I do hereby nominate and appoint my Well Beloved wife Rachel Executrix and my friend Joseph McIntyre and Robert Humphry executors of this my last Will and Testament In Testimony whereof I have hereunto set my hand and seal this 18th day of June A. D. 1827

William McIntyre (Seal)

Signed acknowledged and declared to be the last will of the Testator in the presence of us

Saul Hankle)
R. W. Hirut)
Alexander Ramsey)

Proven in Orhans Court of Covington County, Mississippi the 30th day of December 1830.

WILL OF WILLIS MAGEE

In the Name of God Amen I Willis Magee of Franklin County State of Mississippi, planter, being of health of body and sound mind memory and understanding praise be to God for the same do make this my last will and testament in manner following- I give and bequeath to my beloved wife Asha five negroes to wit Tony, Nancy, Isaac the larger Cherry and Rose, likewise all the stock of any description household and kitchen furniture of what kind soever as also the crop that may be growing at the time of my death or housed on the premises together with all the plantation stock to have hold and enjoy the property above specified during her natural life and after her death to be equally divided among all my sons with the exception hereinafter named with regard to Rose and it is the intent of this my bequest to my wife to enable her to live comfortably during her life to pay all my just debts to board school and clothe the children that are in their minority.

To my son Lewis Magee I give one negro woman named Cherry together with her three children and future increase. I do give to my executors hereinafter named to and for the use and benefit of my three grand children the descendants of my son Jonathan whose names are Needham, Louisa and Frances one negro boy by the name of Samuel and one girl by the name of Delaney. And if the above named grand children die without lawful issue of their bodies, in that event it is my desire that the aforesaid negroes with their posterity be equally divided among my lawful heirs. To my executors in trust for my daughter Penelope I do give one negro by the name of Letty and one boy by the name Cyrus to be equally divided among her children after her death and should her children die without lawful issue the said negroes to revert back to my heirs. To my executors in like manner for the use and benefit of my grand son, Willis Bryd, I give two negroes whose names are as follows to wit Frank and Susan and in case he shall die without an heir lawfully begotten then the aforesaid negroes to revert back to my lawful heirs. To my son Duncan I give and devise one negro boy by the name of Forten and all my land on the South Side of the Creek adjoining Joseph Porter's it being a part of two quarter sections one which I entered the other I purchased from Dan Williams. To Have and to hold to him and his heirs forver. And furthermore it is my desire for them and my executors, are hereby requested to purchase for him in addition to what I have given one other negro of the valuation of six hundred dollars. To my Son William I give one negro boy named Newton and devise to him all my lands lying on the West side of the Homo Chitto River on which there is a small improvement. I also give him one horse bridle and saddle, one bed and furniture. To Have and to hold the said property to him and his heirs forever. To my son Joseph I give one negro named Bob one horse bridle and saddle one bed and furniture. To my son Hugh I give one negro boy called Henry also one horse bridle, and saddle one bed and furniture. To my son Owen H. I give one negro boy Calvin Prance one horse bridle and saddle one bed and furniture. To my son Philip I give three negroes whose names are as follows Maria, Jack and Rose after the death of his mother, to whom I have given a life estate in the said Rose, also one horse bridle and saddle one bed and furniture. All the remainder of my lands I wish to be equally divided between my three sons Joseph Hugh and Owen H. at the death of their mother it being my intention to allow her a life estate in the balance of my land undisposed of. In case any of my negroes that I have left to my wife should become unmanageable my executors have liberty to sell them at public or private sale as they may think most expedient and purchase with the money others in their place My wife is to keep all the property until all my debts are paid- I hereby make nominate and appoint my three sons Lewis, Duncan and Owen H my executors of this my last will and testament and hereby revoking and making void all and every other will and wills at any time heretofore by me made and do declare this to be my last will and testament.

In Witness whereof I have hereunto set my hand and seal this twenty first day of July in the year of our Lord one thousand eight hundred and twenty five.

Signed Sealed declared and published by the above named Willis Magee the testator as and for his last will and testament in the presence of us who at his request and in his presence have subscribed our names as witnesses.

Willis Magee (Seal)

Gabriel Scott
James Harrington
Joseph Scott

THE LAST WILL AND TESTAMENT OF WILLIAM C. MAXWELL, deceased.

I William C. Maxwell of the County of Amite and State of Mississippi being weak in the body, but of sound and disposing mind and understanding, to make and Publish this instrument of writing to be my Last will and testament hereby revoking all former Willis, Codicils and Testaments, by me at any time heretofore made. In manner and form as follows-

Item 1st. It is my will and desire that my Executors pay all my just debts out of the Proceeds of my Estate at as early a day as may be found to be convenient, without injuring the same.

Item 2nd. It is my desire that independant of the common distribution share which may fall to my children in the final distribution of my Estate that the following sum & articles be set apart to them, and each of them, as mentioned in this Item - That is to say - to my son Franklin C. Maxwell, I give and bequeath two hundred and fifty dollars to be paid to, and for him, as he may be educated, also my Rifle Gun to hold in possession by Dr. Alexander F. Dunn for him til he my said son arrives at the age of Fourteen years. Also my saddle horse, saddle & Bridle of the value of one hundred and thirty dollars- and for my Daughter Martha G. Maxwell I give Two hundred dollars- and to my daughter Emily Maxwell I give the sum of Two hundred and fifty dollars to be paid them in and for their Education, also one saddle horse, saddle and Bridle each of the value of one hundred and thirty dollars as they may arrive at the age of eighteen years or marrys. To my Son Willam Carter T. Maxwell I give Four hundred dollars for his Education which may be paid for him as he may be Educated, Also one saddle horse saddle and Bridle of the value of one hundred and thirty dollars-

Item 3rd. To my Beloved wife Martha M. Maxwell I give and bequeath one Saddle horse, saddle and Bridle of the value of one hundred and thirty dollars-

Item 4th. It is then my will that the balance of my Estate be equally divided between my wife Martha M. Maxwell, and Margaret B. Maxwell, Martha G. Maxwell, Franklin C. Maxwell, Emily Maxwell, William C. T. Maxwell and the children of my dec'd daughter Jane E. D. Covington (they my said daughter Janes children totaling the same share that she would have been entitled to were she living and no more) being my two Grand Children.

Item 5th. The property and Estate herein bequeathed to my daughters, are bequeathed to them, for their sole and separate use and to the sole and separate use of them and their heirs of their bodys. And in the event of the death of either of my children without Issue, then their portions, or portions, shall return back to my Estate and be equally divided between my surviving children.

Item 6th. It is expressly understood that, that portion of my Estate which my decend to my two Grand daughters (being the children of my dec'd daughter Jane E. D. Covington) be bequeathed to them for their sole and separate use, and to the sole, and separate use of them and the heirs of their bodys, and in the event of the death of either of them, then the survivor shall inherit the Estate of the dec'd sister and in the event of the death of each of my said Grand Children without Issue, then their portion which was received from me, shall Revert back to the Estate and be equally divided between my sirviving children or their desendants, with this further understanding, that in the final distribution of my Estate my two Grand daughters (being the daughters of my dec'd daughter Jane Covington) is to be charged (with one negro boy called Washington) with the sum of Five hundred dollars as a portion of their distributive shares of my Estate, And the reason of this charge or dedication from them, is that a boy called Washington was taken and appraised as a part of Harbuth Friths Estate which in fact only was a loan by me to my daughter Jane (then Jane E. D. Frith.

Item 7th. In the final distribution of my Estate, I hereby secure to my Beloved wife, Martha M. Maxwell the right of selecting as apart of her distributive Share in my Estate the following negro Slaves viz, a negro woman called Nancy of Dark complexion about thirty years old and her daughter called Sarah about Fifteen years old & of dark complexion and also, that she occupy and enjoy the use of the Plantation on which I now reside, for and during her natural life or widowhood. It is further my will and desire that my Estate be kept together, untill my Eldest child arrives at the age of Twenty one or marries- then to be divided, and each one take his or her share, the balance of the shares to be still kept together by my Executors, untill the next shall arrive at the age of twenty one or marries- and so on untill all my children, shall have arrived at the age of Twenty one years of age or shall have married.

Item 8th. And lastly for the Execution of this my last will and Testament- I hereby nominate, constitute and appoint my wife Martha M. Maxwell Executrix and my friend Nathan Robert W. Brown and Elijah M. Davis Executors under the same and and further I hereby appoint and nominate my friends James M. Smylie and James F. Lowery of the firm of Smylie & Lowery my attorneys and to be the advisors of and attorney of my said Executors.

In Testimony whereof I have hereunto set my hand and affixed my seal this the 3rd day of February A. D. 1844. The names on the first page and the lines on the fourth page all stricken out before signing and sealing.

W. C. Maxwell (Seal)

Signed Sealed Published and declared by the above named W. C. Maxwell to be his last will and testament, and we have hereunto suvscribed the same in his presence and at his request hereto, in the presence of the Testator & in the presence of each other this the 3rd day of February 1844.

John Stribling
F. C. Wren
R. L. Torrance

The State of Mississippi)
Hinds County)

Personally came open Court John Stribling and Robert L. Torrance who being first duly sworn deposeth and saith that they saw William C. Maxwell sign & seal the preceding instrument of writing, and that they heard him declare the same to be his last will & testament, that they together with F. C. Wren the other subscribing witness signed the same as witnesses in the presence of the testator & in the presence of each other.

R. L. Torrance
John Stribling

Sworn to in open Court 29th May 1844 S. R. Davis Clk

WILL OF MARY McDONALD

In the name of God Amen.

I, Mary McDonald of Winston County and State of Mississippi being of sound mind and memory and considering the uncertainty of this frail and transitory life do therefore make, ordain, publish and declare this to be my last will and testament, that is to say, all my lawful debts are to be paid and discharged, the residue of my estate, personal, I give bequeath and dispose of as follows, to wit: To my beloved son Fluellen McDonald my negro man Major and also my negro girl Elizer, to my daughter Martha E. Henry my one negro girl and Liza, I also give and bequeath to my daughter Janie M. Gamblin my negro man Brit and negro woman Esther, also my colt mule and I give and bequeath to my grand daughter Mary E. McDonald my negro girl Dillard to have and to hold, I give to my three children Fluellen M. McDonald, Martha E. Henry and Janie M. Gamblin all my crops of all kinds together with all my horses and mules, cattle, hogs and sheep household and kitchen furniture, plantation utensils &c to be equally divided amongst them, share and share alike.

In witness whereof I have hereunto set my hand and seal this ninth day of September in the year of our Lord one thousand eight hundred and sixty two.

Her
Mary X McDonald (Seal)
Mark

Witness (illegible) before signing
John W. Sudberry
A. T. Humphries

Dated 9th day September 1862

Proved in Probate Court of Winston County October Term A. D. 1862.

MARY NORRIS' WILL

In the name of God Amen, I Mary Norris of the County of Jefferson and the State of Mississippi being old and infirm of body but of sound and discriminating mind and memory and understanding considering the certainty of death and the uncertainty of the time thereof and being desirous to settle my wordly affairs and thereby be better prepared to lease this world when it shall please God to call me hence do therefore make and publish this my last will and testament in the manner and form following that is to say-

First and principally I commit my soul unto the hands of Almighty God and by body to the earth to be decently buried at the discretion of my Executor hereinafter named and after my debts and funeral charges are paid I devise and bequeath as follows towit-

1st I give and bequeath unto Andrew Montgomery my son-in-law for his use and benefit a negro slave named

Liddy that is now in his possession together with her increase and a negro woman Margaret about 38 years old together with her children named Louisa about 5 years old and Henry about 12 months old and all their increase.

2nd I give and bequeath unto said Andrew Montgomery for the use and benefit of his daughter Eliza a negro firl named Henritta about eleven years old also one feather bed all the foregoing property intended by me to be a full portion of my property in slaves.

3rd I give and bequeath unto my daughter Eliza Beck for her use and benefit a negro firl named Maria about 25 years old with her child named Melinda about 4 years old also the boy Church about 11 years old together with their increase. Also two feather beds and bedding all the said negroes named in the 3rd Section intended by me as a full share of property in negroes.

4th I give and bequeath unto my daughter Eliza Beck the following slaves together with their increase from this time towit- A negro boy named Booker about 20 years old a negro man named Sam about 50 years old a negro man named Jesse about 60 years old a negro woman named Caroline about 23 years old a negro woman named Judy about 25 years old with her children named Sarah 4 years old and James about 12 months old A negro woman named Melinda with her children named Mary about 3 years old and Jefferson about 9 months old valued by me at the sum of Four Thousand dollars under the following conditions to Wit the negroes Booker, Sam, Jesse, Caroline, Judy, Sarah, James, Melinda, Mary and Jefferson the valuation last above mentioned as her property and in consideration of which she the said Eliza agrees and becomes bound to pay unto the guardian or guardians of the son of my late son John S. Norris, deceased- that is to say James, Emily and Patrick Norris the yearly sum of Four Hundred Dollars during the minority of the said children the said yearly payment above mentioned is not to commence until after the expiration of twelve months after the said Eliza shall obtain possession of the said slaves being after my decease and further that at the majority of said children James Emily and Patrick Norris or as each of them comes of age the one third part of the principal of Four Thousand Dollars shall be paid to them by said Eliza her heirs Executors etc - to each in proportion of those that survive which amount being paid is in full contemplation of this my will and in event of the death of all the said children before they arrive at maturity or to the age of twenty one years then I devise and desire that the one half of the said principal of Four Thousand Dollars shall be paid to the children of my son in law Andrew Montgomery and the remaining half to the children of my daughter Eliza Beck, or their lawful representatives and it is further my will and desire that the said Eliza Beck shall not be compelled to pay the guardian or guardians of said children James, Emily and Patrick Norris the said yearly sum of Four Hundred Dollars until such guardian or guardians of said children shall fully satisfy the said Eliza that the said sum of Four Hundred Dollars is necessary toward the yearly maintenance and education of said children James, Emily and Patrick and if the said Eliza is not satisfied and does not pay over the sum of Four Hundred dollars yearly the amount shall cummulate in her hands for the use and benefit of the said children on they or each of them coming of age. Also as the said amount of principal being the sum of Four Thousand Dollars is or shall be paid at the time each arrives of age then only a proportionate part of the yearly sum is to be paid to the children then still in their minority or their guardian.

5th I do will and bequeath unto my daughter Eliza Beck a certain mulatto boy named Anderson now about 6 years old to be for her use and benefit as a servant until he arrives at the age of 25 when I desire that he shall be set free by said Eliza and I do further request that said boy shall be learned some mechanical occupation during said term.

6th I do further will and desire that the negroes Tamar and Jack shall have the privilege of choise to whom they shall go to live with between Andrew Montgomery or Eliza Beck and whichever of said parties said negroes may choose to belong to such I do bequeath them to not considering them of any value but wich to place them where they may be content.

7th I will and desire that all my personal property not previously mentioned (save and except a feather bed which I hereby will and desire to be given to Eliza Beck for the use and benefit of my granddaughter Emily Norris to be given to her when she comes of age or sooner if my daughter so wish) to be equally divided between Andrew Montgomery and Eliza Beck.

8th And lastly I do hereby nominate and appoint Thomas W. Beck my Executor to carry out and into effect this my last will and testament without compelling the said Eliza Beck to give any security of any kind whatsoever and I do hereby revoke and make void all former wills by me heretofore made. In Witness whereof I have hereunto set my hand and seal-dated in Jefferson County this twenty third day of April in the year of our Lord One Thousand Eight Hundred and Forty as my last will and testament and written on one sheet of paper.

Her
Mary x Norris
Mark

Signed and sealed in presence of

E. Sisson
R. P. Harmon
Samuel Beck

PETER NELSON'S WILL

In the Name of God Amen I Peter Nelson of Adams County in the Mississippi Territory being of sound mind and memory and considering the uncertainty of human life do make and publish this my last Will and Testament as follows to wit- Item first, it is my that all my just debts be paid by my executor herein after appointed out of my estate.

Item Second After all my just debts are paid I give and bequeath unto my beloved wife, Margaret one half of my whole estate real and personal.

Item Third It is my will that my executor pay out of the remaining half of my estate after the death of my said wife Margaret and with six months thereafter to the following persons-Margaret Sharbino, Mary Carven, Ann Tyler, Sarah Clark and Magdelia Halbrook each five dollars.

Item Fourth I give and bequeath unto my sons Marson Nelson, Peter Nelson, Jr. and my daughter Catherine Nelson all the aforementioned one half of my real and person estate to be equally divided between the said Marson, Peter and Catherine after the payment of the several sums of money aforesaid.

Item Fifth It is my will that immediately after the death of my said wife Margaret my Executors make a friendly partition of my estate if they can do so and if not that they choose each one good man within their neighborhood and authorize those men to make partition of said estate and each legatee aforesaid take its share by lot to avoid waste of said estate through legal proceedings.

Item Sixth It is my will and I do hereby nominate constitute and appoint Marson Nelson, Peter Nelson Jr and Catherine Nelson my lawful executors and Executrix of this my last will and testament.

In testimony whereof I have hereunto set my hand and seal this nineteenth day of December in the year of our Lord One Thousand Eight Hundred and Twelve.

Peter Nelson (Seal)

Signed sealed and Publised in the presence of

James Fort Muse
Daniel Whitaker
Stephen Dunn

Proven Adams Co. Orphan's Court April 8, 1817.

MARGARET NELSON'S WILL

I Margaret Nelson, wife of Peter Nelson of Adams County and in the Mississippi Territory of the United States being of sound mind and memory and considering the uncertainty of herman life, do make and publish this my last Will and Testament as follows to wit-

Item first, it is my will that all of my just debts be paid by my Executors (hereinafter appointed) out of my estate.

Item second, it is my will that my Executors do pay out of my estate (after the payment of my just debts) the following sums of money to persons following, Margaret Sharbino, Mary Craven, Ann Taylor, Sarah Clarke and Magdalin Halbrook each five dollars.

Item third I give and bequeath to my sons Marson Nelson and Peter Nelson and to my daughter Catharine Nelson all my real and personal estate to be equally divided between them, the said Marson, Peter and Catharine after the payment of the several sums of money aforesaid.

Item Fourth It is my will that immediately after my death my Executors make a friendly partition of my estate, if they can do so and if not that they do each choose one good man to make partition of said Estate and each Legatee aforesaid take its share by lot to avoid waste of the said estate by other legal proceedings.

Item Fifth It is my will and I do hereby nominate, constitute and appoint Marson Nelson, Peter Nelson Junior and Catharine Nelson my lawful Executors and Executrix of this my Last Will and Testament. In Testimony whereof I have hereunto set my hand and affixed my seal this nineteenth day of December in the year of our Lord, one thousand eight hundred and twelve

Her
Margaret x Nelson (Seal)
Mark

Witnesses

John McNamee
Josiah Stone
G. E. Doss

Proven in Orphans Court Adams County, Mississippi November Term 1820.

WILL OF JOHN PORTER

In the name of God Amen I John Porter of the State of Mississippi and County of Franklin being weak in body but of sound and perfect mind and memory blessed be Almighty God for the same do make and publish this my last will and testament in the manner and form following-

I appoint my son Jefferson C. Porter and my sons James R. Porter and William M. Porter, as they become of age executors of my last will and testament in manner and form following-

1st I give and bequeath to my beloved wife Mary Porter the negro girl Elizabeth and three other negroes if she should ever marry again to have during her lifetime and at her death revert back to my estate.

2nd I give and bequeath to my daughter Caroline Grisham the negro girl Mary and her children two other negroes and four hundred dollars in money.

3rd It is my will that all my property be kept together except what is otherwise disposed of until my younger children become of age- When that which is disposed of shall revert back to my estate when it shall be equally divided so that which I now dispose of shall return to the same owner.

4th It is my will that my grand child, Lucius I. Hendricks be an equal heir with the rest of my children.

5th I appoint my son Jefferson C. Porter guardian of James R. Porter, William Porter, Albert Q. Porter, Elvira Porter and Lucius I. Hendricks to take care of them and educate them.

Read and acknowledged this 23rd day of November 1834.

George Hollaway
Angus Wilkinson
John G. Middleton
Probate Court
December term 1834

State of Mississippi
Franklin Co.

Personally appeared in open Court George Halloway, John G. Middleton and Angus Wilkinson three of the subscribing witnesses to the foregoing will and made oath that the testator John Porter acknowledged the same as his last will and Testament in their presence on the day and year therein expressed that the said testator was of sound and disposing mind and memory that they subscribed the same as witnesses in the presence of each other.

George Halloway
John G. Middleton
Angus Middleton

Sworn in open Court
15th December 1834
John P. Stewart Clerk.

W. T. PURNELL'S WILL

STATE OF TENNESSEE)
)
Knox County)

Desiring of disposing of my property whilst in the possession of my mutual faculties and wishing to leave some directions as to the manner in which I wish my children to be educated and taken care of I make this my last will and testament-

It is my will then that my Four Sons John H. Macajah F. Martin A. and James C. be educated until they graduate at some respectable college and that my two daughters, Elizabeth H. and Eliza R. be taken to Salem in North Carolina and placed in the Female Institution at that place until they complete their education and that all the expenses of what soever attending their education - Sons as well as daughters be paid by my executors- heretofore to be named-out of my estate.

In order to more certainly secure to my children the kind of education indicated above- it is my further will that neither of them receive any portion of my property more than a necessary subsistance until they acquire such Education But should any casualty prevent either of my children from receiving an education they are still to be entitled to receive their full portions of my estate.

It is my will that my Executors dispose of any of my property at any time they may think it conducive to the interest of my Estate or necessary to the support or Education of the children or for the purpose of furnishing them with portions as they become of age.

I appoint as Executors to carry out the provision of this my will my brother, Henry M. Purnell, Frank Hawkins, and G. F. Neill all of Carroll County, Mississippi.

As a portion of my slaves may not be considered suitable for field or other outside labor I leave it to the discretion of my Executors either to hire such slaves out or to apply them to such labor as they may think proper.

Signed sealed published this 26th day of August in the year one Thousand Eight Hundred and Forty Nine

M. T. Purnell (Seal)

In the presence of

Robt D. Cox
H. Baker

JOHN REMBERT'S WILL

The Last Will and Testament of John Rembert, Decd In the Name of God Amen, I John Rembert of Amite County in the State of Mississippi considering the uncertainty of this life and being of sound mind and memory (Blessed be Almighty God for the same) do make and publish this my Last Will and Testament in the manner and form following.

1st After my funeral rites and all my just debts are paid, it is my will and desire that my Executor hereafter to be named shall keep my estate together both real and personal of whatever nature and the proceeds thereof to be put to the use of maintaining and educating my children which I have had by my last wife, Sarah, now deceased.

2nd When my youngest child arrives at the age of twenty one years then my estate whatever it may be at that time, be equally divided share and share alike, among my children by my last wife, Sarah, and if any of them die before a division of my estate among them their share or shares be it one or more be equally divided between the survivors of them.

3rd I give and bequeath unto James, Zacheas, John Andrew, Judy and Charlotte, children of my former wife, one dollar each to be raised from the proceeds of my estate when it comes to be divided among my other children and not till then.

4th And lastly I do hereby nominate and appoint my Worthy friend, William Sibley McKoy executor of this my last Will and Testament revoking all former wills by me made. In Witness whereof I the said John Rembert have to this my Last Will and Testament set my hand and Seal this 15th day of November, in the year of our Lord, One thousand eight hundred and nineteen.

John Rembert (Seal)

Signed sealed and acknowledged by the said John Rembert in the presence of us to be his last Will and Testament who have hereunto subscribed our names as witnesses in the presence of the Testator.

Middleton Kirkland
Jesse McKoy
Charles McKoy

WILL OF THOMAS B. REED

In the Name of God Amen I Thomas B. Reed of the City of Natchez in the State of Mississippi do make and publish this my last Will and Testament as follows.

1. I give to my Executrix and Executor or such of them as may qualify under this will, full power to sell and convey my plantation near Natchez call "The Vale" and at their discretion to invest the proceeds in the purchase of other lands, bank stock or in such other manner as they may deem most for the interest of my family; and it is my desire that the annual profits of said plantation or of the property purchased with the proceeds of the sale of said plantation as the case may be shall be appropriated in the same manner that is herein after directed in relation to my slave property.

2. Having full confidence in my beloved wife, I appoint her sole guardian of my children, untill they shall respectively arrive of full age desiring that she cause their education now in various stages of advancement to be completed in a liberal and judicious manner and for the better enabling her to discharge this trust I desire that my slaves, farming utensils and stock of every kind to be

continued on the plantation held by her near Gibson Port to be employed there for the joint benefit of my beloved wife and my children. I also give to her for her separate use my four carriage horses.

3. After the payment of my funeral expenses my debts and all expenses incident to the raiging and education of my children it is my will that my estate be equally divided among my children on the youngest becoming of full age and should my wife find it expedient to give off to the elder children or either of them on their marriage or becoming of age respectively their equal portions or any smaller advancements she is invested with full power to do so.

4. I give to my friend Capt Isaac Ross, Senr, a mourning ring (to be procured by my Executors) not that I expect he will wear it but to be procured by him among other momentos consecrated to the memory of the dead.

5. My Will is that my Estate stand charged with an annuity of one hundred Dollars to be paid to my friend Mrs. Elizabeth Ford during her life or until the bounty of her son shall in her opinion render the further payment of the same unnecessary. It is to be understood that the said one hundred Dollars per annum is to go in part compensation for the boarding of my younger sons so long as they may continue to live with her.

6. I give to my friend and nephew John Green my watch which I desire him to keep and wear as a token of my regard. I hereby appoint my dear wife Margaret A. Reed Executrix and my friend Isaac Ross Junr and Alvarez Fish Esqr of Mississippi Executors of this my last Will and testament. Witness my hand and seal this 6th day of November 1829.

Tho. B. Reed (Seal)

Witness

B. W. Dudley
Zebulon Butler
John Green

JAMES RATCLIFF'S WILL

In the name of God Amen I, James Ratcliff of the County of Yazoo and State of Mississippi considering the uncertainty of this mortal life and being now of sound mind and memory, blessed by Almighty God for the same do make and publish this my last will and testament in the manner and form following that is to say,

Fist, I give and bequeath unto my beloved wife Nancy the eighth of land whereon my dwelling now stands to be all cleaned West of the branch down to the dividing line between myself and William Wilson to be her residence to have the use and occupation thereof for and during her natural life time and after her death to descend to all my children in equal parts and also give and bequeath unto my wife a negro man named Curtice aged about twenty one years and two negro women to be selected and chosen by said wife from amongst all the negroes which shall be or may belong to me at the time of my death, one horse and four cows and calves to be chosen by her from amongst all that may belong to me at the time of my death and one third part of my stock of hogs to have the use and enjoyment thereof for and during her natural life and after her death descend to all my children in equal parts and also give and bequeath to her all my household and kitchen furniture to be and remain hers for and during her natural life and after her death to descend to my youngest daughter, Mary H. Ratcliff and her youngest daughter Polly O'Neal in equal parts and should the said negro Curtice the horse or either of the cows aforesaid die during the lifetime of my said wife she is to have another or others of equal value during her life aforesaid and after her death descend as aforesaid.

Secondly It is my will and wish that all my just debts be paid and that my Executors hereinafter appointed make such arrangements therefor as in their descretion may be most advantageous to my Estate.

Thirdly It is my will and wish that my four youngest sons be kept and continued in school until each of them shall have made up the following time including the time they may severally go before my death to wit: Nathan two years, King two years, and six months, James Three years and Joseph three years the expenses of which to be paid out of my Estate and no deductions to be made therefor from their distributive shares.

Fourthly, all the balance and residue of my said estate both real and personal I will and wish to be divided amongst all my children in equal parts except the personal property which I may have gotten by my present wife by intermarriage with her deducting from the distributive share of my son Samuel M. Ratcliff the sum of two hundred and twenty five dollars and from that of John J. Vandenburg and my daughter, Matilda his wife the sum of Five hundred and thirty five dollars which I have already severally advanced them taking into consideration a negro woman belonging to me which is in the possession of the said John J. Vandenburg and Matilda his wife and estimating her as my property and making no deduction from the distributive share of my daughter Lois Ann Corbin for any of the money which I may have advanced or paid to her husband Allen M. Corbin and allowing my son Isaac Ratcliff in pursuance of a contract therefor made with him and independent of his distributive share of my said estate to have the use and occupation of all my improvements (except that part already set aside for my said wife) for the space of three years from the 1st of January 1836 together with all the hands belonging to me upon his putting in and working therewith one third part as many hands as I have or may have and to receive one third part of each of said crops and the two remaining thirds to descend to him and all the balance of my children in equal parts as aforesaid except the entire distributive shares of my said daughters, Matilda Vandenburg and Lois Ann Corbin which I give will and bequeath as follows to wit, that of my said daughter Matilda to my said son Samuel N. Ratcliff in trust for and to and for the use of my daughter for and during her natural life and after her death to descend to the heirs of her body in equal parts and that of my said daughter Lois Ann Corbin to my said son Isaac Ratcliff in trust for and to use for the use of my said daughter Lois Ann Corbin for and during her natural life and after her death to descend to the heirs of her body in equal parts.

Fifthly and as to the personal property which I may have gotten by my present wife by my intermarriage with her I give bequeath and will unto the two youngest daughters of my said wife to wit: Elizabeth O'Neal and Polly O'Neal in equal parts provided my said wife should not claim her dower in any part of my estate and should accept to this will and be content with the provisions of this will otherwise should she dissent from this will and claim dower in my estate then in that case all the property I may have gotten by my intermarriage with her I will and wish to descend to all my children as is ordered for the descent of the balance of my property.

Lastly I hereby appoint my two sons Samuel N. Ratcliff and William Ratcliff and my worthy friend John M. Sharp Executors of this my last will and testament hereby revoking all former wills by me made, In testimony whereof I have hereunto set my hand and affixed my seal this fourth day of May in the year of our Lord One Thousand Eight Hundred and Thirty five.

James Ratcliff (Seal)

Signed sealed and published and declared to be his last Will and Testament in the presence of us whose names are hereunto subscribed as witnesses in the presence of the said testator and in the presence of each other.

Willis Biles
George Fisher
P. R. Young

Proven in Probate Court in Yazoo Co. September Term 1836.

PETER RUCKER'S WILL

This is the last will and testament of Peter Rucker of Adams County State of Mississippi by the grace and blessing of God in sound mind made on Sunday the seventeenth day of November A. D. 1844.

1. I request that all of my debts to whomsoever due to be paid up in full.

2. I wish a good substantial brick wall to be built around the Grave Yard.

3. I bequeath to John Rucker Bisland my watch- to Wm. A. Bisland my book case, to Husdell S. Truly my riding horse.

4. I wish my executors to pay the necessary expenses of supporting my cousin Sarah A. Truly until my estate is able to purchase a girl and boy negro slaves to wait on her and after that should she live and wish my executors to purchase and give her six young negroes whenever my estate is able so to do- I wish the property which I bequeath and bestow on Sarah A. Truly to be given and secured to herself and her bodily heirs should she marry and at her death should she have no issue- it is to go to her brothers and sisters.

5. After the death of my brother Jonothan and as soon as the debts of my estate are paid -I wish my executors to give my negro servants Arch, Tom, Betsy, and David Jr. and any other issue of Betsy to be given with the sum of Five Hundred Dollars in cash to Daniel Smith or in the event of his death to Mrs. Martha Truly or if she be dead to Samuel H. Lambdin or if he be dead to John Rucker Bisland.

6. I request that any land and negroes and stock may be kept together until the death of my brothers Daniel, William and Jonothan (excepting the servants before named) and all my debts being paid off- then I wish ten of my negroes to be given to John Rucker Bisland so divided as not to interfere with the family connections of the

negroes and the balance of my property to be divided between Sarah A. Truly and Mrs. Martha Truly.

7. In the event of Sarah A. Truly dying before the purchase of the negroes for her -then the executors will purchase for the bequest to John R. Bisland ten young negroes in place and stead of dividing the family negroes as above specified.

8. My brothers, Daniel William and Jonothan are to receive a good and sufficient support from my estate as long as they live.

9. I hereby appoint (and desire them to act) William Bisland, Daniel Smith and Saml H. Lambdin my Executors to carry out the provisions of my will above expressed.

Witness my hand and seal this seventeenth day of November A. D. 1844.

Peter Rucker (Seal)

Witnessed and sealed in presence of

John H. Collier
Saml H. Lambdin
Daniel Smith

WILL OF RICHARD SINGLETON

State of Mississippi Wilkinson County Know all men by these presents that I, Richard Singleton of the above named State and County having a sound mind make this my last Will and Testament Item I give and bequeath to my beloved daughter, Mary Singleton all of my real and personal estate and all of my movable property and in case she dies without a lawful heir or heirs my estate is to be divided as follows I mean heirs of her body Item I give and bequeath all of my personal and real estate and all of my movable property to my friends Joshua Childs, Charles A. Coon, Samuel Wright to be equally divided between the three. Item In case my daughter dies without lawful heirs of her body I give as a legacy to each of W. Body's children a legacy of three hundred dollars and to Sarah Singleton a gold ring valued at one hundred dollars Item all of my former acts and conveyances of my estate personal and real I wish to be done away in consequence of the despicable opinion I entertain of Singletons wife and the injustice exercised by Hiram Singleton upon his daughter Sarah Singleton Item I wish my daughter Mary Singleton to have a generous and accomplished education under the government and guidance of Dr. Samuel Wright consulting Col Joshua Child and Charles A. Coon. It is my wish that Mr. Charles A. Coon remain on my plantation for five years. No sale of property to take place. I wish Cinder and Stephen to be free so far as they law shall permit. I constitute and nominate my friends Col. Joshua Child Charles A. Coon Dr. Samuel Wright my lawful Executors to act for me and in my name in all cases which concern my business to act mutually, declaring this and none other my last will and testament In case of my death I appoint and nominate Doctor Samuel Wright the lawful guardian of my daughter, Mary Singleton, who I wish to act as a father consulting the other two. Finally I revoke all wills and testaments and other voluntary disposition of my property real and personal and hereby declare this to be and stand my last will and testament. In case my daughter Mary Singleton dies without lawful heirs of her body and one or more of my executors were to die without lawful heirs then all of estate will go to the surviving executor his heirs forever. Given under my hand and seal the seventh day of March Eighteen hundred and twenty two.

R. Singleton (Seal)

Witnesses:

John Scarlett
David Glover
David Jagers

Proven at October Term Probate Court 1822.

ABNER SHOLAR'S WILL

I, Abner Sholar of the County of Madison and State of Mississippi being in a very infirm state of health and sensible to my liability to sudden death at the same time being in my own apprehension of sound mind do judge it best to make and accordingly do make this my last Will and testament.

It is my will that all my Just debts be paid and discharged by Executors hereinafter named and appointed, out of my estate as soon as conveniently may be after my decease. In order that my debts be paid off as speedily as possible it is my will that all my negroes and other personal property (now on the plantation where I reside) remain where they are and to be worked under the control and management of my Executors until all my debts shall be paid off and discharged. From the proceeds arising from the sale of the crops or other wise and that none of the negroes nor any of the property be removed from said plantation until there shall be a sale of my real estate and personal property not bequeathed or otherwise disposed of according to requisitions of this my Will as hereinafter directed and required. I give devise and dispose of all my Estate both real and personal in the following manner 1St I give devise and bequeath unto my two sons Levi Sholer and Charles Sholar two thirds of my whole estate both real and personal to their own proper use and benefit forever, each son taking share and share alike. It is my will that part of the property to constitute the shares and portions herein devised and bequeathed to my two sons shall consist of the following slaves viz Elijah, Charles his wife Mary and their children Martha, Frank, Eneas, Sam, Pamelia and the children of Martha viz Bowling, Mary Alicia and Evelina and their increase and if the valuation of said above named twelve negroes and there increase should be more than two thirds of the whole of my estate (the manner of which valuation is hereinafter pointed out)

Then in that case my two sons shall equally contribute to make up the other third of my Estate herein bequeathed to my beloved wife out of and from the sale of my Real Estate which is herein directed to be sold.

2nd I give and devise unto my beloved wife one third of my whole estate both real and personal to her own proper use and benefit forever.

In consideration of her being the property of my wife at the time of our intermarriage I give and bequeath Lenilda and her child and likewise Edna to her own proper use and benefit forever. Provided however that the said two women and child are not to be considered a specific bequest to her independent of the one third of my estate already bequeathed and devised but the said negroes shall be valued in the same manner as directed for the valuation of my whole estate left unsold by my Executors and the valuation of said three negroes and their increase at their valuation shall be included in the apportionment of her third.

3rd It is my will that my beloved wife shall remain on my plantation where she now resides until the sale of my real estate as hereinafter directed and that she have the use of the house, furniture servants etc in the same manner as during my lifetime free from any change whatever.

4th It is my will if my Executors shall be compelled to sell any of my negroes to pay debts before the sale of my real estate that they shall sell my negro man Sam, Clarissa and her three children.

5th It is my will that so soon as all my debts are paid off and discharged or as soon as my executors shall deem beneficial for the interest of all persons interested in the distribution of my Estate they shall sell all my real estate and other property not specifically bequeathed herein and cause a final division partition and apportionment according to the requisitions bequests and devises herein before recited. In order to prevent any doubts in the minds of my Executors as to the manner in which my Estate shall be divided according to the bequests and devises herein named I will suggest to them that the plan I conceive less likely to create any misunderstanding in the discharge of their duty viz when all my debts shall have been fully paid off my Executor shall apply to the Probate Court of Madison County in State aforesaid for an order of division according to the directions of this my Will, suggesting at the same time the names of five disinterested freeholders of said County who shall be approved by the court then they shall under the directions of this my will and with my Executors proceed to value the whole of my estate not sold by my Executors including the negroes herein devised to my wife and two sons and after such valuation the said commissioners shall assign and apportion so much of the proceeds of the sale of my real and personal estate as shall be sufficient to make two thirds of the valuation of my whole estate including the negroes hereinafter bequeathed to them at their valuation, Provided that the negroes do not amount to two thirds of the valuation of my whole Estate and in case the said negroes do amount to that much then the said commissioners shall assign and allot to them the said negroes and no more and after the assignment of the two thirds as aforesaid to my two sons- then the said commissioners shall proceed to divide by valuation the property herein devised and bequeathed to my two sons giving to each son share and share alike until the same shall be divided equally between them- and the said commissioners shall in like manner proceed and assign to my beloved wife so much of the property or money as the case may be sufficient to make the one third of my estate as herein before bequeathed and devised to her at the same time assigning to her the said Lenilda her child and Edna at their valuation she having the power of choosing what property she wishes to make up her portion not disposed of or herein bequeathed.

And it is my will that my son Levi shall be the guardian of my son Charles and his property, and is hereby appointed and constituted his guardian until he arrive at the age of twenty one years and so soon as the property of my estate is divided and my son Levi shall take out letters of guardianship from some Probate Court of this State of the person and property of my son Charles, first having given bond and security as the law directs then the said commissioners with the other Executors shall deliver the said and portion allotted by them to my son into the hands of the Guardian so appointed. And after the division of my Estate according to instructions herein specified the said commissioners shall likewise deliver and pay over to my wife or her heirs or representatives in case she dies before the division as aforesaid the one third herein devised and bequeathed to her. And likewise the said Commissioners shall pay over and deliver into the hands of my son and Executor Levi his third portion of my estate herein bequeathed and devised to him. And I hereby nominate constitute and appoint my son Levi Sholar and my friend Charles Smith of Madison County jointly and severally the Executors of this my last will and testament and so that in the case of the death of one of them the survivor shall be sole Executor of this my last will and testament and I give such survivor all the power and direction I have given my said Executors. I also give to each of them all the power and repose in each of them all and every trust I have given them jointly provided and so far as he who shall act have the consent of the other Executor. In witness whereof I have on the fifth day of July in the year of our Lord eighteen hundred and thirty seven in seven leaves or sheets of paper set my hand and seal in the manner following (that is to say) to the first six sheets I have set my hand and to the seventh and last thereof I have subscribed my name and set my seal.

Abner Sholar (Seal)

Signed sealed and published and declared by the said Abner Sholar as his last will and testament in the presence of us in his presence and at his request have hereunto subscribed our names as witnesses.

James M. Baker of Madison Co.
N. W. Whitehead of Madison Co.
Isham Reborth of Madkson County

Proven in Probate Court of Madison Co. September term 1837.

BENJAMIN SMITH'S WILL

I Benjamin Smith of the City of Louisville and State of Kentucky, do make this my last will and testament.

First I give and devise to my daughter Frances E. Smith her heirs and assigns forever my plantation in Washington County and State of Mississippi known by the name of Longwood and my Kilb place in the vicinity thereof containing about one hundred and forty acres with all the slaves on said plantations and my slave William the carpenter and his wife and family now residing elsewhere, with all the stock, farming utensils crops and other effects which may pertain to said plantation at the time of my demise.

Second To my wife, Irene Smith and to her heirs and assigns forever I give and devise my plantation near Port Gibson in Mississippi Evermay containing sixteen hundred acres with all the slaves therever, except thirty to be selected by her and removed to my Urmdle place, with all the stock farming tools and other effects which may pertain to my Evermay plantation at the time of my demise.

Third I give and devise to my said wife and daughter and to the survivor of them her heirs and assigns forever my Urmdle place with the thirty slaves directed to be removed to said place.

Fourth I give and devise to my said wife and daughter and to the survivor of them her heirs and assigns forever the house and lot on which I reside in said City of Louisville on Jefferson Street and conveyed to me by George W. Smith.

Fifth My Black place in Washington County, Mississippi containing six hundred and forty acres with twenty four slaves capable of field service to be selected by my wife and the children incapable of service who may have mother in said selection I give and devise to my said wife and daughter in trust for the sole use of my niece Sarah F. Johnson during her life and to pass in fee simple to her children at her death.

Sixth My Executrixes shall appropriate out of my estate the sum of Four Thousand Dollars to purchase a residence for the family of my brother, George W. Smith The title to be taken to the said Executrixes in trust for the sole use of the wife and children of said George during the life of the said wife and at her death the estate to pass to her two children, Benjamin and Irene Smith.

Seventh My slaves Jacob, Davey and Winston who have hitherto been faithful to me I desire that my wife and daughter shall discharge from service in five years after my decease and pay them fifty dollars each provided they shall, in the mean time behave themselves well.

Eighth All my estate, real personal and mixed not before disposed of by this will I give and bequeath to my said wife and daughter.

Ninth I appoint my said wife and daughter Executrixes of this will and desire they shall make no inventory or appraisement of my personal estate unless they prefer to do so nor shall they give any surety to enable them to qualify as Executrixes.

In Testimony that the foregoing written on three pages marked 1, 2, 3, is my last will and testament I have hereto subscribed my name this twenty fourth day of July Eighteen hundred and forty six.

Ben Smith (Seal)

In presence of

John P. Oldhai
W. H. Pope

LAST WILL AND TESTAMENT OF DAVID SMITH

In the Name of God Amen: I David Smith of the County of Hinds, State of Mississippi being of sound mind and disposing memory do this twenty first day of August 1826 make, ordain and publish this my last Will and Testament revoking and cancelling all others in form following towit

Whereas I have heretofore at different periods of my life given to my children who have grown up and married and those who are acting for themselves (to wit) Sarah Humphrey, Dec'd (late wife of George W. Humphrey) Polly Gipson, wife of David Gipson, Sarah D. Terry, wife of Joseph R. Terry, J. W. A. Smith, Benjamin F. Smith, Josiah C. Smith, Esther I. Crutcher, Deceased wife of George B. Crutcher, and Obedieance A. Runnels (wife of Hiram G. Runnels, their several portions of my estate and in addition to what I have heretofore given them I give and bequeath Firstly to the heirs of my said daughter, Sarah Hunphreys Fifty dollars Secondly to my said daughter, Polly Gipson, fifty dollars, Thirdly to the heirs of my said daughter, Esther J. Crutcher One dollar, Fouthly to my said daughter Sarah D. Terry and Obedience H. Runnels and my said sons John Benjamin and Josiah one dollar each, all of which legacies are to be paid in twelve months after my death.

Article Second:

Whereas my youngest daughter Emeline M. Smith is unfortunate in her reasoning faculties and incapable of managing property in a skillful and beneficial manner and wishing to provide for her comfort and maintenance during her life and for this purpose I wish to establish a fund in a manner hereafter specified and place the same in the hands of my two sons, Benjamin and Josiah as trustee for her with which they may raise an annuity for the said purpose and having full confidence in my two said sons, therefore I give unto them, the said Benjamin F. Smith and the said Josiah C. Smith to hold in trust and control to and for the use and benefit of my said daughter, Emeline, the sum of two thousand dollars in the following manner, towit, One bond on my said son John W. M. A. Smith for seven hundred and fifty dollars and one on my said son Josiah C. Smith for Seven Hundred and Fifty dollars both bearing date the 18th of August 1826 and drawing interest from the date and one on my said Sarah D. Terry and the said Joseph Terry and my said sons Josiah and Benjamin for Five Hundred and Fifty five dollars and forty five dollars interest due thereon bearing date of 19th day of July, 1823 and during the life of her the said, Emeline and afterwards to the use of the heirs of her body, provided she should have any and it is understood that it is the express meaning of this testator that the said Emeline is to be supported and maintained with the interest ensuing from the said sums of money so given in trust as aforesaid and the principal is to stand unbroken as a fund for that purpose.

Knowing that all things in this world are unstable and desirous specially to provide for my said daughter Emeline my will and desire is that my whole estate stands pledged and as security for the payment of the said Seven Hundred and Fifty Dollars and the interest that may accrue thereon placed in the hands of my said son, Josiah and for which is land is given as above stated it being my determination and will to secure to her said Trustees for her use and benefit Two Thousand Dollars for her maintenance during her life and if she shall die without issue the said bequest in this article made with its increase shall at her death be disposed of agreeable to her will and pleasure provided the same be given to any of her brothers or sisters or their children or any of them.

Article Third Whereas my affairs in this life are somewhat unsettled and feeling the utmost confidence in my executors hereinafter named my will and desire is that they dispose of any of my property that they may think advisable for the purpose of discharging all of my just debts and to pay the same after which I do by these presents will give bequeath and confine with my said Executors hereinafter named all of my estate real and personal (not heretofore provided for) to wit, Piety L. Smith, Elias W. S. Smith and David H. J. Smith and my said Executors to have full and lawful power and authority to make use of any part of said estate in providing educating or apprenticing any or all of said Children in this Article mentioned or supporting the family as they may think proper and also at the same time they the said executors in their wisdom may think proper to allot or portion off any part of said estate to any of said children in this article mentioned in such manner as may be an equal division of said estate at the same time having due regard to the interest of my beloved wife Obediance Smith all such gifts grants and apportionments to be same in Love as though I had done it myself during my temporal existence and it is to be understood that my said estate after the payment of my just debts and the legacies in the first article given above and the security of the said Seven Hundred and Fifty Dollars mentioned in the second article and the interest thereof is to remain in the possession and imployment of my said wife Obedience Smith during her natural life or widowhood except such portions as she and my other Executors may think proper to allot to my said children in this Article mentioned it being the meaning and intent of the testator to provide an ample support for my said wife during her natural life.

Article Fourth and Last

I do hereby nominate and appoint my said beloved wife, Obedience Smith my executrix and my two sons Benjamin F. Smith, Josiah C. Smith and my son in law Hiram G. Runnels my Executors of this my last Will and Testament without any security what ever. In witness whereof I have hereunto set my hand and affixed my seal the day and year above written. The words "dec'd" and "Obedience Runnels" on the first page "provided" and "they" in the third page and "the" and "my" in the fourth page was interlined before signed.

David Smith (Seal)

Acknowledged in the presence of

Benj. Hutch
F. G. Hopkins
Thomas M. Nersell

Know All Men by these presents that I do make and ordain this to be my codicil to my Will heretofore made and I herewith publish this my codicil to the same but my will is to stand in all particulars except so far only as this my codicil may alter it, and the reason for making this Codicil is this, that since the making of my Will and Testament my daughter Piety L. Hadley (formerly Smith) has intermarried with J. B. T. Hadley and one of the main objects of this codicil is to allot to my said daughter the portion which I wish her to have out of my estate in lieu of the provision made for her in common with her younger brothers and the rest of my children in my aforesaid will.

Now therefore in full of the provision in my said will make for my said daughter as her full allowance out of my estate both real and personal I give to my sons Benjamin F. Smith and Jackson Smith two negro girls one named Rose and the other Caroline about fourteen or fifteen years of age to have and hold the said slaves hereof to themselves and to the survivor of them and his heirs to and for the use and benefit of my said daughter Piety S. Hadley and her heirs forever.

2nd I further give and bequeath to my said daughter Piety Hadley one quarter section of land to be laid off of my lands as my said Executors mentioned in said will may direct.

3rd I give and bequeath to my sons J. C. Smith and Shelby Smith one negro girl about two years old named

Clarah to hold in Trust to themselves and the survivor of them to and from the use of my granddaughter Esther C. Crutcher and her heirs forever of her body but should she die without issue to revert to my estate and this bequest is in full of the portion out of my estate to the said Esther. Given under my hand and seal this the 4th day of June 1832.

David Smith (Seal)

Test:

J. C. Smith
Benj. Mitchell
Armstead Grant

Filed for Probate Hinds County December Term, 1832

LAST WILL AND TESTAMENT OF WILLIAM S. STRATTON.

I William S. Stratton of the County of Powhatan do hereby make and constitute this my Last Will and Testament in manner and form following to wit:

1st I desire that all of my just debts and funeral expenses be paid.

2ndly I give to my wife, Ann Elizabeth Stratton the land on which I live, together with all the personal and perishable property thereon during her life or widowhood and if she marry it is my will and desire that the same shall be divided according to the law.

3rdly I give to my wife Ann Elizabeth Stratton one third part of the money due me in the State of Virginia and Mississippi.

4thly I give the balance (it being two thirds) of the money due me in the States of Mississippi and Virginia to three daughters, Mary Frances, Ann Eliza and Sarah Eleanor, to be equally divided amongst them and their heirs for ever.

5thly lastly, I do hereby constitute and appoint my wife Ann Elizabeth Stratton Executrix and Henry Gordon, Executor of this my Last Will and Testament hereby revoking all former wills and testaments by me heretofore made. In testimony whereof I have hereunto set my hand and affixed my seal this the thirteenth day of January Eighteen hundred and thirty nine.

William S. Stratton (Seal)

Signed and Sealed in the presence of

Peter F. Harris
William P. Tatum
Ezenas Maxey
Abner Marsh

LAST WILL AND TESTAMENT OF JAMES M. SMITH

I, James M. Smith of Madison Co. Mississippi, of sound and disposing mind and being well aware of the uncertainty of human life it having been appointed of God for all men to die do coolly soberly deliberately of my own free will and accord make and ordain this my last will and testament, first in accordance and accordance with the decrees of heaven that dust thou art and unto dust thou shalt return, I direct that my body be decently intered in a respectable manner free from the pomp and vanities of the world.

Secondly believing that honesty is the best policy and that mankind should deal with each other on the square and level I direct that all of my just debts be paid as soon as a sufficiency for the purpose can be raised from the sale of my crop or crops of cotton.

Next Will and specially direct that my mulatto Girl Angeline and her child a female named Pamelia Octavia be immediately set free after my decease they not to be included in any inventory as a part of my estate and I direct that the sum of five thousand dollars be paid to the said Girl Angeline to be vested by my executors in real estate in the State of Indiana or Ohio the rents profits and

Issues the same to go to the said Angeline during her natural life and at her death to go and devolve to her child said Pamelia Octavia and her posterity. And I further direct that a further sum of five thousand dollars be given and paid to the said Pamelia Octavia (she now being about four years old) so soon as she arrives at the age of eighteen years to be vested in real estate as directed in the case of Angeline the rents profits and issues of the same to go to the said Pamelia Octavia during her natural life and at her death to go and devolve to her posterity if she have any and in event of said Octavia dying without a lawful heir of her body the property hereby entailed upon her is to go at her death (said Pamelia Octavia) and be distributed as my other effects are hereinafter directed. And I further direct that the sum of Five Hundred Dollars be appropriated for the purpose of aiding said Angeline and child in reaching their home or homes in Ohio or Indiana immediately after my decease. I will and direct that my slaves (except Angeline and Octavia) be kept at work and employed on my real estate until they gain or earn a sufficiency to pay all of my debts then I direct that my entire estate both real and personal be equally divided between my brother Cotesworth Pinckney Smith and my sister Elen Cornelia, wife of Henry A. Moore (reserving however at all times the legacies directed for account of said Angeline and Octavia) said property to remain in possession of said Cotesworth Pickney and Elen Cornelia during their natural lives then to devolve to their heirs or representatives and I hereby beg leave to request that my Executors tend strictly to my will in relation to said Angeline and Pamelia Octavia and lastly I do hereby appoint my brother Cotesworth Pinckney Smith and my brother in law Henry A. Moore executors of this my last will and testament made the twenty fifth day of May in the year of our Lord one thousand eight hundred and thirty five.

Witness my hand and seal

James M. Smith (Seal)

Witnesses present
Lorenzo Latham
Major H. Harper
James F. Dixon

Filed in Probate Court Madison Co. Miss Dec 28, 1836.

WILL OF G. M. SMITH

In the Name of God Amen

I G. M. Smith of State of Mississippi and Town of Port Gibson being of sound mind and disposing memory do on this 3rd day of July, Eighteen Hundred and thirty three will, give and bequeath the sum of Ten Thousand Dollars to Virginia Caroline Maxwell of the aforesaid State and Town, to her, her heirs, assigns and administrators to be paid in lawful money on the first day of March Eighteen Hundred and Thirty Eight bearing six percent interest for twelve months after my decease up to the time it becomes due.

The balance of my property consisting of lands in Washington County and negroes, notes, accounts and monies after having paid off the above bequest shall be equally divided between my two brothers Elisha and Calvin and my only sister, Hannah Smith that is one third to each to be paid on the first of March Eighteen Hundred and Thirty Eight. All property to be managed by the Executor until which time without interruption from the legatees. The river plantation I wish managed and kept going until the last installment comes due, the same was planned by myself when in anticipation of life at that time. I further will, give and bequeath to my most particular friend Horace Carpenter my gold watch. I hereby appoint Horace Carpenter my sole Executor.

Given under my hand and seal this third day of July Eighteen Hundred and Thirty Three.

G. M. Smith (Seal)

Witnesses
J. M. Scanland
G. W. Montgomery
Edw. Hall.

WILL OF ELIZABETH LAURENCE

The State of Mississippi
Copiah County

In the name of God Amen. I Elizabeth Laurence being weak of body but of sound mind and perfect memory so make this my last will and Testament revoking all former wills by me made in the manner and form following

I do give and bequeath to James Laurence son of William H. Laurence a certain negro girl named Harriet.

I do also give and bequeath unto my grandchild James Robinson one sorrel Filley two years old one cow and yearling one bed and dressing.

Also I do give and bequeath to my daughter Polly Ann Matilda Chance one mare one bridle and saddle one bed and dressing one half of my wearing apparel the other half of my wearing apparel I bequeath to Rebecca Laurence and lastly I give and bequeath to my son Thomas D. C. Laurence one negro girl named Pricella my crop now growing together with the improvements on which I now live, one bay colt one cow calf and yearling all my farming utensils all my household and kitchen furniture also all of my hogs also a certain tract or parcel of land containing one hundred and forty acres lying and being in the State of Louisiana Washington Parish.

In testimony whereof I have hereunto set my hand and Seal this 7th day of September in the year of our Lord One Thousand Eight Hundred and Thirty Five.

Her
Elizabeth X Laurence
Mark

Test
George Ellis
George Ellis Jnr

THE LAST WILL AND TESTAMENT OF THOMAS C. VAUGHN, DECD

In the Name of God Amen! I Thomas C. Vaughn of the County of Jefferson and State of Mississippi, planter, being of sound and disposing mind and memory and conscious of the near approach of death do make publish and declare this my Last Will and Testament revoking and annulling all other wills by me heretofore at any time made. Item 1st I nominate constitute and appoint as my Executrix and Executors of this my will my beloved wife Harriett Letitia and my friends John Watt, Edward Bradford, Daniel Frisby, and Nathaniel Harrison who in addition to the powers confirmed upon them by the laws of the the land shall have and possess full power and authority at their discretion to sell barter or purchase any property real or personal they may deem it for the advantage of my estate to sell or buy they being the exclusive judges of the time and terms and the manner of making the contract subject however to render an account according to Law showing the condition of the Estate. They shall possess full power to execute all and every contract made by me and laft unexcuted at my decease and add to, vary or diminish the same at their discretion and in all things the concurrence of the majority of those who are authorized to act shall be binding upon my heirs and legal representatives. The survivor shall possess all the powers herein conferred but if all my Executors or Executrix should die before this will shall be fully executed or for any other cause administration shall be granted it is my will and desire that such administrator should not execute any discretionary duty whatever but shall as to them administer my estate as though I had died intestate. Item 2nd I also further constitute and appoint my said Executrix and Executors Trustees for the execution of all the Trusts hereinafter specifically mentioned the survivors being fully authorized to act and a majority of those acting shall have power and authority to execute the Trusts.

And if all of my Trustees shall die before the final execution of all the Trusts herein created then any Trustee appointed by order or decree of any court of competent Jurisdiction shall not be allowed to exercise any discretionary power herein vested in my chosen Trustees but shall be confined to the execution of Direct and Specific Trusts and none other. Item 3rd After the payment of my debts I will and devise that the residue of my estate both real and personal of every kind and description whether purchased before or after the signing of this Will or purchased by my Executors after my death shall be legally divided between my aforesaid wife and all my children then living and the issue of such as may have died if any, who shall represent their deceased parent as follows to wit: The shares or portions of my wife and sons I give bequeath and devise to them respectively in absolute fee simple the several portions of my daughters I give devise and bequeath to my trustees aforesaid in Trust to receive the rents and profits and income thereof and annually to pay over the same to each of my daughters out of her separate share or so much thereof previous to their marriage respectively as may be necessary for their genteel support maintenance and education the surplus if any to vest in stock or other property or loan at interest as my said Trustees shall think best and if the annual income of said Trust shall prove insufficient for the proper support and education for any or either of my said daughters then the said Trustees may in their discretion appropriate to that purpose a part of the principal and the said Trustees shall keep the separate shares of the said Daughters distinct and separate and increase or diminish the funds of each according to the circumstances and when one of my said daughters shall marry my said Trustees shall pay to husband or herself the whole annual income of her portion or share. If any or either of my said daughters shall die before marriage then the portion or share held in Trust for her benefit with all the increase thereof shall return to the mass of my estate and be divided and distributed as is herein directed in the first instance and held subject to the same Trusts in favor of the survivors. And if any or either of my daughters shall marry and die without issue living at her decease leaving a husband then the portion or share held in trust for her benefit shall be equally divided in two parts and one part thereof shall be given to the surviving husband in absolute fee simple and the other part thereof shall be divided and distributed as my estate in the first instance and my daughters portions thereof held in the same manner and subject to the same trusts and if either of my daughters shall die leaving issue living at the time of her death the portion or share held in trust for her benefit shall be given to such issue in equal parts among them when they respectively arrive at the ages of maturity and not until then, and any such issue which shall die before arriving at the age of maturity shall not be entitled to any part thereof and if none of said issue last mentioned shall arrive at the age of maturity then such daughters portion or share shall be subject to the same bequest and directions as if there had been no issue living at the death of said daughter. And it is expressly my Will and desire that this will shall apply to and embrace any posthumous child or children I may have as fully and in the same manner that it does to the children living at my decease. Item 4th It is further my Will and desire that my executrix and executors shall at all times previous to a division of my estate as herein directed appropriate any portion of the income of my estate to the support education and maintenance of my wife and children and my said Executrix and Executors shall be the exclusive judges of the proper time for a division and distribution of my said estate but the same shall be divided in time to deliver my sons their shares upon their arriving respectively at the age of twenty one years. Item 5th The devise and bequest herein contained in favor of my wife is intended to be in lieu of her right of dower and all right whatever to any of my real and personal property.

In testimony whereof I have set my hand and seal this the 28th day of October.

Thomas C. Vaughn (Seal)

Signed sealed and published in the presence of us who respectively subscribed the same in the presence of said Thomas C. Vaughn and at his request he being in his proper senses at the time and also in the presence of each other "until then" 6th page second line interlined before signing.

David Harrison
Andrew Montgomery
David Bulten
Thomas M. Miller
T. G. Bulten

Filed for Probate Fayette, Jefferson County Mississippi January Term 1840.

ELIZABETH WHITTLE'S WILL

In the Name of God Amen, I Elizabeth Whittle of the County Adams and Mississippi State of the United States, of sound and disposing mind and memory but considering the uncertainty of this transitory life do make publish and declare this my last Will and Testament in the manner following that is to say First, I recommend my soul to God and my body to be disposed of as my Executors hereinafter named may direct and for and concerning all worldly Estate I give bequest and dispose thereof as follows that is to say Im Primis It is my will and desire that my old slave Chloe receive her freedom amediately after my decease. Item it is my will and desire that my mulatto girl Eliza serve my daughter Anna Maria Moore two years at the end of the two years she is to have her freedom for her kind and attentive behaviour to me in case of the death of my daughter she is to serve my granddaughter Anna Eliza Gerault and to have her freedom two years after my decease. Item I have secured to my son Samuel Carson and his heirs One thousand acres of land therefore I will and bequeath and devise all the remainder and residue of my real estate to my daughter Anna Maria Moore wife of James Moore and her heirs as she may think proper of before or after her decease, the property to be divided between the children of my daughter Anna Maria Moore. Item It is my will and request that my slaves are valued and one half their value to be paid to my son Samuel Carson for his children. The other half of the slaves I will and bequeath to my daughter Anna Maria Moore and her heirs. It is my will and request that James Moore with the money due me by him as soon as he can make it convenient to my son Samuel Carson Three Thousand Dollars for money lent by me to him some years since. After paying all my just debts it is my will and request that James Moore will give to each of my grandchildren a gold watch and chain in remembrance of their Grandmother E. W.

And do hereby nominate and appoint James Moore Samuel Carson and Doctor A. P. Merrill Executors of this my last will and testament hereby revoking all former and other wills and testaments by me at anytime heretofore made and I do declare this to be my last will and testament.

In Witness whereof to this my said will I have set my hand and Seal this first day of January Eighteen hundred and twenty six.

Elizabeth Whittle

Signed and delivered in presence of

Note:
(No witnesses signed)

WILL OF JOHN B. MOORE

I, John B. Moore do make and publish this as my last will and testament hereby revoking all other wills by me at any time made, First I direct that my funeral expenses and my debts be paid as soon after my death as possible out of any monies that I may die possessed of, or may first come into the hands of my executor. Secondly I give and bequeath unto my wife Delila Moore Two Thousand Dollars which amount I desire my Executor to loan out at interest during her lifetime and for her support. Also one good horse saddle and bridle and also for her to have all necessary furniture to keep house with, a part that I at present own. And I also give to my said wife during her natural life negro woman, Charity. Thirdly I do give and bequeath to my eldest daughter Caroline the wife of James Colbert the following slaves to wit, Daniel and Delpha his wife, Mariah, Sarah and Melvin and their increase. Fourthly I give and bequeath to Colbert Moore as Trustee for the benefit of my daughter Harriet the wife of Pleasant Mosby the following slaves to wit Willis Charlotte, Joe, Manerva, Jane, Jack and their increase. I desire my said Trustee Colbert Moore to take possession of the negroes for my said daughter Harriet Mosby and hire out for her support and benefit and should she die without bodily heir the property as above named to be divided between my other children. Fifthly I do give and bequeath to my daughter, Mary, the following slaves to wit, Matt, Malissa, Jane, Levi, Anacky, Jacob and their increase and also give to Mary my sideboard, carriage and horses. Sixthly I do give and beheath to my daughter, Eliza the following slaves to wit, Isaac age 34 years and his wife Elsey, Cran, March, Jim and Margaret and their increase. Also my clock, bed stead bed and clothing also I desire if I should not purchase for her before my death that my Executor will purchase for her a fine gold watch and also one good horse saddle and bridle, Seventhly, I do give and bequeath to my son John B. Moore the following negroes to wit, Rafe, Adeline, Lucinda, little Malissa, Deek and Ned and their increase and my wearing gold watch fine horse, saddle and briddle, bedding and bedstead.

Eightly I do give and bequeath to my son George C. Moore the following slaves to wit King and Molly his wife, Henry Polly Black Jane, and Wade and their increase, One horse saddle and bridle bed and bedding and one gold watch.

Ninthly I do give and bequeath to my daughter, Martha Jane the following slaves to wit Judy and her son Tom, Albert, Vina and old Molly's son Isaac, Lewis and Judy's youngest child and their increase, bed and bedding, one good horse, saddle and bridle and One Gold Watch. And I further desire and request that all of my lands be sold by my executor at private sale either for cash or on time and the money arising from said sale to be laid out in young negroes and all the expenses for the education of my five youngest children to come out of the proceeds of the sale of said land. And I also desire and give to Colbert Moore, Trustee aforesaid for the benefit of my said daughter Harriet Two Thousand Dollars as her portion of money out of the sale of my land. And I further desire that all remaining money or negroes so purchased by said sale of my land may be equally divided between my children, Mary, Eliza, John B. George C. and Martha Jane and in event of my selling any of the within named negroes the child to whom willed are to be made good by my Executor- and all and everything, money stock, crops, furniture and debts left by me and negroes that I may hereafter purchase. At my death I desire to be equally divided between my children, except Harriet Mosby. And lastly I do nominate and appoint Leander Guy my Executor. In witness whereof I do to this my Will set my hand and seal this 26th day of September 1839.

John B. Moore (Seal)

Acknowledged in the presence of subscribing witnesses of same and date for the purpose therein contained Sept. 26th 1839.

O. D. Sledge
I. M. Sledge

REUBEN WILLIAMS' WILL

The State of Missisippi Pike County

Greeting November the 24th, 1821 In the name of God Amen or be it remembered that I Reuben Williams of the said County being weak in body but of sound and perfect mind and memory or you may say this considering the uncertainty of this immortal life and being of sound mind blessed be the Allmighty God for the Same to make and publish this my last will and testiment in manner form following that is to say first I give and bequeath unto my beloved wife Elender Williams my hole asstate during her lifetime and after her death I do also give and bequeath to my eldest son Nehemiah Williams one third of a half section of land in Township 4 Range 8 Section 8 Northwest Quarter also in Sec 5 Southwest Quarter. I give and bequeath to my second son Floyd Williams one third of a half section of land lying in Township 4 Range 8 Sec 8 North West Quarter Also in Section 5 Southwest Quarter. Also I give and bequeath unto my third son William Williams one third of a half Section of land lying in Township 4 Range 8 Section 8 Northwest Quarter Also in Section 5 Southwest Quarter.

I also give and bequeath unto my three sons Nehe-niah Williams, Floyd Williams and William Williams a negro girl Amey to make an equal division between them. I also give and bequeath unto my daughter Nancy a negro girl named Alsey to her and her bodily heirs. Also after the death of my dear beloved wife Elender Williams the household kitchen furniture and stock and there shall be an equal division maide between the four children Nehemiah Williams, Floyd Williams, William Williams and Nancy Williams.

Hereby revoking all former wills by me made in witness where I have hereunto set my hand and seal this the 24th day of November in the year of our Lord 1821. Signed declared by me Reuben Williams above all named to be my last will and testiment in the preseants of us who at my request and at my preseants have hearunto subscribed our names as witnesses to the saim.

his
Reuben x Williams (seal)
mark

Witnesses:

Samuel Coulson
James Rollins
Ezra Estes

JOHN DAVID WASHAW WILL

I, John D. Washaw, of the County of Franklin in the State of Mississippi being of sound and disposing mind and memory do hereby publish and declare this to be my last will and testament as follows to Wit, Item First, the Negro property which I have heretofore given to Louis M. Hollinger and delivered to him with the increase of the same it is my will and desire that he retain being as I consider a fair and just compensation for services rendered by Hollinger to me.

Item Second In addition to the property deeded by me to Henry Mingee and Frederick Foster as Trustees for my wife Catharine by deed in the form of a marriage settlement dated nineteenth day of March Eighteen Hundred and Forty Three and recorded in the office of the Clerk of the Probate Court of the County aforesaid in Book D. pages sixty five, sixty six, sixty seven and sixty eight I will and devise that after the payment of the debts I may owe at the time of my death and necessary funeral expenses unto her in her own right so much of the residue of my estate both real and personal of which I may die seized as will make her portion one half of the whole estate of which I die seized after the payment of such debts as I may be owing at the time of my death and the discharge of my funeral expenses aforesaid.

Item Third The half of my estate remaining after the payments of my debts and my wife Mary Catharine has received her share I will to be sold by my executor hereinafter in this will to be appointed upon such credit as he in his discretion with the approbation of the Probate Court may seem best and the money arising from said sale to be paid by him to my Sister Doveth E. P. Volckman in case she survives me and in case of her dying before me to her children to whom I hereby will and bequeath the same. She the said Doveth being the widow of Frederick Andrew Volckman and at this time believed to be a resident of the town of Griefwald in Prussian Pinerania.

Item Fourth It is my will and desire that in the case of my dying while I have a crop in the ground that my executor employ some person to take charge of my plantation and hands and make and gather said crop and that my executor sell the same and account for the amount of the crop as part of my estate. It is further my will that if my executor considers that it be of benefit to my estate to keep all of my property together and work the same on the plantation that he shall have power to do so during which time none of the legacies bequeathed by the will shall be delivered but my wife Mary Ann shall have a support out of the proceeds provided he does not work said place more than two years and my will is that he do not.

Item Fifth In case it becomes necessary to paying debts to sell any of my property it is my will and desire that my Executor sell my stock of cattle, hogs, horses and every other species of property of which I may die seized and possessed before he sells the lands town lots and houses in the town of Meadville Mississippi or my negroes allowing my wife however to retain as much of said stock and furniture as she may desire to retain for housekeeping.

Item Sixth It is my will and desire that in case my wife should prefer in having her portion of my estate devised to her by this will sold that the same or such part thereof as she may desire to be sold by my Executor in conjunction with the other property that is the half devised to my sister Doveth E. P. Volckman.

Item Seventh Whatever may be the increase of any of my estate while in a course of administration more than will be absorbed by my debts funeral expenses and costs of administration I will that the same be divided by my Executor equally between my said wife and my sister or in case of her death the heirs of my said sister, I mean the children of my said sister.

Item Eight Having heretofore made a will divising my property to Jacob Christian Washaw since deceased and Louis Hollinger I now hereby revoke the same as will as all other wills by me heretofore made. The treatment which I have received recently at the hands of the said Hollinger in grossly insulting my wife in my presence and many other acts of annoyance and vexation evincing such a bad heart that he has cancelled all those acts of benevolent regard toward him which I once entertained.

Item Ninth I hereby appoint my friend Oscar J. E. Stewart Executor of this my last will and testament. Given under my hand and seal this 28th day of December A. D. 1847.

John David Washaw (Seal)

Signed Sealed published and declared by the testator (after the same was read over to him) in our presence as his last will and testament who signed our names at his request and in the presence of each other December 28th 1847.

P. G. Miller
Wm. M. Porter
A. Q. Porter

GLOSSARY

1. Ad Colligendum- For collecting; as an administrator or Trustee.

2. Administrator de bonis non- of the goods not administered. When an Administrator is appointed to succeed another, who has left the estate partially unsettled, he is said to be granted "administration de bonis non"- that is, the goods not already administered.

3. Administrator with will annexed. Administration granted in cases where a testator makes a will, without naming any Executors; or where the executors who are named in the will are incompetent to act or refuse to act; or in case of the death of the executors, or the survivors of them.

4. Dower. The provision which the law makes for a widow out of lands or tenements of her husband, for her support and the nurture of her children. Dower is an estate for the life of the widow in a certain portion of the following real estate of her husband to which she has not relinquished her right during marriage: 1) of all lands of which the husband was seized in fee during the marriage: 2) of all lands to which another was seized in fee to his use: 3) of all lands to which, at the time of his death he had a perfect equity, having paid all the purchase money therefor.

5. Deed of gift. A voluntary conveyance or assignment is called a "deed of gift".

6. Entailment. An interference with and curtailment of the ordinary rules pertaining to devolution by inheritance; a limitation and direction by which property is to descend different from the course which it would take if the creator of the entailment, grantor or testator, had been content that the estate devolve in regular and general succession to heirs at law in the statutory order of proceedure and sequence.

7. Ex Parte. On one side only; by or for one party; done in behalf of or on the application of, one party only.

8. Feme Sole. A single woman, including those who have been married, but whose marriage has been dissolved by death or

divorce and for most purposes, those women who are judicially separated from their husbands.

9. Heir-at-law- He who, after his ancestor dies intestate, has a right to all lands, tenements and hereditaments which belonged to him or of which he was seized.

10. Intestate- without making a will. A person is said to die intestate when he died without making a will, or died without leaving anything to testify what his wishes were with respect to the disposal of his property after his death.

11. Non Compos Mentis- not sound of mind; insane. Very general term embracing all varieties of mental derangement.

12. Next friend- the legal designation of the person by whom an infant (minor) or other person disabled from suing in his own name brings and prosecutes an action either at law or in equity; usually a relative.

13. Nun Cupative will- an oral will declared or dictated by the testator in his last sickness before a sufficient number of witnesses and afterwards reduced to writing.

14. Relict- this term is applied to the survivor of a pair of married people, whether the survivor is husband or the wife; it means the relict of the united pair (or of the marriage union) not the relict of the deceased individual.

INDEX TO INTRODUCTION

King, Benjamin
Smith, Cotesworth P.
Smyth, George W.
Stafford, John
Stockton, Richard
Stone, Luther
Tarpley, Colin S.
Thatcher, J. S. B.
Townsend, Halsey
Trotter, James F.
Turner, Edward
Shields, William B.
Vandorn, P. A.
Wheaton, Charles
Whitehead, W. W.
Whiting, Amos
Wilder, J. W.
Winchester, John
Winston, Louis
Wright, Daniel W.
Yerger, William

INDEX OF NAMES